Two Texts and I

Two Texts and I

Disciplines of Knowledge and the Literary Subject

Suman Gupta

Madison • Teaneck
Fairleigh Dickinson University Press
London: Associated University Presses

Associated University Presses
440 Forsgate Drive
Cranbury, NJ 08512

Associated University Presses
16 Barter Street
London WC1A 2AH, England

Associated University Presses
P.O. Box 338, Port Credit
Mississauga, Ontario
Canada L5G 4L8

The paper used in this publication meets the requirements of the American National Standard for Permanence of Paper for Printed Library Materials Z39.48-1984.

Library of Congress Cataloging-in-Publication Data

Gupta, Suman, 1966–
Two texts and I : disciplines of knowledge and the literary subject / Suman Gupta.
p. cm.
Includes bibliographical references (p.) and index.
ISBN 0-8386-3806-6 (alk. paper)
1. English literature—Study and teaching. 2. English literature—History and criticism—Theory, etc. 3. Interdisciplinary approach in education. I. Title.
PR33.G9 1999
820'.7—dc21 99-19032
CIP

PRINTED IN THE UNITED STATES OF AMERICA

To Cheng

Contents

Part III The Cautious Text

Acknowledgements

THANKS ARE DUE TO DR. PETER TU, HERR ACHIM BROSCH, DR. ERIK Svarny, and Dr. Cheng Xiao for throwing light upon some of the issues which I have discussed here. I am also grateful to an evaluator for Associated University Presses who made useful and perceptive suggestions.

The Argument

DISCIPLINES, AS BODIES OF KNOWLEDGE, ARE CONSTRUED IN TWO kinds of texts which are characterized by the two ways in which the subject (the "I" of members of a discipline) presents itself. When the subject-position is the focal point from which the disciplinary gaze extends outwards, and expands and assimilates everything in its view as within the purview of that discipline, one has a *cautious* text. Typically this is a text which is self-reflexive, self-interrogative, opaque. The discipline that is based in a cautious text has no boundaries: it is a form of knowledge in which everything is subsumed within a certain sort of gaze. When the subject-position is presented as objective, when the discipline revolves around a comprehension of the subject-as-object (members of a discipline view the "I" as other), one has a *bold* text. Usually this is a text which is assertive, unreflexive, transparent. The discipline founded in the bold text is demarcated by boundaries that permit its placement in terms of other disciplines which are similarly formed.

In practice cautious and bold texts of disciplines of knowledge usually coexist, overlap, and otherwise define each other. But they fail to acknowledge each other as such: the cautious text doesn't recognize the disciplinary boundaries accepted by the bold text, and the bold text summarizes the cautious text as bold and doesn't recognize its lack of disciplinary boundaries.

Part I of this study demonstrates the distinctiveness of cautious and bold texts, and consequently conveys a pluralistic understanding of disciplines of knowledge, by emulating different subject-positions. The cautious texts of the philosophical subject, the literary subject, and the nonscientific subject (thus describing the formation of scientific disciplines as emanating from the practice of scientific subjects) are described. This is done through consecutive emulations of different subjects and therefore enactments of different cautious texts. The manner in which the bold text tries to summarize the cautious texts in terms of subjects-as-object follows. Two modes of placing the subject-as-object in the bold text are discerned. The first, through a *metadisciplinary* perspective, i.e., placing the discipline's description of subject-as-object in terms of quanta of knowledge; the second, through a *macrodisciplinary* perspective, i.e., placing the discipline's description of subject-as-object in terms of the institutional space it occupies. Illustrations for the metadisciplinary perspective are provided in Durkheim's and Weber's sociological, and Foucault's "archaeological," methods. The educationist's and anthropologist's (Tony Becher and Clifford Geertz, for example) descriptions of disciplines are used to elucidate the macrodisciplinary perspective.

Part II extends the examination of the bold text by describing the discipline of literary studies in general and English literature in particular through meta- and macrodisciplinary perspectives. The precise relationship between literary studies in general and English literature is described accordingly. This is done by focusing specifically on the notion of crises in literary studies and English literature. The focus is emphasised by a close examination of the issue of canonicity. Canons are described at several levels: in terms of *self-evident* canons, *accepted* canons, *counter* canons, and *potential* canons. It is argued that at no level of disciplinary description can a crisis be discerned for English literature specifically, though there is a necessary putting-into-place of the academic discipline of English literature.

Part III reverts to the cautious text of literature. The expansive and assimilative nature of this cautious text, with its centralized subject-position, is demonstrated by describing the literary subject's (my) engagement with ostensibly "nonliterary" texts. Two such sets of texts are engaged with to provide exemplary demonstrations: the philosophical works of Wittgenstein, and nonmathematical expositions of the Theory of Relativity. I read both sets of texts as literary texts. Eagleton's literary engagement with, and the stylistic features of, Wittgenstein's *Tractatus* and *Philosophical Investigations* are discussed. Similarly nonmathematical expositions of Relativity are subjected to a literary-linguistic analysis of their use of abstract description, metaphor, example, and historical narrative.

Finally, in a section entitled "Afterthoughts" I take some of the observations made in the course of the above study to two specific discussions of current interest. This is done with a view to demonstrating the pragmatic implications of these observations. The discussions in question address T. S. Eliot's alleged antisemitism, and the possibility of formalizing an Indian English literary stylistics.

Two Texts and I

Part I

Disciplinarity and Interdisciplinarity in Literary Studies

Introduction

THERE ARE TWO SORTS OF TEXTS IN THIS STUDY. FOR THE SAKE OF convenience these could be called the bold text and the cautious text. These are easily differentiated by their visual appearance in this part, though caution and boldness isn't the quality of their appearance. The visual translation shouldn't be allowed to mislead the writer-reader. These are texts we are familiar with already. These are not normally incompatible texts, and not normally distinguished in a marked manner. In fact they coexist, they reflect on each other, they transmit across each other, and often merge into each other. So well-orchestrated is their togetherness that the distinction might seem facile—the product of a theoretician's fussiness which has no practical implications, which cannot be demonstrated through a *pure* example of either. It is true that there are few pure examples of either, but in certain areas of enquiry there are emphases which make the distinction relevant. In this part it is maintained that the distinction is relevant: it is maintained that no comprehension of the precincts of disciplines of knowledge or the spaces between them (interdisciplines) or the place of literary studies in their context is possible without this distinction. It is further maintained that all practice of disciplines, interdisciplines, and particularly literary studies, has this comprehension implicit in it, and the future of such practice depends on this distinction.

The distinction between the cautious text and the bold text can be stated only in the bold text (always keeping in mind that neither are likely to be purely that). This is a bold text. The cautious text questions itself, dilutes itself, dissipates itself, pluralizes itself, ironizes itself, restores itself, attacks itself, till it covers the whole view. It cannot extend outside itself. It is a text with a self-reflexiveness that is all consuming. Anything that comes under its purview becomes a cautious text. The bold text on the other hand consolidates itself by a confidence in itself which negates interrogation, a sense of wholeness, a reluctance to examine its assumptions, a conviction in monological constructions. The bold text usually feels it can reach to the cautious text, summarize and contain it, ostensibly without even transforming it. The bold text revels in its comparative wholeness against the other or with reference to the other. It makes sense of the plurality and slipperiness of the cautious text by its own robust, unreflexive, assertion. But the cautious text characteristically evades the bold text's attempt to comprehend it, contain it, summarize it. The ability of this introduction to assert its boldness is an instance of its impurity.

It is possible to draw an analogy between the familiar notions of opaque and transparent languages and cautious and bold texts. It might be useful to think of opaque language as close to the spirit of the cautious text, and transparent language to that of the bold text. But this is not adequate, because boldness and caution are not merely linguistic variations, though linguistic variations, such as transparency and opaqueness, do play a part. What links the two levels of metaphor used here (opaque/transparent to cautious/bold) is the manner in which the linguistic is linked to the subject (the "I") of the texts. It is also because the subject is the issue that the distinction of the texts becomes relevant to an understanding of disciplines of knowledge (and therefore interdisciplinary spaces and the place of literary studies).

How the subject construes itself is, this part suggests, a necessary way of comprehending disciplines of knowledge (and linked areas). Some disciplines construe the subject in a cautious fashion which can only be expressed in a cautious text (where the opaqueness of language is necessary), other disciplines do so in a bold fashion which can only be adequately expressed in a bold text (where the transparency of language can be expected). [However, the fact that there are no pure instances of a bold text and a cautious text should never be forgotten.] Whether the discipline construes its subject in a bold or cautious fashion has, this section goes on to suggest, profound implications for issues such as interdisciplinarity (in theoretical and practical terms), particularly in literary studies. So there are two texts in this section: cautious and bold. The bold text has begun already.

How the subject construes itself in a discipline is examined by raising the question (in both texts): "What am *I?*"

While I am still within the precinct of the bold text, and before giving myself up to caution, a word of caution for the reader-writer. What follows here is not *a* cautious text, but a multiplicity of cautious texts. Each of these gives way to the other from its own perspectives and excludes all other perspectives. To those who are accustomed to the robust assertiveness and unreflexive common sense of the bold text this sudden falling into a multiplicity of vacillating, self-questioning, auto-perpetuating cautious texts might seem irritating. I would like to exhort such readers-writers to be patient. Their irritation is understandable. What I propose to do in the following cautious texts is outside the normal experience of reading-writing works of critical theory. In the following cautious texts I try to emulate different subjects (*I*) to demonstrate how the subject is constituted in, and therefore constitutes, different disciplines of knowledge. In other words, I introduce a self-examining subject (myself, I) who refuses to maintain an integral presence, and who cannot be effectively objectified, or put into perspective (that would defeat the purpose of the cautious text). This strangely chameleonlike subject would pretend to be the Descartian subject at one moment and then metamorphose into the philosophical subject of Deleuze and Guattari; it would claim to be a narcissistic Barthesian subject at the next moment and then try to move "outside" literature; and then it would be seen hammering the doors of science determinedly only to realize that it is excluded because it doesn't become a practitioner of science. These transformations might seem bewildering, and bold reader-writers may find themselves reluctant to make the effort. Those who find themselves obdurate about their reading-writing strategies would do well to disregard the cautious texts altogether, and move on directly to the bold text which begins by trying to summarize the cautious texts which have preceded it.

And finally (I am about to give myself up to caution) a few words about the range of references the reader is faced with in the following pages. These are eclectic, to say the least. These are also sketchy and eccentric at times. A reader may wonder whether any general point about the constitution of a discipline, the textual nuances of disciplinary expressions, and the status of the subject within the latter, is possible through references to only a very few representative thinkers and their works. "You have only mentioned A and B in your discussion of such-and-such discipline", the reader may argue, "why haven't you made space for C,D,E, etc. who are all equally important?" The reader might also admit in the same breath that following the latter path is the way of endless regress, and that the A and B who are mentioned are possibly familiar to a wider circle of readers than the equally significant C,D,E, etc.

But selectivity, and the specific sort of selectivity to be found in this study, is not merely a matter of pragmatics. This selectivity—the eccentric and eclectic range of references—is the most potent clue to the presentation and self-construction of the subjects (*I*) of the following texts. Selectivity is composite in subjectivity; and since the subject is one of the poles of this study, the range of references presented is itself an *object* of attention. The reader needs to be aware of this range of references to grasp the constitution of the different subjectivities (*I*) which appear in the following texts.

And now, onwards . . .

Cautious Texts

The First Cautious Text

The Philosophical Subject: A Trap

1. I WILL NOT PRETEND THAT I AM WRITING-READING A TRANSPARENT text. This text is not merely *about* an area of enquiry (disciplinarity and interdisciplinarity in literary studies), it *is* within that area of enquiry. The axis of *aboutness* and the axis of *isness* have to converge (a Heideggerian form of epistemological argument) before the area of enquiry and my engagement with this area is *thrown out* for scrutiny. Disciplinarity and interdisciplinarity and my space therein are concepts which are unlocked by the text and which imprison the text.

The *aboutness* of the text is declared. "Disciplinarity and Interdisciplinarity in Literary Studies": there is a domain (disciplinarity and interdisciplinarity) and a discipline (literary studies). It is understood that the discipline is contained in the domain, and yet in the declaration it paradoxically purports to compress the domain in the discipline. A balancing act on the rope of the paradox is anticipated. Another way of looking at the declaration could be to see an open end (disciplinarity and interdisciplinarity) and a closed end (the discipline of literary studies). "In" closes the open end and prioritizes closure. But this is problematic. The declaration is of trying to grapple with this problem. The declaration is also of a voice that makes the declaration, that poses the problem of the declaration, that reveals itself by the declarative statement and prepares to grapple with the problem. This voice is my voice: *I* am the subject of this text.

The declared confrontation and my engagement with it may be considered complete when the *isness* of this text, its appearance in a continuum of present moments, is manifest. This *is* the opacity of this text, a cautious text. An opacity marked by its awareness of its unravelling language, references, formal arrangement; of its possible physical aspect (its papers, print qualities, covers); of its potential physical spaces (on my desk, in the publisher's book list, the bookshop's shelves, the library's catalogues, the private collector's bookcase). The *isness* fixes the placement of the text, disregards the closed and open ends, and simply makes it available with merely the declaration to speak for it.

But this sense of completion is not adequate. This sense of completion happens before the *aboutness* has clarified itself, perhaps even declared itself. It happens before the text addresses itself, is written-read. The space in which the text can make itself available with its declaration is already prepared and predisposed to its reception. This cautious text and I surrender ourselves to the inevitable *isness* which prefigures the text and predetermines its availability and only then opens up its *aboutness.* Only then can I appear and the text explain its declaration.

The convergence of the axes of *aboutness* and *isness* is what's at issue here. Only when this convergence is realized fully, and not merely in terms of one or the other, will the area of enquiry which is declared be thrown out and I will be seen grappling with it.

2. The convergence of *isness* and *aboutness* makes this a cautious text. What does that mean?

Each moment of the reading-writing of this text is an admission and analysis of that reading-writing. Freely admitted and readily analyzed, not the guilty discovery of a transparent language turning opaque. Not goaded into admission by an investigative onslaught at the blurred margins of this text: at the invisible colophon, the visible footnote, the silent phoneme, the resounding polysemy, etc. Instead, for a change, admitted and analyzed in the statement of the text-in-progress itself, in never allowing the completion that is marked by its availability to be enough (as Joyce might have denied that *Work-in-Progress* had ever achieved to *Finnegans Wake).* Admitted and analyzed through the processive nature of reading-writing, and moreover through the reading-writing that knows that it has been written-read already[1]: a particular kind of performance. As in a play where one can hear the author's voice, the director's commands, the prompter's echo, the costume designer's scissors, the background painter's brush, and so on.

This admission and analysis of reading-writing is, further, not the result of an interrogation but the initiation of one. With each step of this text's moving closer to realization, the admission seems to draw back a step; the larger reading-writing looms the more evasive it becomes. The admission of reading-writing in this text pushes reading-writing a step farther: there are questions at every moment which need to be answered only to raise others. In effect the further I proceed the wider and more complex the scene is likely to become.

But there is a direction in this spiral, a swirling towards a tip in the cone—a Yeatsian gyre. It is precisely this performance and regression which is the admission of reading-writing which is also the convergence of the *isness* and *aboutness* of this text. All this is directed towards the throwing forth of the area of enquiry (disciplinarity and interdisciplinarity in literary studies) and my engagement with it.

3. Who am *I*? There are certain accepted ways of dealing with that question. There are certain associations which can scarcely be evaded.

Inevitably, therefore, *I* am a descendent of the Descartian cogito, and am the reiterated conceptual persona of the Idiot. If I have to be seen in third person I am that conceptual persona: the Idiot (this term is drawn from Deleuze and Guattari[2]—see that note for an explanation). The subject of the Descartian cogito, of course, writes itself more simply than I, the Idiot, can. I refer back wistfully to the leanness of that ancestral "I" (the Descartian "I"), a mere wisp of a presence, which wiped itself away only to reappear at the selfsame moment, which at that moment gave birth to itself, which wielded a duster and happily gazed on the tabula rasa of its own mind. Descartes could say:

> I was persuaded that it would indeed be preposterous for a private individual to think of reforming a state by fundamentally changing it throughout, and overturning it in order to set it up amended; and the same I thought was true of any similar project for reforming the body of sciences, or the order of teaching them established in schools: but as for opinions which up to that time I had embraced, I thought I could not do better than resolve at once to sweep them wholly away, that I might afterwards be in a position to admit either others more correct, or even perhaps the same when they had undergone the scrutiny of reason. I firmly believed that in this way I should much better succeed in the conduct of my life, than if I built upon old foundations, and leant upon principles which, in my youth, I had taken upon trust.[3]

This is the moment I am envious of, the sort of birth that was never to take place again, the ancestral birth with its magical advantages. The conduct of my presence is in the writing-reading of this text-in-progress, and I will never be born through the sleight of hand which collapses the foundations of opinions. The *isness* of this text and my space in it are, as I had observed in point 1, prefigured and predisposed already. As I write-read I expect the area of enquiry, disciplinariness and interdisciplinariness in literary studies, and my engagement with it to get thrown out to this prepared space. This is the idiotic claim which marks my ancestry all the way from Descartes to Deleuze and Guattari.

4. I followed Deleuze and Guattari in giving my *I* as the reiterated conceptual persona of the Idiot. In doing this I have entangled myself in the proximity of the reading-writing of their text, the web of its declaration of itself which clearly sets out its *aboutness*. Its declarative title: *What is Philosophy?* Philosophy is "the discipline that involves *creating* concepts,"[4] is the proffered concept. The conceptual persona—the Idiot, the madman, etc.—stands between the concept and the conceptual plane of immanence. This is the *discipline* of philosophy. It can be clearly differentiated from the disciplines of science and art:

> What defines thought in its three great forms—art, science, and philosophy—is always confronting chaos, laying out a plane, throwing a plane over chaos. But philosophy acts to save the infinite by giving it consistency: it lays out a plane of immanence that, through the action of conceptual personae, takes events or consistent concepts to infinity. Science, on the other hand, relinquishes the infinite in order to gain reference: it lays out a plane of simply undefined coordinates that each time, through the action of partial observers, defines states of affairs, functions, or referential propositions. Art wants to create the finite that restores the infinite: it lays out a plane of composition that, in turn, through the action of aesthetic figures, bears monuments or composite sensations.[5]

The differentiation of disciplines, if that is what art, science, and philosophy are, is fixed here in the *aboutness* of the text which *is*, for me, so close. The fixing takes place at the beginning, when the aboutness is declared not merely in the title but in the first lines, in the distinction between philosophizing and thinking about philosophy, in the vocalization of the philosophical subject—"only in old age . . ."

This mainly means that by following the normally accepted associations of the question "What am *I?*" I find myself entrapped in the condition of the philosophical subject, in the vehemence of the territorialization of philosophy. No reader-writer (certainly not the ostensible signatories) would mistake the subject of *What is Philosophy?*: it *is* philosophy *about* philosophy. Whatever claim one makes to an element in its aboutness (say, conceptual personae) would inevitably entangle it into the web of what it calls the discipline of philosophy.

Unintentionally I am knee-deep in a part of the area of enquiry (disciplinariness and interdisciplinariness) already. A quagmire of contradictions: for I have shifted from my declaration and its exquisite and potential arrangement ("Disciplinarity and Interdisciplinarity in Literary Studies") to another one with its own exquisite and elucidated arrangement ("What is Philosophy?"). Is this in any way a revealing shift?

5. Since my conceptual persona so far is conceived with the associations stated above there has not been any significant shift at all, no discernible movement, or rather only a small gesture has taken place, like shifting from one foot to another as I stand. From the foot of declarations with potential arrangements to the foot of declarations with elucidated arrangements. In fact, the impossibility of more discernible movement is a condition of my idiocy: there is no escaping the space between the plane of immanence and the concept, I am bound in my very announcing of *I* in the totality of the philosopher's quest. In that sense as soon as I announced myself ("I"), I had loaded that signifier with philosophical significance, and was already within the conceptual totality of a philosophical definition of concepts (the answer to the question "What is Philosophy?").

There is no escape from what Deleuze and Guattari would describe as the *discipline* of philosophy at this point of my enactment (doing, happening) of reading-writing. Any attempt to reaffiliate the conceptual persona associated with "I" would be to falsify it, to misunderstand concepts, to misrepresent philosophy. This philosophical "I", in which I am trapped, makes everything else either a nonphilosophical other or a philosophical itself. Philosophy is the inevitable standpoint where I stand now, however far afield I try to venture. Here, the concept in advertizing is not a concept,[6] the literary person can only be a *partial* philosopher in exceptional circumstances,[7] the examination of propositions is not an examination of concepts (it is science), the construction of a composite of sensations is not a construction of concepts (it is art). One can only say that if one is a philosopher creating a concept of philosophy (or science and art). Philosophy crowds in, expands, subsumes.

So, when I set about constituting the *isness* and *aboutness* of my reading-writing hoping to throw the area of enquiry (disciplinariness and interdisciplinariness in literary studies) forth, I found myself in the midst of philosophy.

6. This seems to disturb the declaration of this text. The open (disciplinarity and interdisciplinarity) and closed (literary studies) ends of the declaration are subsumed in the undeclared third party of philosophy. It would not be thrown out again except as a speck that affirms only philosophy as happening. If I try to affirm my separateness and throw out the area of enquiry (disciplinariness and interdisciplinariness in literary studies) all that appears is the subdued Jonah inside the whale of philosophy. Which leads to a necessary question:

> If philosophy has always intended, from its point of view, to maintain its relation with the nonphilosophical, that is the antiphilosophical, with the practices and knowledge, empirical or not, that constitute its other, if it has constituted itself according to this purposive *entente* with its outside, if it has always intended to hear itself speak, in the same language, of itself and of something else, can one, strictly speaking, determine a nonphilosophical place, a place of exteriority or alterity from which one might still treat of *philosophy?* Is there any ruse not belonging to reason to prevent philosophy from still speaking of itself, from borrowing its categories from the logos of the other, by affecting itself without delay, on the domestic page of its own tympanum [. . .], with heterogeneous percussion?[8]

The dislocation of the question in this text from Derrida's *Margins of Philosophy* is the dislocation from the intention of "treating of philosophy" in the specific sense which requires the presence of the continuous metaphor (the tympanum). The ostensible answer, however, is available because of its "anteriority": which is offered with the appearance of the *a* in *différance,* with its sheaf of directions. By its elision of oral enunciation and phonetic writing, by merging the play of semiological differences with the unending deferral of the presence, by constantly presenting the trace of nothing but itself, *différance* moves into the anterior of the ever-assimilative Being (which is philosophy's inability to hear anything but itself and the trap it lays for the self-interrogating subject):

> Since Being has never had a "meaning," has never been thought or said as such except by dissimulating itself in beings, then *différance,*

> in a certain and very strange way, (is) "older" than the ontological difference or than the truth of Being. When it has this age it can be called the play of trace. The play of trace which no longer belongs to the horizon of Being, but whose play transports and encloses the meaning of Being: the play of the trace, or the *différance,* which has no meaning and is not.[9]

But this quotation is still a dislocation within this text, and *différance* is the (probably necessary) unmentionable "before" which this text need not mention. Not yet. Probably not at all. The area of enquiry has not been written-read yet, thrown out as it was anticipated. It is potential. I had been deluded into thinking I was knee-deep in it. I was knee-deep in philosophy as the discipline of concepts, and Derrida (and others) have hammered at, frayed, the limits of that. I suspect they have violently made the philosophers hear themselves.[10] I note it but it is not my thing. Yet, who am I? What can I write-read? When will the area of enquiry be thrown forth? Should I say "thrown forth" any longer?

7. I should not say "thrown forth" any longer. When the margins of philosophy are frayed, and the anterior of an ever-assimilating Being is suggested, Heidegger is at the center of this deconstruction. But I could still say "thrown forth" because I am still the potential *I* of this text, the conceptual persona ("philosophy" as Deleuze and Guattari puts it), the focal point of an ever-assimilating Being ("philosophy" as Derrida puts it). Is not that why I have not, can not, perhaps would not mention the sheaf of directions of *différance?*

I am the area of enquiry now.

I am writing-reading. The performative and regressive writing-reading.

As seen above in terms drawn from Deleuze and Guattari *I* could be a conceptual persona, the Idiot, shifting from foot to foot between the concept and the plane of immanence, frozen in the inescapability of philosophy. Extending the concept within which *I* am trapped, *I* could probably be reconstituted as the others of philosophy. Let's say the others of *I* could be the propositional persona (trapped in science) or the personified aesthete (trapped in art): all ultimately projections of an extensive concept of philosophy. But all also mutually exclusive, in planes that never meet, cutting across (as Deleuze and Guattari would affirm) the brain and chaos. In a relationship which would render interdisciplinarity impossible.

But in a relationship which is the lack of one, in an exclusion where exclusion is not definitive but constituted, in a mismatch of ontological surfaces where a match cannot even be attempted. This is the point I am driven to write-read. This is where the *I* and the others of *I* stand within the concept of philosophy (a discipline) constituting its others (nonphilosophical or antiphilsophical disciplines).

There is no escaping this impasse unless I rewrite-reread myself again. This is not regression but renewal. Let's say I hark back, in a *ritualistic* fashion, to a birth of the other of the cogito. This is the moment when I unwrite-unread myself here and now, the inconceivable withdrawal when the last letter of this sentence will touch the beginning of a palimpsest.

The Second Cautious Text

Inside and Outside Literature

1. This palimpsest is darkened slightly by what was and has been erased. On it I inscribe anew my declaration of a field of enquiry: "Disciplinarity and Interdisciplinarity in Literary Studies." And I read it.

What passes when that happens is the realization that I shouldn't begin by asking "What am *I?*", because I know that I am the *literary* subject. I have been educated as such, and I posed my declaration because that is what I am. It would be more sensible to ask "What is a literary subject?". But I know that as well, because . . .

What passes between the act and the pause of reading-writing my declaration of this text ("Disciplinarity and Interdisciplinarity in Literary Studies") is the longing for adventure, the thrill of anticipation, the relief and the wonder of what is inscribed, what the text has opened up, the vertigo of infinite freedom. That is the desire of the scriptor, and the desire of the reader for scripting, the longing for that split between the semes promising the agonizing consummation, which Barthes speaks about.[11] In this moment of anticipation, promise, excitement, I have placed this text at the closed end of my declaration of a field of enquiry—disciplinarity and interdisciplinarity are inevitably drawn into the vortex of literature and its language. I am still following Barthes, in a fashion. I have given myself up to the language which writes itself, without any sense of the instrumentality of language, with pleasure.[12] This surrender can only be to the autoeroticism of the writing-reading of this text, which manifests itself in a self-adoring gaze, narcissistic passion; in trying to perpetuate its performance; in regressing into its own warm depths. Call it the pleasure and liberation of literature and its pursuit (literary studies).

Without reflection therefore I find that I am a Barthesian subject and inside literature. Barthes has (and by his example, I have) claimed this freedom and pleasure (when not "bliss"[13]) at the expense of what is inconceivable to the literary person: the complete instrumentality of scientific language. The very possibility of this instrumentality has to be denied, cannot be understood. The intrumental pretensions of language, as it now seems, lies in the descriptive matrices which deny pleasure (formalism, structuralism, normative definitions, etc.) and ideological affiliations which constrain literature (Marxism, bourgeois culture, nationality, racial assertions, gender assertions, colonial construction, etc.[14]). These are pretensions since they impede the recognition of pleasure and freedom in the text. These are pretensions because their instrumentality applies to literature as science. These render literature inconceivable to itself as *literature.* So I assert the atopic text. The text (which transfers itself in its singularity to the reiteration of itself as one, the Text—but more of that later) can only lend itself to a poetics of text (the extent of freedom) and an erotics of text (the extent of pleasure/the ecstasy of bliss). The poetics of the text is Barthes performing and regressing (writing-reading, or rather writing as reading/ reading as writing) into the connotative plurality, even infinity, of *Sarrasine:* withholding itself and declaring itself (as the castrato of Balzac's text is withheld and disclosed) as *S/Z.* The slash of the Z transfers itself to Barthes's text. The erotics of the text are the spurts of readerly writing that are declared as *The Pleasure of the Text,* that performs its own coming at the end. If the atopic text is released and received through its poetics and erotics as such, there is literature; otherwise something false and incomprehensible is in the offing. The text that is not. Something nonliterary, self-effacing, probably born dead.

Does the atopic text allow a Barthes (or *I*) to exist? "Exist" is surely the wrong word. But what does it mean when Barthes says *I* (as I say *I*)? Barthes says *I,* and I continue to follow his example, at various strata of engagement within the text. The irony of labeling these shifting manifestations of *I* as at different "strata" cannot escape the literary historian. It is the ironizing of the phenomenological approach to the text, referring and undercutting the four strata of the phenomenal literary work of art that Roman Ingarden discerned before introducing the reader's concretization of the text.[15] There the stable deposits of the subsequent strata were released to the fluidity of the reader's "perspectival foreshortening"; in Barthes the infinity of the *I*'s perspective hints at the fluidity, the metamorphic nature, of the strata wherein it construes itself.

First, *I* could be construed in the substance of the text itself, as a narrator who by being so withdraws his/her name in favor of *I* in the narratorial act (the various narrators of *Wuthering Heights*, for example), or a narrator who doesn't take the trouble of offering a name but *I* (the narrator of *Sarrasine*), or the narrator who cannot offer a name but *I* and even that verges on disappearance (the voice of Beckett's *The Unnamable*):

> In principle, the character who says "I" has no name (Proust's narrator is an outstanding example); in fact, however, *I* immediately becomes a name, his name. In the story (and in many conversations), *I* is no longer a pronoun, but a name, the best of names: to say *I* is immediately to attribute signifieds to oneself; further, it gives one a biographical duration, it enables one to undergo, in one's imagination, an intelligible "evolution," to signify oneself as an object with a destiny, to give meaning to time. On this level, *I* (and notably the narrator of *Sarrasine*) is therefore a character.[16]

Second, *I* could construe myself on the margins of the text, wrench myself from its substance and place myself on the fringes and folds of the text (the authorial interlopers who appear gently in Jane Austen's and George Eliot's novels, assertively in Henry Fielding's novels, violently in Thackeray's *Vanity Fair*). Third, *I* could savage the substance *and* the fringe and folds of the text, tearing the text apart even as its pieces grasp for the whole (the *I* of Laurence Sterne's novels: *I* the tourist [*Sentimental Journey*] or *I* Tristram Shandy [*Tristram Shandy*] and *I* in the digressions). Fourth, *I* could slip out of the text in the area of invisibility, become the *I* of the reader as the reader "lends, by proxy, to the discourse" when he/she reads "As though terror-struck" in *Sarrasine.*[17] Fifth, *I* (a dislocated other voice) could impress myself on the reader through the authorial signature which draws the text into the text of the signature: as *Sarrasine* may be drawn into the Balzacian text (and *S/Z* into the Barthesian text).[18] Sixth, perhaps *I* could assert myself as author even without the signature (a moot point), so tacitly there that it is almost no assertion at all, as one might find the "arranger" in Joyce's *Ulysses.*[19] Seventh, *I* could be located in the metatext of the reader who reads the text, who lets readers into a vicarious pleasure/bliss of reading the text, of groping between its semes—the *I* of the critic.[20] *I,* a denotative or connotative signifier, an erect intelligence rendering and rerendering and withdrawing and erasing, the marked presence or absence within or without or on the surface of the text. Eighth, *I* could simply be nothing but self-referential as the atopic text opens the locks of infinite freedom and pleasure/bliss:

> If I agree to judge a text according to pleasure, I cannot go on to say: this one is good, that bad. [. . .] I cannot apportion, imagine that the text is perfectible, ready to enter into a play of normative predicates: it is too much *this,* not enough *that;* the text (the same is true of the singing voice) can wring from me only this judgement, in no way adjectival: *that's it!* And further still: *that's it for me!* This "for me" is neither subjective nor existential, but Nietzschean (" . . . basically, it is always the same question: What is it *for me?* . . .").[21]

The atopia of the text, the erotics of the text, the poetics of the text, ebbing from the singularity of an existential or subjective or conceptual *I,* dissolving the stratifications within which *I* construes itself even as it does so, cascading over the surface of definitions, formulations, norms so that it corrodes the resistance of science, drawn into the whirlpool of the reader writing and the writing of the reader . . . there is an overwhelming emergence here. The emergence of the signifier which refers itself, merges itself where it is written-read and merges all writing-reading in itself, and therefore seems to offer an unquestionable oneness: the Text. It is this capacity for perpetual self-emergence and absorption which Barthes refers to when he sees the Text in the focus of interdisciplinarity:

> *Interdisciplinary* studies, of which we hear so much, do not merely confront already constituted disciplines (none of which, as a matter of fact, consents to *leave off*). In order to do interdisciplinary work, it is not enough to take a "subject" (a theme) and to arrange two or three sciences around it. Interdisciplinary studies consists in creating a new object, which belongs to no one. The Text is, I believe, one such object.[22]

In this context, interdisciplinary studies is an anomaly in the constitution of disciplines as understood by the literary subject, the Barthesian *I.* It is moreover the anomaly perpetuated by science—

or sciences (arranged around a "subject")—which is unacceptable given the all-subsuming fluidity of the Text which *I* perceive. Science, which insists on an instrumentality of language, which has no pleasure/bliss in offering this language, which constrains instead of liberating, cannot be the purveyor of "interdisciplinarity" because the literary subject cannot understand it. This is beyond understanding for Barthes (or I), it is the deceptive, the inscrutable, other which is constituted as the unspeakable other because it is in Barthes's (or my) gaze. This gaze only assimilates and reassimilates the Text; there is no space for science there, only the absence of its exclusion. So what is interdisciplinarity as reaffined to the Text? Is it *inter*disciplinarity as *between* already constituted disciplines? It cannot be. Not if there is any exclusion in the focus of the infinite and assimilative Text. If the Text is a newly constituted object of interdisciplinarity it is in defiance of already constituted disciplines. It is, in fact, the interdisciplinarity which acknowledges the infinity and the assimilativeness of the Text, not the interdisciplinarity which is the meeting ground for traditionally constituted physics, say, and linguistics. It is the interdisciplinarity which grows outward from the Text. That is why the Text, according to Barthes, "cannot be allotted to the traditional realm of "Literature."[23] But the Text probably has to be found in the realm of a *new* understanding of "Literature" (which receives the poetics and erotics of the text), and is certainly not science. The interdisciplinarity Barthes advocates is the infinity and assimilativeness of the Text: the plurality of a new "Literature" (a megadiscipline?).

In my own way, *I*, the Barthesian literary subject, am as expansive and all-embracing as the philosophical subject I have unwritten-unread. Ultimately, my vision subsumes everything as literature only, and collapses everything into the poetics and erotics of the Text. I acknowledge my others only as Texts and refuse them a discrete subject-position independent of me and charitably call this "interdisciplinary." But if the others refuse this construction I fail to understand them.

2. There are times when Barthes (and I, as above) has to contend with ideological references, metalinguistic jargons and systems. Contenders are inevitably overcome by the all-inclusive text of literature; the text is the great leveler. It "liquidates all metalanguage," "destroys utterly, *to the point of contradiction,* its own discursive category, its sociolinguistic reference," and "attack[s] the canonical structures of language itself"[24]; literature is "deceptive,"

and bliss is the "powerful underside of writing."[25] The text's mode of contending is therefore through both frontal attack and evasion. To appear as a text, with a poetics and an erotics which is written-read in it, is evasion (of all ideological references) and attack (destruction of its sociolinguistic category); evasion is attack. But evasion and attack are also, if one flicks the page of this discourse suddenly, if one, so to say, lets the fluid *I* do a volte-face, moments when the text and the Barthesian subject become vulnerable, may be captured within the contending discourse. If the literary subject deserts Barthes at this point and rereads-rewrites itself from the other side, the evasion and attack of the text could turn into a capture within ideological references, a containment in sociolinguistic categories. One can see this as a relocation of reading-writing from its infinity and assimilativeness (from pleasure/bliss and freedom) by a violent thrust to an anteriority or posteriority, an "outside." The violent thrust which wrenches the relocation into place is not reconcilable with the happening of literature and its pursuit (literary studies). It is in effect a radical renovation of the happening of literary studies: it presents itself as a chaining, a subjecting, of literature.

The violent thrust, the wrenching of the relocation, is momentarily felt, and felt in retrospect, in Tony Bennett's *Outside Literature.* The enigma of the title (for the erstwhile Barthesian) is predicated by the enigma of its beginning:

> there is no outside of literature—no way of writing about it that can be external to it in the sense of being unaffected by, or without consequences for, the way in which the field of literature is currently constituted. Nor, even supposing one could be fashioned, would there be any point of writing from such a position.[26]

The wrench is momentary and retrospective, I said, because it *seems* to be located elsewhere. It seems to appear at the bottom of that page where Bennett describes the sense of literature outside which he purports to stand: "'literature,' that is, as a category of aesthetic discourse." This is where it *seems* to stand; it cushions the wrench which dawns on the erstwhile Barthesian writer-reader (particularly reader) as she/he progresses down the page. The deja vu of this encounter with the sense of literature outside which one can apparently step is that stirring of the wrench, the violent thrust, which has taken place somewhere anterior to the text. It is retrospectively felt: the erstwhile Barthesian had started reading the text, the enigma of the beginning ("there is no outside of literature . . . "), with the somnolence of the aftermath of this violence. Probably somewhere between the enigma of the title and the enigma of the beginning the erstwhile Barthesian reader (the I of 1.) has done the volte-face, has reconstituted itself so that nothing more than a retrospective sense of what has happened, a sense of remote reiteration of something apparently new, is possible. I return to the enigma of the beginning with the confidence that I am outside literature already, outside literature even as I read it: how else could I have accepted that literature is *currently constituted* (where did the closure of context come from?) so that I can write *about it* and inevitably *affect it.* I have prodded the skin of literature, standing outside its complete organism, when I read that. The organism moved. But that is not the affect, the consequence, that Bennett presents. What does a shifting from one foot to the other matter? A more marked affect for literature has occurred somewhere anterior to the text, when I violently thrust myself outside its organism and touched its skin. Needless to say, Bennett is not ignorant of the violence that has already taken place. Having given the sense of literature outside which he intends to stand after the fact, he envisages and performs the violent thrust after the fact as well:

> It is to this process of extricating—wresting—from aesthetic discourse materials which might be of service in constructing a discursive space external to it that this study addresses itself.[27]

Bennett has a remarkable talent for placing the retrospective as the prospective. Of course, this is not surprising. The linearity of reading-writing the text demands it. This space outside literature has to be anterior or posterior or on the surface of the text; the sheer happening in the text, its poetics and erotics, is now inconceivable. The wrenching outside the organism of literature to behold it can only present itself as happening after the fact. This sort of text is the shadow of its happening, the simulacrum that has written itself complete before it appears to write itself.

Was I amidst an aesthetic discourse as *I* in 1. (above)? No. To say "aesthetic discourse" is to place myself outside. In its enunciation I am reconstituted, or rather, constituted anew. Its enunciation is a recognition which fixes me in a conception of the approximate repetition, of the almost reiterative, and therefore of contextual (historical) location: the recognition of *I now.* Being thrust in this position outside literature now I feel that literature and its ostensible aesthetics stands before me for me to examine from without. Patterns and symmetries become visible to me from this outside view of literature; patterns and symmetries which begin to exist, of course, because I now perceive near reiterations, near repetitions, within the body of literature (in terms of literary history, in terms of aesthetic ideas and expression, in terms of social-cultural impact and intent) and gaps between these reiterations. These patterns and symmetries become my way of recognizing my position with regard to literature. The gaps which divide reiterations could be thought of as virtual distances: "virtual" because they are not simply spatial-temporal, these are gaps allotted by the subject's (mine now) conception which allows the near-reiterative or almost-repetitive to be discerned.

Therefore, I now am at the virtual distance that is separated from the distances that separate Winckelmann from Hegel and Hegel from Pater, and their placement of beauty in a naive and fulfilled culture that could only be in antiquity. Parallel texts shoulder each other, ready to eliminate each other: Pater's textual enactment of *la Gioconda*'s beauty and the reading-writing of Leonardo's time, for example, is itself separated not only from Winckelmann and Hegel, but also from Leonardo's own parallel texts of ideal beauty and the ideal of nature in *Trattato del Pittura*.[28] Virtual distances stretch across from the touchstones of Arnold to the touchstones of Pound and the touchstones of the Leavises. The virtual distances of separation are the measure of the almost reiterative which makes a conceptual frame of reference, a literary historist placement, a thematic or formal contextualisation, possible. It is tantamount to saying that there is a space before the text (say, the conventional literary history) and a space after it (for instance, the receptive literary history of Jauss or Slawinski[29]) in which the text is reflected and rereflected and rerereflected and so on (the causes of the text and the transmissions of the text). I now am separated from all the virtual distances which give me my present, and this is the necessity of my being outside literature. There is the distance of Plekhanov's placement of *art for art's sake* at the moment of societal discontent, and the distance of the members of the Frankfurt School beholding art (Walter Benjamin's assessment of the emancipation of art from its "parasitical dependence on ritual" in an age of mechanical reproduction, Adorno looking *at* the negativeness of modern art with relation to modern society), the distance of Sartre's impassioned argument for freedom in every element of the writer-text-reader nexus enclosed into the situation of 1947[30] . . . The list of separations could carry on ad infinitum. The virtuality of the separation is also an admission of the literary subject's (mine now) inconstant position. The inconstant position I possess now, outside literature, is a product of the exhaustion of selecting the references which affirm their virtual distances (let me not confuse myself with the ambiguity and possibility of conceiving a Riffaterean "Super reader"[31]).

In other words, the "aesthetic discourse of literature" outside which I now find myself is an announcement of distance which allows "aesthetic" to be construed as such. When "aesthetic" is construed the distances, the contexts, the ideologies, the entire horizon of expectations around and expanding away from the text are visible, and the erotics or poetics of the text cease to be effective any longer. The inside of the aesthetic is unavailable from this standpoint, aesthetic is the construction within, so to say (as in Eagleton's *The Ideology of Aesthetics*). An aesthetic ideal is either irrelevant then, or pushed into a distant past (as for all neoclassicists), or projected in the distant future (William Morris's notion of handicraftsman as artist, Herbert Marcuse's aesthetic ethos[32]—most utopians).

3. Now that I am outside literature (however unstably located) do I find a greater degree of coherence than the Barthesian I? Does 2. above convey a sense of a coherent I? *I* am outside literature—what does that mean?

Of course, the manifold stratifications of literature through which I appear now are not less pluralistic than the Barthesian I. Whereas stratifications were an irony in the context of the Barthesian I, it is my sober experience now. Ingarden's four strata which are concretized by the reader's (writer's?) perspectival foreshortening are indeed gradually concretized. If I behold the organism of literature from outside I can perceive the strata appearing gradually, concretizing, through my persistently myopic or hypermetropic vision. These are serious observations. At no stage can I leave myself in the comfort of an ineffable self-signification: at every stage the outwardly construed text and its environment is apparent as distorted by my vision. Every stage is the nausea of my myopia/hypermetropia which cannot be corrected by any lens.

But that description is not complete, just as Ingarden's phenomenology of the text can't be deemed conclusive (despite the late appearance of the concept of concretization). A more devastating schism now appears inevitably. The reader-writer of literary studies (and I am reading-writing of literary studies) is torn asunder. Or, to be more accurate, literary studies itself is torn asunder in a manner which renders a complete change in the *sense* of (or agreement regarding) this term ("literary studies"). And therefore of the literary subject ("I") as well. Standing outside literature now I cannot refer to literature and the pursuit of literature as one composite of "literary studies"—an outside confirms an inside. The ever assimilative and infinite Text gives way to a perpetually realigned and proliferating (ideologically, contextually, etc.) text: i.e., respectively the inside and outside perceptions. I now call the unrealizable space of the inside the "aesthetic discourse of literature" from the retrospective/prospective outside, I think of it as a metaphysical space, I conceive of it as a space so subjective that it is beyond expression. In other words, I now defer an awareness of the *creation* of reading-writing constantly (relegating it to an inside which is evasive, beyond expression), and foreground the *criticism* of the apparently complete reading-writing. The inside (creation of reading-writing) of the organism of literature is unavailable to me now, and being outside I am fixed at a distance from that organism. I can only touch its surface, I cannot but see it whole and identify myself accordingly. This schism in the erstwhile "literary studies" means, as I said before, a change in the very *sense* of that term. In fact, a more complex duality of terms now seems obvious. The space of the inside, that which is called the "aesthetic discourse of literature" from my retrospective/prospective outside, which eludes me and yet, strangely, fascinates me because it is there on the other side of what I can touch—it gives shape to the organism which allows me to know myself (in all senses) from within: this is now "literature." It is the creative aspect. Whenever I cease to be a creator reveling in the poetics and erotics of the Text (as I have now), I am expelled into the retrospective/prospective outside, from where I can only touch the organism of literature: this is now "literary criticism" or "literary studies." That is why Wordsworth speaking of "recollection in tranquillity" is an acceptable critic when he says it, and Lawrence a creator (with a dream) who is not being critical when he speaks of writing a "poetry of the immediate moment." I can either be a creator of literature or I can be a literary critic or student of literature. There is no middle ground on the outside of literature, that is all that this text can say.

The schism is well recognized and explained elsewhere. Such recognitions and explications need to be placed in the environment where they appear for the full import to become available. I refer to recognitions and explications such as Pierre Macherey's:

> [. . .] either literary criticism is an art, completely determined by the pre-existence of a domain, the literary works, and finally reunited with them in the discovery of their truth, and as such it has no autonomous existence; or, it is a certain form of knowledge, and has an object, which is not a given but a product of literary criticism. To this object literary criticism applies a certain effort of transformation. Literary criticism is neither the imitation nor the facsimile of the objects; it maintains a certain separation between knowledge and its objects. If knowledge is expressed in discourse, and is applied to discourse, this discourse must by its nature be different from the object which it animated in order to talk about it.[33]

The "certain separation between knowledge and its objects": but both knowledge and its objects in this case are, as Macherey points out, discourse (literary discourse). From the outside of literature, from the perspective of literary criticism or literary studies (my anterior/posterior perspective now), the inside of literature, the inexplicable area behind "aesthetic discourse", hides a distant subject (now "other") as well. The discourse (knowledge) about a discourse (object) may not be an imitation or a facsimile, but the separation has in it the anxiety of a confusion of that sort. I now, therefore, carefully try to exteriorize that I, from which there was a wrenching apart, a violent thrust, by giving it the sign of the "other" (author, narrator, reader, etc.). This is the difference between the Barthesian reader (always *I*) and, say, the reader of reader-response theory (*I* becoming "other"). The latter is the constant surrender of the subjectivity of the reader to the otherness of the reader: Fish reading *Paradise Lost* to the "informed reader" reading; Iser reading *Tristram Shandy* to the "implied reader" reading; Riffaterre reading *Les Chats* to the "superreader" reading; Norman Holland's experience of reading to the psychology of the reader.[34] This is I now outside literature quelling the echo of the distant I inside literature by trying to exteriorize and silence it as the "other," by giving it a sign of the "other." The need to exteriorize and silence as "other" is the containment within the horizon of expectations within which the text is now placed: the appearance of the notion of community in reader-response theory is never a surprise but a necessity (hence David Bleich's "classroom," Fish's "interpretive community"[35]). The schism of literary criticism/studies and literature needs to be reaffirmed to overcome the anxiety of standing outside literature, to announce the outside of literature itself. All those who thrust themselves there reiterate it, as Macherey does, as Terry Eagleton does[36] . . . and so on.

4. Why anxiety when one is safely outside literature? Why reaffirm the obvious?

I suppose literature exerts a sort of gravitational pull, a force that threatens to suck me up into the very center of the organism of literature. It is marked by lines of reference which bind me to the organism and the manner in which my movements subtly change the shape of the organism. These place me, and yet to retain my place I have to resist them. I try to withstand the attraction of literature. I try to do so by standing very still so that no inadvertent movement of mine would affect the shape of literature or by keeping such movements rigidly controlled. These are difficult. I am always in the field of literature, so to say, and I am seldom successful in standing still or controlling my movements (and therefore the shape of literature) sufficiently. There is responsibility involved in my position. I have to be sensitive to the implications of what I do. And yet I cannot help but do something which will influence, however indiscernibly, the flexible organism of literature since I am in its field. The organism of literature is a bit like an amoeba with only partially voluntary movement, and partially involuntary movement which is controlled by external volition. If I thrust myself violently, as I did from the inside, to tear myself away from literature (even its outside) I would cease to be *I* any longer—I would cease to speak in this space, this space would be silent. If I pretend to look at other organisms, the organism of philosophy, the organism of physics, I find that these have become, like me, objects in the field of literature. However hard I try to enter their fields I fail because their fields fail to manifest themselves. I realize that only a violent thrust which bars me from this space where I speak would render me capable of discerning those other fields. All I can see and say within this space is the strange phenomenon of other organisms apparently subdued by the field of literature; inevitably whatever I try to say about physics and philosophy are literary discourses of physics or literary discourses of philosophy. They never escape the space. They might escape the space of the field, but not without violence, not without silencing literature first. Interdisciplinarity seems potential but evades practice, slips away from the grasp.

With that multiplication of metaphor I should draw myself to a close now and here. I do not wish to mince words. What has emerged here is this: whether I construe my subjectivity as inside literature (in an expansive and assimilative Text, in an aesthetic discourse), or whether I construe my subjectivity outside literature (in a realigning and proliferating Text, splitting the creator's discourse from the critic's), I am inescapably in the cautious text of literature. The cautious text of literature emanates from me, the literary subject, however and wherever (inside or outside) I present myself.

The Third Cautious Text

On Not Being a Scientist

1. I am not a scientist. This statement is not an awareness of difference, it is a knowledge of complete exclusion. I am not outside science as I may be outside literature. My being outside literature defines me, I am inevitably in the field of literature, each of my gestures affects the shape of literature. None of these happen when I believe I am beholding science. The only attraction I feel towards the organism of science, the only conviction in my ability to affect something there that I can entertain, are the ones that are bound to be thwarted. I am constantly reminded that what I perceive to be science is a kind of mirage, generated from the subject-position which I occupy in exclusion from science (the conceptual persona, the Barthesian I, I now outside literature). This mirage vanishes before the scientist's petulance, the scientist's rejection of the "validity" of my perception, the scientist's rejection of the "usefulness" of my perception, the scientist's inability to see my mirage or hear my joyous exclamation. More importantly, I am excluded by the constant activity of the scientist which he/she is at a loss for words to explain, or which is explained only at the cost of losing comprehensiveness, wholeness, and "beauty," a fractured explanation. The oasis of science is always just outside my ken, I can only grasp at the mirage which repeatedly slips away. My thirst is the impossibility of an interdisciplinarity which I hope to extend to a scientist. One either is a scientist or is not a scientist and I am not a scientist.

Sometimes scientists explain their pursuits for the "common enthusiast," they offer popular or simplified versions of their achievements which are actually as much a withholding as a giving.[37] This is more a recognition of the reader-writer as banned from the oasis of science than a reaching out to him/her. Sometimes, very rarely, scientists can be goaded into responding to the literary person or the philosopher (the "I"s), to their curiosity and their assertions, but the result is not actually a response. This is a reminder of their deafness (or is it a mutual deafness?). An irate clash of two "I"s which are confusingly demarcated by the same slim signifier and which are too different to even accept the other as the other. The impatience and dismissiveness which mark such encounters is inevitable. The following exchange (a misnomer) between Albert Einstein and Rabindranath Tagore is characteristic. (I do not explore the invisible mediations of the "note-taker" or commentator in the following quotation):

> *E:* "There are two different conceptions about the nature of the universe—the world as a unity dependent on humanity, and the world as reality independent of the human factor.
>
> *T:* "The world is a human world—the scientific view of it is also that of a scientific man. Therefore, the world apart from us does not exist; it is a relative world, depending for its reality upon our consciousness."
>
> A little later Einstein took up the point again:
>
> *E:* "Truth, then, or beauty, is not independent of man?"
>
> *T:* "No."
>
> *E:* "If there were no human beings any more, the Apollo Belvedere no longer would be beautiful?"
>
> *T:* "No."
>
> *E:* "I agree with regard to this conception of beauty, but not with regard to truth."
>
> *T:* "Why not? Truth is realised through men."
>
> Here, according to a later account by the note-taker, there was a long pause. Then Einstein spoke again very softly:
>
> "I cannot prove my conception is right, but that is my religion."
>
> After some further discussion—in which Einstein asserted, "I cannot prove, but I believe in the Pythagorean argument, that the truth is independent of human beings"—Einstein became concrete: "The mind acknowledges realities outside of it, independent of it. For instance, nobody may be in this house, yet that table remains where it is."
>
> *T:* "Yes, it remains outside the individual mind, but not outside the universal mind. The table is that which is perceptible by some kind of consciousness we possess."
>
> *E:* "If nobody were in this house the table would exist all the same, but this is already illegitimate from your point of view, because we

cannot explain what it means, that the table is there, independently of us. Our natural point of view in regard to the existence of truth apart from humanity cannot be proved, but it is a belief which nobody can lack—not even primitive beings. We attribute to truth a superhuman objectivity. It is indispensable for us—this reality which is independent of our existence and our experience and our mind—though we cannot say what it means."

T: "In any case, if there be any truth absolutely unrelated to humanity, then for us it is absolutely non-existing."

E: "Then I am more religious than you are!"
(Here, said the note-taker, Einstein "exclaimed in triumph.")[38]

I have quoted this exchange at length because it subverts its form of exchange by not being an exchange at all; it explores the juxtaposition of two discrete discourses which only manage to exclude each other. The following are the positions which seem to elucidate the differences, but actually comprehend two separate and uncomprehending discourses which are inevitably at cross purposes.

a. Einstein makes two related statements about ways of *conceptualising* the world ("a unity dependent on humanity," "reality independent of the human factor"). Neither concept makes any fundamental difference to Einstein's *world:* it manifests itself to him as a scientific phenomenon irrespective of either concept. In that sense, Einstein's world *is* independent of how it is conceived. Or, simply, Einstein's world *is.* To say "world" doesn't immediately or necessarily indicate how it is conceived.

Tagore makes one statement *about* the world ("This world is a human world"). This is a qualified statement regarding the world: not about *conceiving* the world, but about Tagore's *world* itself. The conceiving is therefore not an independent operation but contained within the very enunciation of "world." To say "world" is to say it is conceived by humans.

In other words, Einstein and Tagore do not understand what the other means by "world." There are two distinct semantic units used here (Einstein's "world" and Tagore's "world") though it appears as one lexical unit (simply "world").

b. Einstein picks two terms which can *qualify* his world: "truth" and "beauty." He is inclined to see them as independent of the different ways of conceiving the world too. These could say something *about* his world. Einstein is not sure that "beauty" is entirely independent of conceptualization (the scientific notion of beauty is given below in Steven Weinberg's terms) so he concedes the point—though he clearly begins by implying that both "truth" and "beauty" should be independent of concept. Einstein is quite sure that "truth" however is: for Einstein "truth" is the quality of the unqualifiable Einstein's world, it is that which makes it independent of concept.

Tagore sees beauty and truth as *products* of his world which is, in its very positing, an emanation of its conceptualization; which is already qualified by its humanness. Because Tagore's world is conceived can "beauty" and "truth" become possible.

In other words, Einstein's "beauty" and "truth" bear no connotative resemblance to Tagore's "beauty" and "truth," except in bearing the same denotative significations.

c. Einstein's "table" is *equivalent* to his world: it *is*, irrespective of how it is conceived. Einstein expresses his indifference to modes of conception as an indifference to human presence, which is misleading. Einstein is not saying that human presence is excluded from his world, Einstein is merely asseverating that it is irrelevant to his world. This becomes clear when he paradoxically claims "our natural point of view" (same as conceptualization surely) as the justification for his belief. His point is that none of this matters to his scientific explorations of his world, which just *is*, like the table whether it is seen or not.

Tagore's "table" is *within* his world. Since the world is conceived, the table within has to be conceived as well. Since the world is not an individual's conception, the table within it cannot be a purely individualistic conception either (hence the unfortunate metaphysical term "universal mind"). One could say, Tagore accepts the initial view which leads to Husserl's search for pure essences but not the possibility of an actual realisation of pure essences.

To put it otherwise, Tagore's "table" cannot be found where Einstein situates his, and vice versa.

d. Einstein's final triumphant exclamation is the irate rejection of exchange, the resounding deafness of science, the serene enclosure of science on which no Tagore can hope to make a dent however consistent and persuasive he may be. The quotation demonstrates the indifference of science to Tagore's world and the impregnability of Einstein's world to Tagore's curiosity. Politeness no doubt created the illusion of exchange. There is no exchange: Einstein and Tagore are, so to say, worlds apart.

But are these fair observations? Could it not be argued that in the quoted exchange neither Einstein nor Tagore are speaking *as* scientist or *as* poet? They are perceived as such popularly, they have received sufficient recognition in their fields by this time to justify their being perceived as such, they are speaking before an audience (the invisible notetaker is of the audience) in that capacity, and they meet as scientist and poet. And yet, as far as the dialogue goes, it might be suggested that they are not at that moment representative practitioners of science and literature respectively; they are making, however unsuccessfully, "common ground." This might be regarded as philosophical ground, not scientific or literary. This is the meeting, it could be asserted, of Einstein's post-Machian naive positivism (the navetê of his arguments is apparent when the philosophical debate on this issue—on sense, sense data, sensibilia—in Bertrand Russell's and J. L. Austin's works, or between Machian socialists and Marxist-Leninists, is considered), and Tagore's odd (or perhaps not so odd) amalgam of mysticism, liberal humanism, and German idealism. It is not, to put the argument in other words, a debate between scientist and litterateur; it is a debate between two philosophical points of view.

And yet I have no hesitation in maintaining that despite these arguments the quotation presents precisely the characteristics of an exchange between scientist and nonscientist. The point is in the dialogue of cross-purposes, in the fact of there being no exchange, in, so to say, Einstein's deafness or refusal to understand. Einstein simply refuses to understand Tagore's position though Tagore actually wins the argument; Tagore corners Einstein to the extent of the latter's admitting he can't prove his assertion. It is that deafness which is outside the realm of a purely philosophical debate. It is asserted with the entire force of their respective standings as scientist and nonscientist. There are plenty of acknowledgements of this in the quotation. Tagore brings in the "man of science" in a deliberate fashion fairly early. Einstein concedes Tagore's point regarding "beauty" with an air of deferring to Tagore's authority in aesthetic matters. Much more concretely, Einstein's sense of *doing* science, speaking for the *practice* of science, comes through most emphatically when he admits that positivism is his "religion," an act of faith. Philosophy doesn't accept faith qua philophical argument, nor does a *theory* (philosophy) of science allow faith within its discourse; but the *practice* of science does stick religiously to its empiricist paradigms.

Who has presented that analysis of the illusory exchange between Tagore and Einstein? I, the nonscientist, of course. I now. What I have said makes no difference to the happening of science.

My presentation of Einstein's views is the presentation of my inability to enter Einstein's world, is my resignation to seeing nothing but Einstein's refusal to qualify his world (as independent from conceptualization). I perhaps circumvent the confusions of Tagore's perspective (of using the same word differently) but I am as excluded as Tagore from the science of Einstein's world. And Einstein as excluded from the literature of Tagore's world, or mine. The exclusion is complete, even a discussion of the exclusion is unnecessary, is a polite gesture rather than a hope of reconciliation, is an irritatingly polite gesture. When the lack of necessity is recognized, is posited, irritation flares up momentarily: the irritation and the abrasiveness with which this exclusion is maintained by the scientist. This is made apparent to the nonscientist (I now) rarely but it is clearly put sometimes. Particularly clearly put when the scientist makes the fractured effort of speaking out to the "common enthusiast." It is the irritation which Steven Weinberg expresses regarding philosophy which is apparently pertinent to science:

> This is not to deny all value to philosophy, much of which has nothing to do with science. I do not even mean to deny all value to the philosophy of science, which at its best seems to me a pleasing gloss on the history and discoveries of science. But we should not expect it to provide today's scientists with any useful guidance about how to go about their work or about what they are likely to find.[39]

The irritation behind this statement is not the spurt of stubbornness with which the spoilt boy who asks "why?"[40] refuses to be sidetracked: the spoilt boy who insistently asks "why?" also rationalizes his insistent want and therefore the space for answers which do not satisfy. Philosophy is the answer which cannot satisfy the scientist who follows the path of the why, privileges a certain sense of "why"[41] (not "where" or "when" or "what" or the other senses of "why," which would allow philosophy or literature to intervene). Philosophy or literature are always evasions. "Beauty" and "truth" are the functions of that certain sense of why: the instinct of symmetry and simplicity which gives shape to the desire of the scientist: the answer to all "whys," a final theory.[42] The scientist doesn't wonder what is "truth" and "beauty," the scientist knows that the answer to the "why" which will satisfy is "beautiful" and "truthful." If the scientist didn't know this, if a scientist didn't insistently ask "why" in a certain sense, if a scientist strayed into the path of the "what"/"where"/

"when"/other senses of "why," he/she would cease to be a scientist. Anyone who asks "why" in the scientific sense and apprehends "beauty" and "truth" accordingly would be a scientist, reach the oasis and forget the mirage.

To say "this is science" (which is the tendency of my observations here) is irrelevant to the scientist. Science is (to affirm the tendency of my observations) the soaking up in the "why" which doesn't allow for the "what" that would allow me to say, "This is science." A scientist does science. The scientist responds with exasperation to those who are able to say "this is science" without being soaked up in the "why," when these thinkers make themselves heard. The scientist hears them rarely, and responds even more infrequently. Weinberg does. And others sometimes in odd spaces, when the scientist is called upon to do more than science, more than a fractured rendition of science for the "common enthusiast."

The literary student and the philosopher understand the difference of science. The conceptual I of Deleuze and Guattari sees the impenetrable plane of undefined coordinates of science, the Barthesian I cannot conceive the desire of the scientific text and cannot comprehend the transparency of the scientific text, and I outside literature feel no attraction from the organism of science and see no way to affect its shape. But that is an understatement. I, not being a scientist, feel the prudish turning away of science, a force shield of rejection, a deafness and a blindness which (despite my difference) is a turning away, rejection. This rejection fascinates, and I look closer at the rejection of science. I try to embrace it but inevitably fail. Literary studies in all its heterogeneity and complexity reaches towards scientific ideas (the concept of time in narrative, psychoanalysis in literary criticism, science provides metaphors, reconstructs canons, etc.[43]) but in this reaching out nothing *scientific* happens. It's all literature, within or without. There is no attraction from science to meet the reaching out of literature. This is the condition of my not being a scientist or, more aptly perhaps, this is the condition of my relation to literature.

Perhaps the philosopher feels the rejection more powerfully, at least expresses it more powerfully at times. I, not a scientist, can see the conceptual persona of the philosopher reach out towards science, I feel the *emotion* of the reaching out and the strength of that rejection . . . say, in Althusser's *Philosophy and the Spontaneous Philosophy of the Scientist.* But Althusser's conceptual persona, admittedly not a scientist, presents a critique which undercuts the emotional drama of this rejection; which, in other words, actually addresses the emotion. That is a sophisticated point of view which I, in Althusser's wake, address below. The emotional drama is exposed, so to say, when the conceptual persona who is not a scientist attempts to expose science.

2. In addressing the "whatness" of science, i.e, in addressing the philosophy of science, the ability to affect science is surrendered. Consider Karl Popper and Thomas Kuhn, both of whom, in contrary ways, engage with the "What is science?" question. But why do I turn to the Popper-Kuhn debate yet again? Why not reach outside the cliché—reach into the less stereotyped philosophy-of-science ventures of Rudolf Carnap, Carl Hempel, or Ernest Nagel in the logical analysis of scientific method camp (like Popper) or the history of science based examinations of scientific method as in N. R. Hansen and Paul Feyerabend (like Kuhn)? Or perhaps try to present a thematic-encyclopaedic view of issues in the philosophy of science: tackling realism and antirealism in scientific theorization, the issue of constructive empiricism, pragmatic truth, Bayesianism, etc.? Once again *I* am in danger of trapping myself in the cautious text of philosophy, in this case the philosophy of science. I can talk about philosophy and science or literature and science but not exclusively from the midst of a philosophical discourse or a literary discourse. The point of this section is not what I *am* but what I *am not.* I am not a scientist. This admission of *not being* is best located, not firmly in the camp of the philosopher of science or the litterateur of science (for reasons I clarify below), but on the fringe of my negativeness. My negativeness is marked by the renovation of clichés—so Popper and Kuhn. What follows is not so much about the issues raised by Popper and Kuhn ré science as about their own dissociation from the praxis of science.

Both Karl Popper and Thomas Kuhn engage with the "What is science?" question and provide two models which are perceived as being contending models. Popper accepts scientific enquiry as an ideal model of the pursuit of knowledge.[44] As his body of works unravel the reader-writer finds Popper's "I" asserting himself more emphatically. Popper gradually clarifies his position by designating his role as within philosophy and in relation (usually by opposition) to philosophers. There is a growing egotism as Popper moves from, say, the statemental *The Logic of Scientific Discovery* to the reassertive *Objective Knowledge* to the autobiographical *Conjectures and Refutations.* The growing egotism is the gradual realization of the opaqueness of the ego (the conceptual persona) within the transparent text of conjecture and testability (ostensibly scientific). It takes the shape of a disenchantment with his readers-writers who do not hear him and do not respond as he expects—but he locates the ego by identifying the readers-writers as predominantly philosophers and only rarely scientists. This gradual assertiveness of the opaque self, which is always incongruous in his transparent text, which always textualizes itself on the periphery of the text, reveals the emotion of the reaching out to science and the rejection of science. The rejection of science is not an unambiguous shake of the head, it is a turning away, an indifference which seems to withdraw the object from Popper's scrutiny.

Kuhn in *The Structure of Scientific Revolutions* is the philosopher who begins at the point where he withdraws from the doing of science, surrenders his identity as scientist, and invites the rejection and indifference of science. There is a sort of martyrdom in this, an air of the missionary who moves away from the precincts of Christendom and finds himself "going native" in some exotic land. Kuhn's is the conceptual persona of the hero.

> Those conceptions [held previously as a theoretical physicist] were ones I had previously drawn partly from scientific training itself and partly from a long-standing avocational interest in the philosophy of science. Somehow, whatever their pedagogic utility and their abstract plausibility, those notions did not fit the enterprise that historical study displayed. Yet they were and are fundamental to many discussions of science, and their failures of verisimilitude therefore seemed thoroughly worth pursuing. The result was a drastic shift in my career plans, a shift from physics to history of science and then, gradually, from relatively straightforward historical problems back to the more philosophical concerns that had initially led me to history.[45]

The shift of Kuhn's "I" through the boundaries of history and philosophy are established by *his* turning away from the practice of science, being a scientist. His turning away should not be mistaken for a volitional act. That the turning away is located in the self is heroic enough. Kuhn's "I" *has to* turn away from science once the scientific perspective has been dislocated; Kuhn's "I" has to be cut adrift by the questions which he poses himself; and the description above is one of being adrift (but righteously so if one ceases to be a scientist). Clearly, in asking "What is science?" and trying to answer it Kuhn had, in that context, lost science.

The most familiar (to their readers-writers) concepts associated with Popper and Kuhn regarding science are also the concepts which render science inaccessible to their conceptual personae and the philosophical space which they therefore occupy. The practice of science shifts from the pursuit of scientific knowledge (perpetually in process towards a hypothetical final theory) to the dynamic interrelationship of discrete examples. By their quality of pastness (and therefore projected futureness) the examples of the practice of science are left with no relation to the practice of science, which is perpetually in process. The interpolation of the dynamic relations between the examples are the prerogative of the person who believes he/she beholds science but is not a scientist. The interpolation of dynamic relations locates the conceptual persona of the philosopher (therefore non-scientist), the "I" of Popper and Kuhn, both in terms of the absolute exclusiveness of science (from not-science) and in terms of the inadequacy of the area they occupy to intervene in science.

The most familiar concepts . . . these are probably Popper's concept of falsifiability and Kuhn's concept of the scientific paradigm.

Popper's concept of falsifiability is also his "solution" to Hume's problem of induction:

> I formulated Hume's logical problem of induction as follows:
>
> L_1 Can the claim that an explanatory universal theory is true be justified by 'empirical reasons'; that is, by assuming the truth of certain test statements or observation statements (which, it may be said, are 'based on experience')?
>
> My answer to the problem is the same as Hume's: No, we cannot; no number of true test statements would justify the claim that an explanatory universal theory is true.
>
> But there is a second logical problem, L_2, which is a generalization of L_1. It is obtained from L_1 merely by replacing the words 'is true' by the words 'is true or that it is false':
>
> L_2 Can the claim that an explanatory universal theory is true or that it is false be justified by 'empirical reasons'; that is, can the assumption of the truth of test statements justify either the claim that a universal theory is true or that it is false?
>
> To this problem, my answer is positive: Yes, *the assumption of the truth of test statements sometimes allows us to justify the claim that an explanatory universal theory is false.*[46] [Popper's italics]

This mode of stating Hume's problem (compare this with Hume's own statement, or even with Popper's earlier statement of Hume's logical problem[47]) is a response, he claims, to Bertrand Russell's fear that Humean scepticism would make science impossible. His mode of persuading the reader-writer of this theory of falsifiability is to show how it works in science by drawing on examples in *The Logic of Scientific Discovery.* Popper's theory of falsifiability as a solution to the problem of induction is dependent on the understanding of the practice of science in examples, on being able to relate these examples in terms of *his* theory, which is his mirage of the conviction that in the oasis of science science works in practice. In this process the exclusiveness of science is inadvertently revealed because, of course, his solution to the Humean problem is not a solution at all. In fact, he doesn't address the Humean problem; he demonstrates the exclusiveness of science by showing that it doesn't need to address the Humean problem at all. The Humean problem would problematize the very ability to propose "universal explanatory statements," to attribute "truth" or "falsity." The Humean problem has an implicit conceptual persona of the madman in it, at complete odds with all reason. The "solutions" that can be offered are always after the fact of the concept of the problem which is what renders the notion of "solutions" dubious: Humean scepticism draws responses of opposition, not solutions. This response could be Hume's psychological observations, could be Ayer's contention that induction constitutes rationality and the problem is self-defeating, could even be Saul Kripke's Wittgensteinian "form of life" to a Wittgensteinian-Humean scepticism.[48] The practice of science is indifferent to Hume's problem of induction, it proposes explanatory statements despite this problem, it finds and surrenders conviction despite this problem; in accepting the practice of science as seen in examples Popper shows its complete exclusion from the realm of the philosophy of inductive explanation/problematization. Inspite of this he refers to the Humean problem to make his exclusion from science clear: this can only be an (inadvertent?) admission of the inadequacy of the space he occupies. This inadequacy gradually becomes clearer by the assertiveness of the "I" who fills in the space of the failure to address science except as exclusive, the space left by the failure to acquire a space from where the practice of science can be entered. In other words, the inadequacy of not being a scientist, or the inadequacy of being the philosopher who asks "What is science?" So, "I" propose a theory of testability, a theory of verisimilitude, "I" refuse to be seen as a positivist, to consider the question of meaning, "I" don't believe in the instrumentality of science, the end of science . . . "I" keeps speaking persistently and hopelessly amidst the echoes of the space which "I" occupy.

Kuhn's concept of scientific paradigms is introduced as different from "established usage":

> In its established usage, a paradigm is an accepted model or pattern, and that aspect of its meaning has enabled me, lacking a better word, to appropriate 'paradigm' here. But it will shortly be clear that the sense of 'model' and 'pattern' that permits the appropriation is not quite the one usual in defining 'paradigm.' In grammar, for example, '*amo, amas, amat*' is a paradigm because it displays the pattern to be used in conjugating a large number of Latin verbs, e.g., in producing '*laudo, laudas, laudat.*' In this standard application, the paradigm functions by permitting the replication of examples any one of which could in principle serve to replace it. In a science, on the other hand, a paradigm is rarely an object for replication. Instead, like an accepted judicial decision in the common law, it is an object for further articulation and specification under new or more stringent conditions.[49]

Withdrawing the established usage of paradigm gives the word a character which is specific to science and definitive only through the illustration of scientific practice. This illustration takes place in terms of numerous examples from the discovery of oxygen to the discovery of quantum mechanics. The concept of 'paradigm' gradually takes shape as the practice of science is seen in this retrospective view: the culture of normal science and paradigm-changing science is described, the interrelatedness of paradigms and the fluidity of paradigms is pondered, the limitations imposed by paradigms and the anxieties implicit in new paradigms is examined, the role of scientific education therein is observed. As the reader-writer progresses through the book paradigms defy definition (not a set of laws, not a catalogue of rules, not a compendium of dictates) and become the very shape of scientific practice: Kuhn's 'paradigm' takes a renewed shape because of its infinite assimilativeness of all examples of science, and its foregrounded difference from areas of practice which are not science (established usage). The likeness with judicial decision drawn in the above quotation loses tenability in this process: paradigms comprehend the very modus operandi of scientific formulation or affirmation which are, by being scientific, different from the nonscientific. If that was not the case Kuhn's paradigms would not be confined to science alone. 'Paradigm' simply signifies 'scientific practice': there is nothing one could do as the latter which is not referentiable as the former. And that is where the exclusion of the heroic "I" of Kuhn is located. To refer to an "act" is not to do the "act" in any sense, to say "scientific practice" has no implications in scientific practice, to assimilate all examples of scientific practice in saying "paradigm" is to remove any intervention in scientific practice as happening and to see an indifferent science which has always happened. The leaving of the oasis to finally see nothing but a mirage. Kuhn's voice merges into mine here, the voice of the person who is not, in this context, a scientist, who is rejected by the happening of science. Of course, Kuhn's "I", like me, knew this at the onset—as I had mentioned before it was *he* who turned away from science. But still there is emotion in this rejection, there is emotion in the realisation that a concept like 'paradigm' can have no implication for science (always disappointing the fascination of the not-scientist): and this emotion manifests itself in Kuhn's 1969 postscript to *The Structure of Scientific Revolutions.* The postscript is an attempted withdrawal of the term 'paradigm' from the infinite assimilativeness and scientific exclusiveness of the original usage mainly by affiliating it to an ancillary concept of discourse communities.[50] I take this to be an admission of the inadequacy of a scientific exemplar-based concept of paradigms. It seems to me that in the postscript the entire shape of the notion of 'paradigms' offered earlier is withdrawn to be replaced by a term which does not remain exclusively scientific, and therefore doesn't address the "What is science?" question any longer: the negation of the nonscientist fascinated by science.

3. The exclusiveness of science cannot be addressed except as exclusive. I can address the *exclusiveness of science* in those terms. I have here. I am not a scientist if I do that. I cannot answer the question "What is science?" but I can ask the question, I can recognize what the question involves, and in asking the question mark my difference, my own exclusion, by simply saying "I" in a recognisable manner. Not the "I"s that are disappointed by their scrutiny, who believe they have answered "What is science?" so that the scientist can hear and comprehend it and shape their practice accordingly. Science doesn't allow the question, only a mode of practice. The nonscientist can ask the question and fail to answer it, but also thereby announce his/her excluded space, announce him/herself as included somewhere else. I, who am not a scientist, may be the Barthesian I facing the scientific text; I now

outside literature can see the turning away of the organism of science which at best offers me the fractured communication from behind a shield of deafness; I the conceptual persona can mediate from a plane of immanence towards the concept that I am not a scientist:

> All *objective* knowledge of philosophy is in effect at the same time a *position within* philosophy, and therefore a Thesis in and on philosophy; that is why you felt, on the contrary, that *I could speak of philosophy in general only from a certain position in philosophy:* demarcating myself, by distancing myself from *other* existing positions. There is no objective discourse about philosophy that is not itself philosophical, and therefore a discourse based upon certain positions *within* philosophy.[51] [Althusser's italics]

This "I" is Althusser speaking to scientists about *Philosophy and the Spontaneous Philosophy of Scientists.* I refer to Althusser here without referring to the concepts (or theses) he presents in speaking thus to scientists—the thesis of the deception and appearance of ideology which is contained in an Althusserian Thesis that stretches beyond this particular text. I refer to Althusser only in the spirit in which he speaks to scientists as "I", a philosopher. Althusser addresses scientists with the assertion of not being a scientist, with the recognition of the scientist's rejection, by:

a. Understanding the scientist's presence with relation to him as a malicious presence, awaiting the philosopher's fall on the face;

b. Demonstrating the impenetrability of science and philosophy even when the scientist listens with positive interest, even when the scientist becomes a philosopher at a moment of crisis (which is always a surrender of science);

c. Denying interdisciplinarity as a working concept at all levels, because of its ideological expediency behind its assertion which deceives the actual working of disciplines;

d. By drawing a plane of philosophy which sees a spontaneous philosophy existing silently within science, which, though withdrawn from the "exploitation of science by philosophy" (and other similar interventions and exploitations), is itself a philosophical thesis.[52]

The constancy of the awareness of rejection, the raising of the rejection of science ré the nonscientist to the level of explicitness described above for Althusser (or for me, here), is a different drama from that of Popper's or Kuhn's. It is not a drama of sadness, of disappointments, of being set adrift. It is a drama (Althusser's when he talks to scientists, mine as I read-write this text) which finds a curiously comprehensive view of science in not being a scientist, in the very rejection of science, in its evasive practice, its petulance and irritation, its turning away.

The Bold Text

1. THE CAUTIOUS TEXTS ENDED ABRUPTLY. ARGUABLY, THE CAUTIOUS texts didn't end but cut themselves off from a possibly indefinite charting out of the autoconstruction of subject-positions within different disciplines. That is, disciplines which are inherently cautious, which cannot but produce some sort of cautious text, where "I" is the focal point of the disciplinary space and the view before "I" is always a disciplinary landscape which can expand indefinitely.

I am obviously in the midst of the bold text now. Only in the bold text can I stop worrying about my subject-position and start looking *at* the statements of cautious texts and their regressive and performative preoccupations. If I do that and throw caution to the winds I can (or assure myself that I can) actually withstand entrapping views which nevertheless expand indefinitely. Disciplines which cannot but find themselves in cautious texts, which cannot express themselves outside their precincts (or planes, or spaces—whichever is easier to visualize) can be put into perspective, thrown into relief, so to speak. In effecting this the bold text fulfils its boldness, finds in itself the region from where most disciplines can be construed as *out there,* as comparable, as presentable in terms of certain unities which permit comparison. These unities are discussed below. In this venture, in the very success of putting disciplines into perspective, the bold text:

a. Loses any relevance or understanding within the cautious texts: becomes unrecognisable, and certainly inexpressible, within the cautious texts; and

b. Might begin to present itself as a discipline in itself, a kind of discipline of disciplines, as in Emile Durkheim's sociology of knowledge, Michel Foucault's archaeology of knowledge, Clifford Geertz's ethnography of knowledge, etc., and as in institutional fora of history of ideas, critical theory, culture studies, social sciences, education, etc.

Further, sometimes when the bold text loses relevance or understanding within the cautious texts and construes itself as a discipline of disciplines, it does so in terms of a practice which is modelled on the enclosed and cohesive practice of science, which is indifferent to, in fact repels, the subject of the cautious text. And in doing so it excludes itself much as the discipline construed in the cautious text does. But more of that later.

Let me begin with the prerogative of the bold text: let me summarize what the preceding cautious texts have apparently stated. In doing this a region beyond the comprehension of the cautious texts will emerge, or, more accurately, the summary of the cautious texts in the bold text will become unrecognizable and inexpressible in the cautious texts. Let's try to summarize and see how this happens.

The cautious texts are focused on the subject-position of literary studies: "What am I?" asks the investigator of conditions of disciplinarity and interdisciplinarity in literary studies. In asking this it is implied that the subjectivity of the literary student is at stake; if that is understood the nature of the discipline of, and therefore the scope for interdisciplinariness in, literary studies would become evident. This leads to an investigation of different subject-positions of "I" as conceived in a disparate collection of sources and ostensibly owing allegiance to different disciplines which seem pertinent to the literary student. The sources seem to comprehend mainly texts of different branches of philosophy and literary theory. There is no explanation for this choice except perhaps the limitation of the investigator who is a student of literature. The fact that these seem pertinent to the literary student is enough to justify their selection. According to the investigator, the manner in which he/she interrogates "I" cannot be supplemented by texts outside the selections he/she can make and is aware of. Very well. The investigator starts with the obvious questioning and placing of the "I" in terms of philosophical expositions. It soon becomes apparent that philosophical expositions construe "I" only to reify an ever-assimilative and expanding discipline of philosophy and philosophical Being. The only escape from it which can be offered within its precincts is by a gimmick, the insertion of the a of *différance* which oddly enough can become "anterior" to Being and fray the margins of philosophy. But this still isn't an entry into the disciplinariness of the literary student, though *différance* undoubtedly possesses infinite potential in the attack on margins. But the margins have to be recognized. The investigator then shifts to tracing "I" in the investigative region where literature seems most closely aligned: the pleasure of reading, the erotics of reading, the very subjectivity of reading which withdraws the text from the instrumentality and dryness of science. In other words, he/she turns to the area which seems to be dominated by Roland Barthes. This is fruitful: to say "I" in the fluid manner of Barthes is tantamount to saying "I read-write, construe literature around me and am inevitably in literature." But does it suffice? The investigator obviously thinks not. How efficacious is this placement of the subject in literature for those who seem to stand outside literature, who write outside literature and nevertheless change the shape of literature? The subject of the outside literature is also literature, the investigator observes. He/she presents, through a series of metaphors, the idea that outsideness with regard to literature might imply a radical displacement within the discourse (the split of literature and literary studies, for instance) but is still dependent on the reification of "I" as literary subject. It becomes apparent that with the two broad subject-positions that can be occupied as a literary student, and given their fluidity, the margins of literary studies as a discipline become manifest. These margins are, it simultaneously appears, as exclusive and extensive within their enclosure as those of philosophy. As a final way of distinguishing the exclusiveness of the subject-positions which have been discerned, the different locations of "I" which are nevertheless all assimilative in their own terms, the investigator tries to place his/her "I" with regard to science. He/she begins with the realisation that this cannot be done except as excluded from science, i.e., as "I am not a scientist." The notion of the subject excluded from science itself becomes a position of differentiability of the discipline of science, allocates a margin to science. The interrogation of science in terms of literary subjects and philosophical subjects (particularly philosophical subjects in the preceding cautious text) clarifies this.

In the course of this investigation of the cautious texts the following probably become clear to the investigator.

a. The trace of the subjectivity of "I" is a useful way of seeing how the discipline of literary studies is construed. This is different from philosophy and excluded from science, and one can surmise that the examination of difference and exclusion can be extended to other disciplines as well.

b. Conceived in this manner all disciplines can deal with all conceivable facets of knowledge but only as that discipline. Everything that can be conceived by a philosopher would be a philosophical concept, everything that can be conceived by a literary student becomes a literary area, and so on. From the point of view of a philosophical or literary or nonscientific "I" there is nothing that is not philosophical or literary . . . and if there is it ceases to be comprehensible. Or, putting it otherwise, from the position of the literary, philosophical, etc. "I"s their disciplines are endlessly assimilative and stretch in all directions.

c. This follows from b: there is no subject-position, no "I", from which interdisciplinarity is possible. Disciplines are impenetrable, fluid, assimilative, enclosed and open at the same time, in a manner which allows no space between them, no comparative standpoint which can perceive a space between. In the cautious text interdisciplinarity is an impossibility.

That's the summary of the cautious texts. This is obviously not a cautious text. This is the bold text; the contradiction in the statement of point c at the end of the summary leaps to the eye. It is the culmination of a subtext which has in fact done precisely what point c doesn't permit. It has apparently leapt across the boundaries of disciplines, it has apparently construed a text without admitting to a literary, philosophical, nonscientific, etc., subject. The cautious texts proceeded by fixing the subject inescapably within a discipline, and each moment of transfer was a moment of violence, an erasure of the other discipline, even an inconceivability of the other discipline. But not so in the summary of the cautious texts in the bold text. This is possible because in its reading-writing the assumptions of the bold text are adopted and transmitted. The assumptions of the bold text are easily delineated:

i. The subject is always held at bay, is continuously pushed away by an inflection of grammar. This does not necessarily imply that the subject is invisible, though that may well be the case. Generally it is accepted that even if I feel reluctant to say it, and take recourse to "*it* is seen . . ." or "*one* sees . . .," it is in fact *I* who does say it. But I am not the subject any longer around whom the discourse is centered, from where the text expands, from which the disciplinary margins can gradually become apparent. On the contrary I am constructed by the discourse, posited by the text, placed by the discipline. I am not the subject who sees (perhaps I do, but the bold text boldly disregards this), I am the subject seeing myself as object. I am an objective subject. I am a formulated subject. I am held at bay by my own gaze on myself. I see myself because the bold text interposes as a mirror. This mirror, I have said, is an inflection of grammar. It is in fact the third person of the bold text. I may appear to speak as first person, but the bold text wields itself so that a third person is implicit in "I". So, in the summary, "I" and the "investigator" become indistinguishable. ii. The summary of the cautious texts in the bold text assumes that the cautious texts reveal across their frames certain constants, some continuities, specific unities. It is suggested that the subject-position itself is such a continuous factor in the cautious texts, whereas the reader-writer of the cautious texts is aware that the subject is in fact the most disjunctive of all factors, discontinuous to the degree of reconstituting disciplines at different points of its assertion of self. The summary suggests that the cautious texts follow a search, develops with a purpose (comprehending disciplinarity and interdisciplinarity in literary studies), whereas in reading-writing the cautious texts one recognizes different purposes depending on which subject is manifest, which disciplinary voice is adhered to. The summary suggests that the concept of disciplinarity (and therefore interdisciplinarity) is the unifying factor in the cautious text, that in the cautious texts a kind of disciplinary concept is created whereby interdisciplinarity seems impossible. But the reader-writer of the cautious texts has experienced different disciplinary concepts, and when interdisciplinarity was denied at different points in the text there was no recognition of repetition or reiteration. The bold text might insinuate that reading-writing is the great continuity of the cautious texts. But the reader-writer of the cautious texts knows that in the cautious text he/she wasn't one reader-writer but many. The cautious texts have many readers-writers coherent with many subjects, who are compressed into an individual objective subject by the assumption of continuity in the bold text. It is this compression of the individual objective subject that allows for the first time the possibility of interdisciplinarity. Interdisciplinarity is permissible only in the bold text, is in fact entailed by the assumptions of the bold text.

Have I then, in initiating the bold text, in summarizing the cautious texts, transcended the disciplinary space? Have I found a metadisciplinary space where all disciplines are, as the subject is, held at bay: where interdisciplinarity is not only possible but imperative? That is one way of putting it. The more recognizable view would be that this is a space which constitutes itself as new disciplines. In these new disciplines a metadisciplinary role is adopted, the bold text becomes its natural element—these could be identified as sociology, culture studies, history of ideas, education, critical theory, etc. These might adopt a metadisciplinary space, but the word "metadisciplinary" shouldn't be allowed to mislead the reader-writer. The bold text of these disciplines hides what the cautious texts reveal of different disciplines (the disjunctions, discontinuities, and instabilities). These disciplines are available to the penetrating investigation of disciplines construed through the cautious texts. In the same way that the bold text has summarized the cautious texts, the cautious texts can subsume the bold text.

2. The continuities, unities, constants which appear in metadisciplinary bold texts comprehend a range of research and contemplation which it would be impossible to summarize in this bold text. Arguably it isn't necessary either. The continuities, unities, constants allow a metadisciplinary methodology, a particular approach to the investigation and organization of knowledge as such, but do not contribute to the construction of the new or metadisciplinary discipline. If one says, for instance, that a mode of synthesis which is aligned to areas of social phenomena is to be found in the works of Karl Marx, Max Weber, Emile Durkheim, Karl Mannheim, etc. one doesn't thereby imply that they are all sociologists (i.e., are placed in a disciplinary space) because of the mode of synthesis. It would be generally agreed that they are all sociologists because they deal with social phenomena. Or conversely, if it is stated that Riffaterre and Lévi-Strauss based their studies on a structuralist frame of analysis this would not imply that they are placed in the same discipline. One would look for an *objective field* with regard to which the structuralist analysis is aligned.

In other words, the metadisciplinary areas which constitute themselves as new disciplines and naturally emerge in the bold text may have the appearance of being metadisciplinary by dint of certain continuities, constants, and unities which they accept, but these are not the criteria through which they appropriate their disciplinary status. The disciplinary status is appropriated and asserted through another assumption of the bold text: the objectification of the subject, the third person distancing of the first person, which implies a field of objects which subsumes the subject and becomes the focus of the discipline. The disciplines which are able to exert a metadisciplinary methodology constitute themselves as disciplines by aligning this methodology to a defined field of objects. The method which might permit us to realize the self-constitution of these metadisciplinary disciplines is that of discerning how the subject is surrendered to a field of objects. This in turn is best done by considering some instances of the perfect antithesis of the subject—the concept of the basic object, or (since the loaded term "object" might be misleading) the basic quanta to which these disciplines turn their gaze.

As illustrations of the above, and to continue from the above, the following (sufficiently disparate) descriptions of such quanta can be considered: Durkheim's notion of "social facts" (or Weber's notion of "action") in sociology and Foucault's notion of "statements" in his "archaeology" (which finds its special role by the interplay with "history of ideas" as a discipline).

a. Social facts

The third person "I" appears at the beginning of Durkheim's *The Rules of Sociological Method:* the bold text withdraws the voice which initiates the investigation of sociological method and relocates it as posterior to a field of sociological investigation.

> When I fulfil my obligations as brother, husband, or citizen, when I execute my contracts, I perform duties which are defined, externally to myself and my acts, in law and in custom. Even if they conform to my own sentiments and I feel their reality subjectively, such reality is still objective, for I did not create them; I merely inherited them through my education. [. . .] The system of signs I use to express my thoughts, the system of currency I employ to pay my debts, the instruments of credit I utilize in my commercial relations, the practices followed in my profession, etc., function independently of my own use of them. And these statements can be repeated for each member of society. Here, then, are ways of acting, thinking, and feeling that present the noteworthy property of existing outside the individual consciousness.[53]

The field of sociological enquiry which is anterior to the subject, which defines the subject, which empties the subject, which consumes the subject, cannot appear in a text which is regressive and performative, a cautious text. This text cannot say "I read-write this and therefore this exists"; on the contrary it maintains "I read-write this because it exists". The subject is defined, emptied, and consumed till only a surface remains, a surface without the core which makes a subject the point of emanation in disciplinary discourse. This is only a subject which can be *seen,* rather like Madam Merle's concept of human beings as shells in Henry James's *The Portrait of a Lady.*

But seen from where? Where are the eyes that see, the nonsubjective eyes? Somewhere anterior to "I"; these are not even sentient eyes. The gaze seems to emanate from *things:* things that populate and indeed construct the social world which contains (as inclusion and as confinement) the individual (all subjects). These construct every aspect of the world, are extensive of every aspect of the containment of the individual, and are given as "social facts." "Social facts," Durkheim maintains in his first methodological stipulation, should be treated as "things."[54] Social facts are, so to say, the quanta which constitute every facet of the humanistic disciplines. They are defined as that which contain (as inclusion and as confinement) the individual human being and therefore have to be the basic units, the quanta, which underlie the "objects" (different facets of human existence as expressed in the bold text) of all humanistic disciplines.

> *A social fact is every way of acting, fixed or not, capable of exercising on the individual an external constraint;* or again, *every way of acting which is general throughout a given society, while at the same time existing in its own right independent of its individual manifestations.*[55] [Durkheim's emphases]

This twofold definition of "social facts" comprehends the twofold connotation of containing the individual (all subjects): "constraint" is effective confinement; being "general throughout a given society" implies inclusion (deindividualization). "Social facts" are therefore the quanta that constitute the "objects" (as the bold text would have it) of all humanistic disciplines—language, wealth, kinship, politics, law, religion, education, etc., etc. If "social facts" are defined to become the "object" (the direct antithesis of the subject, now simply the contained individual) of a discipline like sociology, that discipline, naturally arrogates for itself a "metadisciplinary" role. Sociology becomes the discipline which mediates between all humanistic disciplines, sociology becomes the discipline of interdisciplinariness.

The nonsentient gaze of sociology, emanating from amidst those things, "social facts," might occasion some discomfort. The containing of the individual (all subjects) means the locus of intelligence has to shift elsewhere. This is a problem with no answer, this is the moment at which the boldness of the bold text is manifest. The boldness of proposing (because it is dangerous and because Durkheim permits the dangerous opening without demur) a concept of *représentation collective.*

There is another element in this process of the unraveling of the bold text of Durkheim's sociology which should be noted. It proceeds beyond the point at which the cautious texts abruptly cut themselves off. The cautious texts above drew a picture of the drama of the subject who is not a scientist, who looks at science and tries to understand science and in the process is inevitably repulsed by science. Science irritably turns away from the subject who says "I am not a scientist," and consolidates itself in the closure of its practice. The metadisciplinary sociological gaze, constituted as it is in the bold text, refuses this rejection. It does not say "I am not a scientist," it asserts "This is science." It does so however while looking at science, trying to understand it as a field of practice at a distance, modeling itself on the model of science which it can see whole. This is a paradox which the cautious text would find impossible to resolve: for the subject who is not a scientist the very act of looking at science, ascertaining its practice as a model, is to invite the indifference of science; even for the subject who was a scientist the attempt to do this propels him/her into the area of the nonscientist. In the bold text of sociology, however, this is irrelevant. The sociologist is *in* the practice of science, and simultaneously affirms this by standing *away* from science and using it as a model. There is no paradox in this. This is the shape of the bold text. In *The Rules of Sociological Method* the being in the practice of science is maintained by its own turning away from the nonscientific perspective (all the demystifications and emendations which Durkheim recommends with regard to past sociological practice); and the standing away from the model of science provides the rationale for the methodological recommendations which are made.

A more complex, though basically similar in so far as the constitution within the bold text goes, quanta approach in sociology is presented in Max Weber's concept of "action." The breadth of his preoccupations and the consistency (and inconsistencies) of his quanta-outwards construction render a detailed analysis of the build-up from "action" to "social action" to "economic action" and so on untenable here. However a cursory consideration of the definition of basic terms with which he introduces his *Economy and Society* would show the similarity to the quanta approach of Durkheim. Whereas Durkheim actually presents the surrender of the "I" to a third person usage, Weber begins with a third person "subject." The non-sentient gaze is not a problem—somehow it is resolved before the argument is initiated, with the announcement of the "subject" itself. There is no painful transition from "I" to subject-in-society. Weber casually begins with the "subject" and moves rapidly to subject-in-society. Weber's placement in the bold text is firmer. In a sense, Weber fills in the blank spot of Durkheim's thinking; he clarifies why the already third person "subject" is translatable in the bold text to the subject-in-society, whereas Durkheim leaps directly from the "I" to the subject-in-society without remarking the textual peculiarities of the intermediate process.

Consequently the process through which Weber develops his basic terms beginning with an already third person "subject" to the subject-in-society is also a process of the consolidation of the bold text. He begins with the bold text and goes on to affirm its boldness. There is no wrenching from the first person to the third person, there is simply a clarification of the rationalization between the third person singular and the third person collective (in Durkheim the collective consciousness was a dangerous assertion). This rationalization is done through the agency of the continuity and integrity of the term "action." "Action" is introduced at a stage of "subjective meaning" and "subjective interpretation" and then expanded out to the metadisciplinarity of sociological contemplation. The expansion process consists largely in the attribution of a progressively more definitive meaning to the term "action" (by fixing a norm of rationality from which deviations can be measured, by gradually moving out to the place of subjective meaning in a collective, by declaring the precision of the charting out of "ideal types" and "averages" of action, etc.[56]). One gradually realizes that the use of the term "action" to bridge the gap from the already third person subject to the subject-in-society is merely a gradual and friendly assertion of the underlying notion of continuities and unities which lies at the heart of the metadisciplinary bold text. The continuities in the sociological bold text is not merely a *result* of the construction from the quanta of "action" outwards, it is *contained in* the conception of the quanta of "action." Weber describes in the initial part of his *magnum opus* not merely the construction outwards from the quanta of "action" but also a progressive clarification of the implication of "action" in this process.

b. Statements

Foucault's *The Archaeology of Knowledge* possesses an even more complex positioning of the subject and of quanta than the above: a complexity which is an index of the gap of knowledge which separates them. This is, of course, a temporal gap, but that's only one element of it. It is also the gap of a realignment of (to use Foucault's terms) discursive formations, of the pulsing surfacing and drowning of the subject, of the reification and expansion of the objective space, of the loss and appearance and change of disciplines. Foucault's construction of his "archaeology" is still within the bold text (as we shall see) but a bold text which concedes a shape of knowledge which is against its nature: the text concedes the fractures in the shape of knowledge, the existence of discontinuities, ruptures, transformations. Foucault's bold text therefore teeters so precariously on the completeness and isolation of its autoconstruction, it piles itself up in such a brilliant expansion of self-qualification and amendment, that its fragility becomes apparent. If one of its bricks is removed the entire structure collapses. Foucault's text isn't quite regressive and performative as a cautious text would be but it stretches the self-awareness of the bold text to its limits. The compiled brilliance of this autoconstruction presents its own isolation, and becomes therefore a model of the simulacrum for Baudrillard.[57] It is, in other words, a construction which has to create its own evidence, its own analysis, its own base.

That is why the ostensible first person subject in Foucault's construction is the author, the signature which pulls together a Foucaultian Text—the writer of *Madness and Civilisation, The Order of Things,* and *The Birth of the Clinic* (these are brought to bear on *The Archaeology of Knowledge*), as of *Discipline and Punish,* and *The History of Sexuality.* But beyond gesturing towards the subject of the Foucaultian Text by reference, the force of the construction is to displace the subjectivity of the authorial "I", of subjectivity itself, through the delineation of quanta (this term itself has to take on more complex connotations in this context), or "statements." To lead towards what this entails I quote Deleuze on this point:

> [. . .] Foucault echoes Blanchot in denouncing all linguistic personology and seeing the different positions for the speaking subject as located within a deep anonymous murmur. It is within this murmur without beginning or end that Foucault would like to be situ-

> ated, in the place assigned to him by statements. And perhaps these are Foucault's most moving statements.[58]

The quanta position of statements seems implied in so far as Foucault begins with an assumption of their ubiquity in *The Archaeology of Knowledge.* In the vertical plane of the space of statements, i.e., when statements are seen to lead towards the construction of specific discourse formations, the straightforward quanta nature of statements appears to be accepted. It is only in the, so to say, horizontal plane of the space of statements, i.e., when statements are examined as general components of all discourse formations, that the problematics of the quanta nature of statements become apparent. Then, the continuities or unities in different discourse formations have to be accommodated in the space of statements, have to be rendered possible by the space that a concept of statements in discourse formations permits. It is observed then that the definition and description of statements effectively withdraws from the simplistic idea of a definitive, stable, basic quanta, the idea of the monad. A process of withdrawal is encountered: i.e., withdrawing the descriptive models of statements from grammar, logic, or contextual analysis which would encourage a monadic conceptualization.[59] Not that any of these descriptive models are considered irrelevant to statements, it's simply that none of them are seen to comprehend statements satisfactorily any longer. Statements become in a sense even more basic but less confined to *a* plane of discourse than the descriptive models of statements mentioned above (grammar, logic, etc.) would suggest; i.e., statements are liberated to accommodate disjunctions and ruptures that transcend the limitations of a discrete, or a segment of a discourse formation. This accommodative presentation of statements can be said to provide the *functional* aspect of Foucault's project.

The *substance* of statements is charted out in the examination of their enunciative function. According to Foucault the enunciative function of statements can be understood through the following observations:

a. Statements relate to a domain (which is different from the relation between signifier and signified, the proposition and its referent, the sentence and its meaning) which

> forms the place, the condition, the field of emergence, the authority to differentiate between individuals or objects, states of things and relations that are brought into play by the statement itself; it defines

the possibilities of appearance and delimitation of that which gives meaning to the sentence, a value as truth to the proposition[60];

b. The subject of the statement is not an author/individual but a vacant space which can be filled by different individuals, which can not, in fact, be fixed at any moment, but in which "the position of the subject can be assigned"[61];

c. The enunciative function of a statement, which raises the domain to which the statement relates, can operate in this fashion because of the existence of associated domains; and

d. Statements have a material existence, and

> The rule of materiality that statements necessarily obey is [..] of the order of the institution rather than of the spatio-temporal localization; it defines *possibilities of reinscription and transcription* (but also thresholds and limits), rather than limited and perishable individualities.[62]

Each of the above observations are predicated by a series of evasions. Evasions seem to be characteristic of Foucault's style (beautiful, most of his critics agree), and these evasions are to avoid the onslaught of expectations engendered by the reader-writer of bold texts. *The Archaeology of Knowledge* denies, as observed above, one of the conditions of the boıd text by accepting rupture, disjunction, discontinuity; the evasions serve as constant reminders of the futility of looking for underlying easily traceable unities and continuities in and between discourse formations. Nevertheless, when Foucault does present a substantive account of statements (in the above four points), as opposed to evading expected accounts, he effectively aligns his text with the recognizable bold text. At the substantive level, Foucault's statements are developments of Durkheim's social facts, for example, and the development is nothing more than what is rendered imperative by the gap of knowledge between them. The gap of knowledge between them meant that Durkheim was inevitably less aware of the implications of the bold text (in a sense he was in the position of founding the basis from which the implications could become evident) than Foucault, and therefore formulated a simplistic quanta and a less coherent metadisciplinary stance. Foucault knows what to evade and what to modify. The result is that:

a. Whereas Durkheim's social facts were to be seen as "things" Foucault's statements have a more accommodatively defined "material existence";

b. Instead of surrendering the subject to an objective space and being left with a non-sentient sociological gaze as in Durkheim, Foucault allows a space in which the "subject is assigned" (therefore still contained in the sense of confined and included);

c. Whereas Durkheim would find it necessary to replace the distantiation of the subject with the dangerous and problematic concept of a collective unconscious Foucault would propose a safer picture of intra- and inter-play of domains.

Though Foucault does persuasively allow an assignable space for the subject in his presentation of statements (an assignability which itself removes the primacy of the subject and places him/her into a virtual third person position), reference to the larger Foucaultian Text, his body of works, reveals that this space cannot be occupied except by implication. It is almost a metaphysical space, a space so quiet as to be almost invisible. It cannot be otherwise in the bold text. This is done at the expense of the subject's body. The subject's body is torn asunder and placed at a distance to become an objective surface for a scrutiny so intense, a working-upon of power so pervasive, that the deindividualisation/desubjectivisation is total.[63] There is an unmistakable echo of Durkheim's comprehension of the individual subject as a shell. The assignable subject of Foucault is a nonentity.

The result of the perspective offered from the statement as quanta, exercising its enunciative function with reference to a domain and by interplay with other domains, forming a network in and across discourse formations, absorbing other networks we are familiar with and undercutting networks we are comfortable with, evading the continuities and unities normal to discourse formations in the bold text . . . the result of all this is Foucault's "archaeology." Archaeology has an air of totality as an approach to knowledge: totality would however offend Foucault's careful sensibility. Totality in this context is not a reinstatement of the underlying continuities of knowledge, not a holistic view of knowledge, not a harmonious apprehension of knowledge in some disciplinary arena. Totality in archaeology is an apprehension of knowledge from a kind of still point. Not that knowledge is seen as an apprehension of the static, quite the contrary, but the apprehension itself has a completeness, a comprehensiveness, a coherence about it which is possible only in stasis. Which cannot be undercut itself, moved, shifted, displaced. Which would always underlie whatever appears. It is this stasis which Foucault's text suggests by its choice of labels. "Archaeology" is the name chosen for this approach to knowledge; it celebrates the monumentality of discourse, its stillness if you please, rather than the shifting ground of its interpretations. The corpus that this "archaeologist" applies himself to is the "archive" of discourses—one can visualize the sense of its being all there, ready to be picked. The thrust of the archaeologist's endeavour is *description* of things as they are; faithful, rigorous, persistent description. The archaeologist's knowledge is a knowledge of stillness.

It is this kind of totality which finally permits Foucault to distance himself from science. He doesn't get involved in the Durkheimian paradox of being in science and using science as a model. The indifference of science to the nonscientist, the focus on practice in science, doesn't appear as comprehensive in a bold text which realises its own ruptures and discontinuities. Science doesn't accommodate the metadisciplinariness which the statement as quanta would necessitate. Metadisciplinariness, like Durkheim's sociology, is what Foucault's archaeology (in his bold text) moves towards. But this is not with science as a model. Foucault's archaeology is conceived as more basic than science. He carefully locates it in the balance of *savoir,* whereas science (the usual model) and the history of ideas (the discipline archaeology is most likely to be confused with) are in the balance of *connaissance.*[64] That the points of distinction for Foucault's archaeology should be the history of ideas and science is significant. The careful differentiation between archaeology and the history of ideas is natural in view of the fact that the latter would be the usual institutional category Foucault's work is likely to find a place in. The cautious differentiation from science is, I believe, a recognition of the role science has played as appropriated practice and model in other metadisciplinary areas.

That Foucault's archaeology is confessedly located in the balance of *savoir,* and forwards a relation with all *connaissances* not as overview but as underlying base, is an announcement of its metadisciplinariness—i.e., its interdisciplinary potential.

3. A recapitulation: the bold text works with assumptions which allow potentially interdisciplinary spaces to open up, unlike the closure and accommodativeness of cautious texts. The interdisciplinary potential within the bold text can be demonstrated by its ability to summarize cautious texts. The assumptions which enable this are, first, that the subject can be pushed into an objective space, and second, that certain traces of unities

and continuities can be found across knowledge. With these assumptions certain disciplines can be constituted (Durkheim's sociology and Foucault's archaeology, for example) which open up the way to interdisciplinarity by adopting a metadisciplinary approach. The metadisciplinary approach consists of using the distancing of the subject that the bold text permits to the fullest extent, thus shifting the immanent locus of disciplinary enquiry to an antithetical concept of quanta of knowledge. Knowledge is comprehended as constituted by these quanta in different and complex networks (Durkheim's "social facts" and Foucault's "statements," for example). The culmination of the constitution of quanta are, of course, in institutions. Simplistically understood, institutions contain (as confinement and inclusion) the subject by legitimizing certain networks of quanta. The metadisciplinary perspective normally proceeds to elucidate how networks of quanta are generated and how in the proliferations of this web institutions find their impetus and assimilate and disperse power (Durkheim on education and religion, for instance, and Foucault on the clinic or the prison). The disciplines which *emerge* from (are not constituted by) such metadisciplinary perspectives are seen as institutionally validated. The elucidation of the dynamic between quanta of knowledge and institutions is normally examined, within this perspective, as a dynamic of chronological development (I include in this all the reformulations of history which appear here). Thus, it is inevitable that Durkheim's concern with the role of education in the perpetuation of generality and constraint of social facts should lead to *The Evolution of Educational Thought*,[65] just as Foucault's preoccupation with discourse formations which contain the body (of subjects) leads to the social-historical *Discipline and Punish* and *The History of Sexuality*.

There is another approach which naturally grows from the bold text and offers potential interdisciplinary spaces. Though not unrelated to the above metadisciplinary approach it should be distinguished from it. To render the distinction clear I propose to call it a macrodisciplinary approach. Like a metadisciplinary approach a macrodisciplinary approach may also constitute itself as an independent discipline (education, politics, anthropology as academic disciplines, for example). To put it briefly, a macrodisciplinary approach concentrates entirely on the level of the institution instead of the dynamic between quanta of knowledge and institution. The institution is seen as a self-contained and given area; institutional varieties and inter-relations, internal mechanisms, regions of affect, disseminations of power, discourse structures need only to be described adequately to grasp the space of knowledge which is available. The necessity of the assumptions of the bold text for the expression of a macrodisciplinary approach is obvious: the subject has to be held at bay, has to be contained within the precincts of institutional demands; and the organization of the institution delineates the continuities and unities that can be traced across knowledge, that render the bold text necessary. The distinction between, and therefore the relation between, a metadisciplinary and a macrodisciplinary approach can be comprehended in the following manner: the metadisciplinary approach tries to fill in the dynamic process between quanta (a micro level) of knowledge and the institution (a macro level); the macrodisciplinary approach simply describes the institution as given and as delineating the precincts of knowledge. While the metadisciplinary approach usually comprehends the dynamic which it addresses itself to in terms of chronological development, the macrodisciplinary approach is generally marked by a synchronic descriptive mode even when it is applied to the institution in different historical contexts.

The macrodisciplinary approach is best illustrated in terms of its disciplinary practice. In fact, this study can be taken a step further. This bold text can be taken into the macrodisciplinary discipline which actually deals (to a large extent) with the institutionalization of disciplines of knowledge: I refer to "education" as an academic discipline. The following therefore has two levels of significance: 1. *illustrative* of the macrodisciplinary approach that is necessarily constituted as a discipline in the bold text, and which is distinct, though related to, metadisciplinary approaches; 2. *descriptive* of the effective view of disciplines as they are defined and constructed within the institution.

I have used the term "institution" in a broad and undefined manner so far. A single definition of institution in this context would be to assume a unitary and basic term which cuts across approaches (metadisciplinary or macrodisciplinary). It should be clarified here that this is not the case. In the bold text the term institution is corollary to the adopted approach. In the metadisciplinary approach the institution is the "end product"; i.e., is understood as consequent on the quanta. In the macrodisciplinary approach the institution is given; i.e., is understood as the beginning point. Definitions would be conditional to this placement, and to the specific kinds of placement. The senses of institution coherent with the different disciplines considered here are illustrated accordingly.

In considering the macrodisciplinary discipline of education the given institution is, of course, the academy and educational institution. Since the focus here is on concepts of disciplinarity and interdisciplinarity, I consider (some) educationists' perspectives with regard to the place of academic disciplines in the educational institution. Further, since arguably the academic discipline is constructed and placed within the educational institution in a top-down manner, since the section concerned with higher education (which reaches into the academy) deals with the academic discipline at its margins (accommodating, readjusting, modifying, questioning, reiterating, dispensing, adopting), or at its frontline, so to say, the observations here are pertinent mainly to the institution of higher education. It is usually agreed (though this isn't necessarily so) that disciplinary knowledge propounded in primary and secondary educational institutions lead up to the accepted margins of that discipline in institutions of higher education, and therefore the academy. I do not deal with the academy as an independent body (i.e., the institution as pertinent to specialization and research and information gathering, and the exchange between specialists and specialisms) because it seems to be understood among educationists that descriptions of academic disciplines and specialisms do not necessarily coincide, and that a complex relationships exists between the two. Disciplinary descriptions have evidently a specific relationship to the process of induction of students into a field of knowledge.

As an illustrative/descriptive example of an educationist's understanding of academic disciplines I begin with the following relatively simple statement by King and Brownell:

> [. . .] we undertake that most dangerous game—the pursuit of *isomorphic* features of the several autonomous disciplines. We find these isomorphic aspects:
>
> A discipline is a community of persons.
> A discipline is an expression of human imagination.
> A discipline is a domain.
> A discipline is a tradition.
> A discipline is a syntactical structure—a mode of inquiry.
> A discipline is a conceptual structure—a substance.
> A discipline is a specialised language or other system of symbols.
> A discipline is a heritage of literature and artifacts and a network of communications.

> A discipline is a valuative and affective stance.
> A discipline is an instructive community.[66]

This is given as preparatory and ancillary to a theoretical model for devising school curricula: as an academic discipline "education," of course, feels compelled to yield to applicability (in educationist jargon it is a *soft applied* discipline). The description of academic disciplines proposed here is the slippery base, dangerous game, which is expected to lead to a comfortable stage of applicability. The slippery base is the given base, i.e., the givenness of the institutional space described by academic disciplines in an educational institute. This is the uncontrollable object of description, and this may lead through description to a controllable macrodisciplinary practice.

The givenness of the institutional space occupied by academic disciplines is exposed through another device: the use of the term "isomorphic," and the revealing footnote which is attached to it:

> An isomorph is something identical with, equal to, alike, or the same as something else in form, shape, or structure.[67]

But that's a partial explanation. An isomorphic relation would normally entail not only an identity, equality, alikeness between "something" and "something else," but also suggest that the "something" and the "something else" derive from different ancestry or origins. If King and Brownell choose to give a partial explanation of "isomorphic" this is probably because a partial explanation is appropriate to their usage. And so it is—the isomorphisms which cut across disciplines from the educationist's point of view cannot reveal anything about the ancestry or origin of disciplines. There is nothing more basic, more fundamental, more elemental than the given institutional space for the macrodisciplinary approach. There are no quanta. In this case the institutional space is that of academic disciplines; nothing precedes them, there is no common source, merely the isomorphic features which are thrown up by the description of this institutional space. In a sense, these are isomorphic *because* nothing precedes them: the descriptive isomorphisms cannot be qualified or explained in terms of ancestry or origin because in the educationist's context origin or ancestry is not the issue. This sense of givenness in the educationist's appraisal of the institutional space held by disciplines gives rise to an air of coincidence, almost accidentalness, in the identification of isomorphic features. There is no underlying method in the educationist's ability to come up with this particular set of features apart from the fact that they are given, they simply are there. The educationist's description of disciplines (or, in the broader sense, the macrodisciplinary appreciation of disciplines) emerges from a gaze which apparently divests itself of presumptions and expectations. It is a persistent gaze which charts out, compares, categorizes. Rationales, if provided, are after the fact.

Obviously, the educationist's gaze has to begin, end, and be circumscribed by the bold text. Continuities, unities, constants, which are inherent in the very shape of the bold text, are unquestioningly present (or found, or searched) in King's and Brownell's account of academic disciplines—the isomorphisms, for instance, which exist almost accidentally, without reference to ancestry or origin. The gaze which merely observes and describes (charts out, compares, categorizes) is not a gaze which has any origin outside the institution it examines. Nothing precedes the institution. It seems to be given just as the institutional space is given. It is not a gaze that can be located to a subject, which is as it should be in a bold text. On the contrary, the givenness of the institution (whereby the givenness of the unanalyzable macrodisciplinary gaze) is expressed by parameters which render an individualized subject irrelevant, where it disappears somewhere in the folds and becomes invisible. The isomorphic aspects of academic disciplines identified by King and Brownell—community, human imagination, domain, tradition, syntactical structure, etc.—contain the subject in a manner which doesn't even need to be discussed any longer (unlike the metadisciplinary approach). The subject disappears in the acceptance of the institution as available only outside the precincts of individualized subjective considerations. The bold text of the macrodisciplinary approach doesn't even provide a gesture (however perfunctory) of self-questioning; it is the bold text at its most brash.

An expansion in the range of descriptive modes to assimilate the institutional space occupied by academic disciplines, a more complex grouping of unities, continuities, constants than isomorphic features, doesn't change the quality of the educationist's bold text. Such expansion is not merely because the educationist's gaze becomes more searching, more discerning, more sensitive, though that does undoubtedly happen. Nor can it be attributed solely to an increasing degree of complexity in the object of description, the institution. That also indubitably occurs, but the expansion often occurs faster than if it were initiated by historical change alone. The expansion, whether the gaze grows more searching or whether the object grows more complex, should be restricted by the dependence on the givenness of the institution, and therefore by what the institution offers as pertinent information, what is made available as pertinent information. If the educationist wants to examine, with a macrodisciplinary approach, the institutional space accorded to academic disciplines in general he/she would normally depend on what the institution designates as of interest or as relevant to specific disciplines or disciplines in general. This is the natural conservatism which attends an approach which establishes itself by its capacity for acceptance (of what *is* the educational institution, for instance). The preceding observation is not intended to denigrate the "radical" stance that some educationists adopt with regard to application; the comment reflects on the descriptive basis of education. So educationists would generally accept the institutional designation, and for an expansion of terms to occur he/she has to find a locus from which the centrality of the institution under observation is displaced. A locus in fact from which the centrality and givenness of the educational institution is dislocated, but from which the educational institution continues to be observable and the macrodisciplinary approach applicable. This would bring to bear in the attribution of the institutional space of academic disciplines factors which are not designated by the institution but which nevertheless do play a part. This would add to the institutionally sanctioned factors and analyses, the factors and analyses which have a bearing on this area but which the institution can not perceive or wishes not to sanction. Such a dislocation clearly occurs in Clifford Geertz's analysis of the ethnography of thought, and expands on the features which have a bearing on, say, academic disciplines but which are not designated as such by the educational institution (and therefore missing from, for example, the work of King and Brownell).

Clifford Geertz has the advantage of investigating the precincts of one macrodisciplinary discipline (education) from the perspective of another (anthropology). The shift in locus and therefore the expansion of terms follow as a matter of course. Clifford Geertz sees the function of an anthropologist describing thought "ethnographically" as being one of "describing the world in which it makes whatever sense it makes"; and the most obvious implication of this is that

> as thinking in this view is a matter of trafficking in the symbolic forms available in one or another community (language, art, myth, theory, ritual, technology, law, and the conglomerate of maxims, recipes, prejudices, and plausible stories the smug call common sense), the analysis of such communities is ingredient to interpreting it, not ancillary.[68]

If one wishes to simplify the difference between Geertz's (the anthropologist's) and King's and Brownell's (the educationist's) macrodisciplinary approaches one could say the former describes an aspect of any given institution (nation, tribe, village, school, university, etc.) while the latter describes all aspects of a given institution (the educational institution). The anthropologist describes the communal character of all institutions and does this in terms of certain predetermined criteria for organizing communal character (described briefly within parentheses in the above quotation). The educationist usually focuses on the criteria offered by the given institution of eduction to describe its components and processes. One could justifiably maintain that the anthropologist has a presumed methodology for examining the institution, while the educationist has a prechosen institution to examine its affects. I need hardly point out in this context that the macrodisciplinary approach takes very different directions in the two disciplines while retaining strictly speaking their macrodisciplinary character: the idea of "macrodisciplinariness" should therefore be left open and not closed by any finite number of illustrations. Coming back to the point however, the differences imply that if the educationist chooses to examine an aspect of the educational institution he/she would not normally go beyond the terms sanctioned by the institution, i.e., King and Brownell would accept that disciplines are defined by academic discourse communities but won't therefore examine the complex constitution of discourse communities in that context. Whereas if an anthropologist chooses to examine an aspect of the educational institution he/she would bring to bear the entire methodology for examining communal character on this, i.e., Clifford Geertz would examine the complex constitution of discourse communities to show how definitions of disciplines follow accordingly. The educationist and the anthropologist are not at odds here, but an expansion of terms is imminent. That is precisely what Clifford Geertz does: he expands the connotations of seeing disciplines according to academic discourse communities by introducing factors of communal definition which the educationist wouldn't consider relevant at first. Clifford Geertz looks at the language, the career patterns, the maturation cycles of members of academic discourse communities to make his point.[69]

The dislocation from the terms given by the institution in the macrodisciplinary approach of education, or, in other words, the expansion of terms necessitated by the different macrodisciplinary approach of anthropology, can be reassimilated in the characteristic bold text of education. This occurs, for instance, in Tony Becher's *Academic Tribes and Territories,* a work which admittedly draws inspiration from Clifford Geertz's observations on the ethnography of thought. The influence of the anthropological method is evident in both the statement of intention and the selection of material (often exceeding that which is institutionally sanctioned as relevant to descriptions of disciplines). The stated intention:

> The contention I advance, and here set out to substantiate, is that the ways in which particular groups of academics organize their professional lives are intimately related to the intellectual tasks on which they are engaged. In practice, the two seem to be inseparably intertwined; but in attempting to explore the characteristic features of their relationship it is necessary to separate the first analytically from the second. I therefore seek to draw a distinction between the social aspects of knowledge communities and the epistemological properties of knowledge forms, and also to look closely at how the two influence one another.[70]

The need to distinguish and relate the social aspects of disciplinary communities to the epistemological considerations of disciplines, the necessity for portraying a disciplinary culture which comprehends both, marks the expansion in terms beyond the disciplinary description of, for example, Brownell and King. Behind this statement of intention lies a tacit recognition of the need to disentwine normally received (institutionally sanctioned) notions of epistemological considerations taking precedence over and subsuming the social condition of a disciplinary community. The recognition is tacit since it does not, in this quest, attempt to comment on the policies of educational institutions: the onus of making the distinction and drawing the interrelations is within the educationist's gaze. It is understood that the intention is to expand the scope of what the educationist perceives of the institution, not to materially alter the shape of the institution itself. An effective change in the shape of the institution may be corollary to this perception, but the perception is not conceived with that intention. Applicability is usually posterior to the consolidation of the educationist's acceptance of the given institution, as was observed in my examination of Brownell's and King's contentions. Nevertheless, in the statement of intentionality there is clearly an expansion of terms.

Consequent to the expansion of terms there is an expansion of material which mold the gaze. The material expands in several directions: it explores received notions both in the form of past research and in the shape of testimonies by representatives of certain disciplines; it considers received notions from these sources not only with regard to accepted practices and epistemological considerations of disciplines but also with regard to the general social existence of their members (professional ambitions, opinions unrelated to disciplines, behavior patterns and responses to colleagues, etc.).[71] However, as observed in the case of Brownell's and King's work, the educationist's gaze doesn't emanate from a subject (an educationist's "I") though it ostensibly seems to do so. In the above quotation the appearance of the "I" is merely provisional, and soon disappears in the folds of the proliferation of institutionally available voices—voices of representatives of other disciplines, the mediation of other descriptive macrodisciplinary voices which simply categorize, elucidate, delineate. It becomes paradoxically the collective voice of the institution (a collectivity which is defined by its existence in the institution of higher education) which examines its own condition and affirms its status.

The result of the expansion in Becher's encyclopaedic work is a macrodisciplinary text where the compendium of observations appear as if by accident. Moreover, they are brought together after the fact of their appearance by means of organizational criteria which are not argumentative but referential (typical of the encyclopaedia). There is no underlying method for the description, no basic methodology as in Geertz's ethnographical approach. With the brashness which can be expected of the macrodisciplinary bold text observations proliferate and are set down through the perseverance of the descriptive zeal, the persistence with which the nonsubjective gaze of the educationist delves into the institution which is its *raison d'etre.* What replaces the basic methodology is the expectation in the educationist's bold text of continuities, constants, coherences across the field of knowledge which are encompassed by disciplines in the institution of higher education. It is much like the isomorphisms of King and Brownell—it is adopted in a similar "given" fashion, in the shape of "*characteristic* features of their [epistemological considerations and social aspects of disciplines] relationship" [my emphasis].

4. Interdisciplinarity becomes conceivable only in the bold text, and potentially realizable through metadisciplinary or macrodisciplinary approaches to knowledge. Whether a realization takes place in either approach is a matter of consensus. To members of disciplines which are constituted along meta or macrodisciplinary lines interdisciplinarity would be realizable whenever they wish to concede it. Some may wish not to concede it and desire exclusive proprietary rights over a disciplinary space with a metadisciplinary or macrodisciplinary perspective. They would have to defend themselves constantly through a bold text which seems bent on defeating them, which spreads out continuities and unities by nature, against the onslaught of other disciplines. To the subject of the discipline which can only expound itself in a cautious text interdisciplinarity would seem irrelevant. This doesn't imply that such a discipline is, in some sense, limited—on the contrary, within its margins it is likely to be infinitely assimilative and expansive.

Clearly, this is a rather schematic set of observations. I would like to reiterate (this point had been made at the beginning of this part) that no discipline, or no approach to knowledge, can constitute itself in terms of a purely cautious text or a purely bold text as they have been presented here. For the sake of contrast the distinction has been exaggerated (through the choice of examples, for instance, and the selection of examples within examples). As a case in point, the notion of the subject being "outside literature" as described in the cautious text is unlikely to be completely immune to the assumptions of the bold text: a close analysis of any outside literature critical work would reveal that subtle shifts between the bold and the cautious texts, the former containing and summarising the latter, the latter excluding and retreating from the former, occur more often that not. All those who are familiar with works of literary criticism which possess, say, a sociological bent would also be familiar with the appearance of multi-layered texts which struggle against each other within the same covers. The reading of a specific literary text

(Eagleton reading Emily Brontë's *Wuthering Heights*), the presentation of a sociological perspective (Eagleton providing a Marxist sociological analysis of England in the early nineteenth century), the placing of the text in context which prescribes a rereading or an informed reading or a reading from "outside literature" (Eagleton rendering the former dependent on the latter and thereby transforming the former)[72] are distinct processes. They move between layers of cautious text and layers of bold text with apparent ease, without remarking on the separate rationales involved, and without reflecting on the synthetic assumptions and the disjunctive hypothesisations evoked. I do not embark on a closer analysis of this here. The point is that, despite such shifts, such a work of literary criticism is predominantly a work of *literary* criticism, and has a stronger inclination towards the cautious text.

Further, though the term "discipline" has been used undiscriminatingly across the bold and cautious texts it should not be understood to encompass a specific meaning all through. In the bold and cautious texts here the term "discipline" does not possess a unitary or basic meaning which remains unshaken by the names it adopts, the functions it arrogates for itself, or the texts it manifests itself in. If that were the case, "discipline" would itself become some kind of quanta (like "statements" or "social facts") and this book an example of a metadisciplinary approach. As it stands, this book is a collection of fragments which barely form a collage, some bits and pieces of which become apparent only at the expense of others, and each discrete fragment threatens to consume the whole. If it appears to be schematic it is so only at the danger of ceasing to be so or being so in a very tenuous fashion. The term "discipline" therefore is completely fluid in this text. Each discipline described, whether in a cautious or bold text, whether inside or outside within the cautious text, or whether with a metadisciplinary or a macrodisciplinary approach within the bold text, comprehends and presents a slightly differing concept of "discipline." The above did not assume a fixed meaning of "discipline," the above has tried to show the shifting status and nuances of the term under different modes and forms of conceiving and pursuing knowledge. The notions of interdisciplinarity which become potential here are conditional (in its appearance or inability to appear) on the status and nuances of the corresponding notions of disciplinarity, which are not bound together by anything more basic than being forms of conceiving and pursuing knowledge.

To put it in other words, interdisciplinarity cannot appear by the simple consensus of a group of persons, who identify themselves as belonging to different disciplines, to create a joint forum. The relations between the separate conditions under which they assume their disciplinary status need to be drawn. This may be outside the purview of certain disciplines which constitute themselves primarily within the cautious text. This may be the sole concern of certain disciplines which constitute themselves primarily within the bold text with a meta or macrodisciplinary approach. The former and the latter need not overlap at any point—in fact it is unlikely that they would. Within the latter the kinds of relations drawn by metadisciplinary and macrodisciplinary approaches need not overlap either—indeed they probably would not. It seems that extraordinary difficulties would have to be surmounted before an unequivocal interdisciplinary area, a space between different but monologically defined disciplines, can appear. Possibly, an unequivocally interdisciplinary area is not really wanted, has never been wanted, has never been conceived. There are no unambiguous and distinct spaces between disciplines which contribute to the accumulation and pursuit of knowledge.

So, what goes under the name of interdisciplinary? What happens in an interdisciplinary conference? An interdisciplinary journal? An interdisciplinary research paper or book? What sort of idea does a funding body have when it makes an award conditional to interdisciplinary content? What is the radical academic looking for when he/she tries to break out of disciplinary boundaries and go interdisciplinary?

The following cover the range of activities which the above questions gesture towards.

i. An obvious instance of "interdisciplinarity" occurs when the disciplines which adopt meta or macrodisciplinary attitudes and constitute themselves primarily through the bold text actually bring these attitudes to bear upon what they consider to be different disciplines. From a sociologist's, educationist's, etc. perspective a monological and schematic description of disciplines is possible which consequently permits the spaces between them to be investigated. For instance, if the sociologist defines different disciplines according to some sort of quanta ("social facts" or "action" for example) this necessarily implies that at some micro level interrelations can be traced out. Similarly, if the educationist contends that all disciplines are defined by the relative spaces they occupy within an institution of higher education this also implies that they are correlated through the conception and administration of the institution as a whole. However this mode of monological definition which allows something like interdisciplinarity to appear is, as observed above, inevitably problematic. The disciplinary definitions adopted by the sociologist or educationist need not coincide with those that prevail within the paradigms and practices of other disciplines. The careful sociologist and educationist would, no doubt, consult representatives of other disciplines, but the synthetic approach which allows them to collate the disparate results lie within their own meta or macrodisciplinary approaches. It seems to me that most educationists and sociologists (among representatives of other meta or macrodisciplinary disciplines) are aware of the problems. In their "interdisciplinary" quests therefore the term is usually used tentatively, used with a dispensable model in mind, used with justifiable trepidation. The models of interdisciplinary discourse, the relationship between quanta and structure, are constantly redefined and reformulated. Similarly, it is recognized that departments and universities function on their own agendas which coexist only through constant negotiation, and the code of conduct of the negotiations is perpetually under scrutiny—by those educationists interested in the question of academic freedom, for instance. Educationists are also generally aware that a cohesive definition of "academic community" is difficult to propose and perhaps not desirable, where "academic community" designates the communal character of all members of the institution of higher education (or education at any level) and cuts across disciplinary self-definitions even when these are related in a monological fashion. The group of essays collected recently under the title *Academic Community: Discourse or Discord?* and edited by Ronald Barnett illustrate this clearly. The concerns of this group of essays is admirably summed up in the introductory essay by Barnett.[73] The mode of argument is twofold: a. that interdisciplinarity is possible and perhaps desirable if a sufficient change in the organizational structure of the institution and the society which surrounds it is made; b. that the organizational structure in place cannot be abandoned without an alternative which will allow the institution to continue as such.[74] Both these steps are consistent with the educationist's macrodisciplinary approach. Regarding the realization of interdisciplinary efforts the tone is one of watered down optimism, and the need for change (when it rises above the purely theoretical) only permits of what Tony Becher calls "incremental change" within the institution.[75]

Further, it should be noted that the notion of realizing interdisciplinarity from a meta or macrodisciplinary approach is not one and the same thing. The two approaches obviously differ and do not necessarily overlap, though serious and useful discussions often mix up the two concepts of potentially realizable interdisciplinarity in a confusing manner. The enlightening debates in the not-yet-dated *Interdisciplinary Relationships in the Social Sciences* edited by Sherif and Sherif, the proceeds of a symposium in 1969, is a case in point. It presents the mix of meta and macrodisciplinary approaches to the issue within the apparently theme-centered development which the editors emphasize. The kind of interdisciplinarity that Sherif and Sherif envisage and wish to discuss is consistent with the quanta approach of metadisciplinarity, and is by and large the approach adopted by most other contributors.[76] The last two contributions by Roose and Campbell take a completely different approach in speaking of the organizational difficulties of interdisciplinary investigation, and prioritize (typically of a macrodisciplinary approach) the institutional assumptions.[77] Close reading shows that these constitute two rather different (and in many ways irreconcilable) senses of the term "interdisciplinary," though they are assumed to be the same with merely complementary emphases within the organisation of the text, as no doubt on the floor of the conference room.

ii. It is not unusual for the subjects in disciplines which are normally constituted in the cautious text to turn their attention to areas which normally do not come within the precincts of their discipline: the results may, inappropriately, be thought of as interdisciplinary. This is, as I have argued above, not a correct designation but it does seem to have some currency. From this perspective the philosophy of science or the use of psychoanalysis in literary criticism would be understood as interdisciplinary. As maintained above the philosophy of science does not have any implication for the paradigmatic or practical conduct of the scientific discipline, and the position of stepping outside literature in the cautious text of literary criticism has implications only for the conduct of reading-writing within the discipline of literary studies. These are symptomatic of the assimilativeness and expansiveness of the discipline in the cautious text as it emanates from a fluid subject position and gaze. To designate this kind of intellectual activity interdisciplinary is to misconstrue the process at work: these areas do not interrogate the spaces between disciplines, these are concerned with the extension of the discipline within the cautious text. From the point of view of literary studies and philosophy, for instance, in so far as they are construed within the cautious text they can only refuse interdisciplinarity.

iii. Scientists speak of interdisciplinarity *within* the sciences, or rather of old pure and applied disciplines and new interface disciplines. I have observed in the cautious text that science seems to exercise the exclusiveness of the discipline within a sort of cautious text but in terms which are not available to the subject of the humanistic discipline. Science seems to possess a field of practical and paradigmatic criteria of disciplinary definition and interdisciplinary interaction which are simply not available to the nonscientist. The meta or macrodisciplinary approaches would, no doubt, like to contain the repulsion, or at best the indifference, of science but even these approaches cannot offer monological definitions of scientific disciplines and interface disciplines with conviction. The indifference persists, or the repulsion is all the more emphatic. The notion of "interfaces" and disciplinary self-definition in the sciences seem to be beyond the scope of this study: only a scientist can deal with them. Deal with them probably does not mean vocalize them in relation to the activity of the pursuit of knowledge (as in this text). The scientist would probably deal with them by his/her practice of them, his/her challenge, consolidation or change of their paradigms (in Kuhn's sense).

iv. The most common use of the term "interdisciplinary" appears with reference to fora which are shared by representatives of different disciplines (irrespective of their bold or cautious textuality, of their meta or macrodisciplinary approaches, etc.) who discuss a set theme. The interdisciplinary space is associated with the negotiations between representatives with regard to the common theme; it is necessary that the theme should be common for the negotiations to actually take the shape of exchanges. The library is well stocked with the documentation of such interdisciplinary negotiations. Those that do actually take the shape of interdisciplinary exchange, it seems to me, do so not because the set theme is common in the broad sense of cutting across all disciplines but because the forum accommodates only an alliance of investigative prerogatives which share common ground. Such common ground could be either in terms of (i), (ii) or (iii) above. Even in such instances the problems attached to (i), (ii) or (iii) surface constantly. With the assumption of the "common" term as the sole criteria for bringing the forum together, where the "common" term is expected to cut across a broad range of disciplines, interdisciplinary *exchange* is seldom effected. Edited publications of the discussions of interdisciplinary symposia like the Ciba Foundation Symposium *The Future as an Academic Discipline* (1975) or Higher Education Council consultations on *Reductionism in Academic Disciplines* (1985),[78] amongst numerous others, illustrate mainly the lack of exchange in such forums. These enlighten one as to the widely divergent understandings and significances attached to common terms like "reductionism" or "future", all of which are valid in discrete disciplinary discourses, and very few of which can be given interdisciplinary licence. Negotiations are generally at cross-purposes.

5. And therefore the final questions, the culminating interrogatives of this part, and the path to the next: in what sense could interdisciplinarity be brought *into* literary studies? How far is the discipline of literary studies cognisant of interaction with other disciplines? In asking this I "complete" the regressive progression with which this part had begun and return to the beginning. These are questions with which this part had begun.

I now have a schema within which this question can be comprehended and an exposition attempted. The schema is not too complex. There are disciplines which are constituted within cautious texts and those within the bold text. In the first the disciplines tend to be exclusive, assimilative, and seem to emanate from a subject-position (science seems to appear in a sort of negative cautious text which is also exclusive). In the second continuities and unities are assumed to exist across all disciplines, the subject is transferred to an object position, and interdisciplinarity becomes potential through meta or macrodisciplinary approaches within a more fluid structure of disciplines. Metadisciplinary approaches fit into the bold text by prioritizing a notion of quanta of knowledge, while macrodisciplinary approaches begin with a focus on the institution.

I have observed that the discipline of literary studies normally constitutes itself within the cautious text, whether in terms of being "inside" or "outside" literature. I have also observed that interdisciplinarity can appear tentatively only through meta or macrodisciplinary approaches within the bold text. It has also been pointed out above that the term "interdisciplinary" is used in four senses, all of which are problematic and most of which are inappropriate.

In this context the questions regarding interdisciplinarity (and the necessary relation to disciplinary definitions) in literary studies can be resolved in two ways which are consistent with (i) and (ii) of section 4 above.

(i) Literary studies could be brought within the bold text as a monologically defined discipline amongst others from a meta or macrodisciplinary perspective. Its disciplinary margins and interdisciplinary potential can be realised in the process. Literary studies could be seen in terms of quanta: the sociologist or historian of ideas, for example, may try to understand literary studies in terms of the "social facts," "actions," or "statements" which construct a literary discourse. Or literary studies could be understood in terms of the institutional space that it occupies in relevant institutions: the educationist may try to discern the space that literary studies holds in an educational institution. Strictly speaking none of these do come under the self-definition or practice of literary studies: these would be understood as a sociology of literary studies or the educationist's perspective of literary studies respectively.

The next part (Part II) of this study examines an educationist's/sociologist's perspective of literary studies. It does this in terms of the specific example of English literature, for reasons which are elucidated there.

(ii) Literary studies can be left within the cautious text where it normally appears, while the scope and focus of its gaze can be extended to include discourses and objects which do not usually come under its purview. This is neither an identification of the margins of literary studies, nor a realized interdisciplinary effort. On the contrary, this merely demonstrates the assimilability and expansiveness of the cautious text of literary studies and dissolves the notion of its possessing disciplinary margins with relation to other disciplines. But it may, in current usage, be mistakenly thought of as interdisciplinary.

Part III of this study illustrates this in terms of two examples: a literary engagement with the philosophical texts of Wittgenstein; and a literary-linguistic analysis of non-mathematical expositions of relativity.

I need scarcely remind the reader that there are no pure cautious or bold texts, only predominantly cautious and bold texts. This is apparent in Parts II and III.

Part I Notes

1. The activity marked by the joint reading-writing as engagement with the text: "reading-writing" acknowledges the placement of the active and creative component of an engagement with a text across both ends of the phrase. This particular sentence combines paradoxically Wolfgang Iser's concept of the processive nature of reading with a view to consistency building [*The Act of Reading* (London and Henley: Routledge and Kegan Paul, 1978), chapter 5], and Stanley Fish's notion of the preemption of the shape of reading and writing in the context of interpretive strategies ["Interpreting the *Variorum*," *Is There A Text In This Class?* (Cambridge, Mass.: Harvard Univ. Press, 1980), p. 171].

2. Gilles Deleuze and Felix Guattari, *What Is Philosophy?*, trans. Hugh Tomlinson and Graham Burchill (London and New York: Verso, 1994), pp. 61–62:

> Is there something else, in Descartes's case, other than the created cogito and the presupposed image of thought? [. . .] In the present case it is the Idiot: it is the Idiot who says "I" and sets up the cogito but who also has the subjective presuppositions or lays out the plane. The Idiot is the private thinker, in contrast to the public teacher (the schoolman): the teacher refers constantly to taught concepts (man-rational animal), whereas the private thinker forms a concept with innate forces that everyone possesses on their own account by right ("I think"). Here is a very strange type of persona who wants to think, and who thinks for himself, by the 'natural light.' The Idiot is a conceptual persona.

The use of the conceptual persona of the Idiot in this cautious text is not to limit the breadth or assimilativeness of Deleuze's and Guattari's concept of the conceptual persona. It serves another purpose which is peculiar to this text—it presents, at the very crux of modern philosophy, the distinction between the bold text (the schoolman's text, summarizing philosophy, presenting the subject as third person, as shall be demonstrated in the latter section of this part) and the philosophical cautious text (the Idiot's text).

3. René Descartes, *A Discourse on Method*, trans. John Veitch (London: Everyman, 1986), p. 12. This is probably one of the best illustrations of the public teacher and private thinker (bold-cautious) dichotomy mentioned by Deleuze and Guattari (and maintained in this text). It also hints towards the constitution of the bold text as being affine with the "state," with education and the "body of sciences" propagated therein. These are themes I dwell on later.

4. Deleuze and Guattari, *What is Philosophy?*, p. 5.

5. Ibid., p. 197.

6. Ibid., p. 10. The rejection of the concept in advertising is, of course, indicative of the specific connotations that this word has in philosophy. What Deleuze and Guattari do not clarify here is that the "concept" in advertising is not false but different. The concept in advertising is not cohesive, assimilative, or expansive enough to be acceptable within the cautious text of philosophy. But in the bold text of advertising the concept is available as synthesizing a complex of ideological trends [as in Judith Williamson's *Decoding Advertisements* (London:

Marion Boyars, 1978), for instance, or in Raymond Williams's "Advertising: The Magic System", *Problems of Materialism and Culture* (London: NLB, 1980)]; manifesting certain continuities and unities across its discourse formations [discussed by Geoffrey N. Leach in *English in Advertising* (London: Longman, Green and Co., 1966), for example, and Guy Cook in *The Discourse of Advertising* (London: Routledge, 1992)]; and leaving the trace of these through the subtle shifts of its history [see, for example, Jennifer Wicke's *Advertising Fictions* (New York: Columbia Univ. Press, 1988)].

7. Ibid., p. 67.

8. Jacques Derrida, *Margins of Philosophy,* trans. Alan Bass (New York: Harvester Wheatsheaf, 1982), p. xii.

9. Ibid., p. 22. I hardly need to labor here that "anteriority" has more complex connotations in the context of the "sheaf" of meanings of *différance* than the simplistic notions of being *outside,* or somehow *before,* or even *behind,* that are favored here.

10. Alluding to the complex play of meanings of "tympanum" used by Derrida.

11. Roland Barthes, *The Pleasure of the Text,* trans. Richard Miller (London: Jonathan Cape, 1976).

12. The opposite, in Barthes's terms, to the writing of science. Roland Barthes says in "From Science to Literature", *The Rustle of Language,* trans. Richard Howard (Oxford: Basil Blackwell, 1986):

> For science, language is merely an instrument, which it chooses to make as transparent, as neutral as possible, subjugating scientific matters (operations, hypotheses, results), which are said to exist outside it and to precede it: on one side and *first of all,* the contents of the scientific message; and on the other and *afterwards,* the verbal form entrusted with encompassing these contents, which is nothing (p. 4).

13. Richard Miller's translation of *jouissance* in *The Pleasure of the Text.* I feel that in mentioning this Richard Howard's observations in "A Note on the Text" (i.e., Miller's translation) regarding the translation of *jouissance* and *jouir,* which I have freely adopted here , should be kept in mind (pp. v–vi).

14. This sweeping compression of complex planes of discourse is not to hide them under the carpet: this is merely an indication of what this region of the cautious text is not able to comprehend, what is alien to the subject (to me) at this moment of reading-writing. These will, of course, reappear in the bold text when it becomes possible.

15. Roman Ingarden in *The Literary Work of Art,* trans. George Grabowicz (Evanston: Northwestern Univ. Press, 1973), identified and examined the following four strata of literary works of art: (a) the stratum of linguistic sound formations; (b) the stratum of meaning units; (c) the stratum of manifold schematised aspects and aspect continua and series; and (d) the stratum of represented objectivities and their vicissitudes. The reader's concretization of these is described in Chapter 13 ("The 'Life' of a Literary Work").

16. Roland Barthes, *S/Z,* trans. Richard Miller (London: Jonathan Cape, 1975), p. 68.

17. Ibid., p. 151.

18. Ibid., pp. 211–12.

19. David Hayman (among others) has done so in *Ulysses: The Mechanics of Meaning* (Englewood Cliffs: Prentice-Hall, 1970). He described the "arranger" as:

> a figure who can be identified neither with the author nor with his narrators, but with

one who exercises an increasing degree of overt control over his increasingly challenging material (p. 70).

20. Roland Barthes, *The Pleasure of the Text,* p. 17.
21. Ibid., p. 13.
22. Roland Barthes, "Research: The Young", *The Rustle of Language,* p. 72.
23. Ibid.
24. Roland Barthes, *The Pleasure of the Text,* pp. 30–31.
25. Ibid., p. 39.
26. Tony Bennett, *Outside Literature* (London and New York: Routledge, 1990), p. 5.
27. Ibid., p. 7.
28. Walter Pater's description of (among other paintings) *la Gioconda's* beauty is presented as the aesthete's appreciation of timelessness ["Leonardo da Vinci", *The Renaissance* (1973; rpt. Oxford: Oxford Univ. Press, 1986), pp. 79–80]. This paradoxically shoulders the continuous description of Leonardo's historical, cultural, and personal context. The paradoxical juxtaposition is continuous with and (as the cautious text constantly reminds) distinct from parallel placements of timelessness and context ("culture") in Hegel's theory of art and Winckelmann's observations on Greek sculpture. In this case the paradoxically juxtaposed points of continuity/distinction, context/timelessness, real/ideal (which are some of the indexes of "virtual distance") might remind us of the parallel in Leonardo's own theory of painting. The nexus of imitation and selection in Leonardo's theory of art poses a similar paradoxical juxtaposition [see Leonardo da Vinci's *Treatise on Painting* (Cordex Urbinas Latinus 1270) Vol.I (Princeton: Princeton Univ. Press, 1956)]. However, Erwin Panofsky's comment on this in *Idea: A Concept of Art Theory* (New York: Harper and Row, 1968) is also worth keeping in mind: "[. . .] from the standpoint of the Renaissance both of these demands (imitation and selection), incompatible only in later terms, seemed like parts of a single postulate: the demand that the artist confront reality anew in each work of art, be it as connector or imitator" (p. 49). Can a similar point be made for 18th and 19th century thinkers?
29. I refer to Hans Robert Jauss's "seven theses" to relocate literary history from the aesthetics of production and representation to the aesthetics of reception and influence in "Literary History as a Challenge to Literary Theory", *Toward an Aesthetic of Reception* (Minneapolis: Univ. of Minnesota Press, 1982) pp. 3–45. And, along similar lines, the "five shifts" proposed by Janusz Slawinski in "Reading and Reader in the Literary Historical Process", *New Literary History,* vol.19, no.3, Spring 1988, pp. 521–39.
30. G. V. Plekhanov, *Art and Social Life* (London: Lawrence and Wishart, 1953), p. 172, 158. The specific reference is to Walter Benjamin's essay "The Work of Art in the Age of Mechanical Reproduction," *Illuminations* (London: Jonathan Cape, 1968), p. 226. The essay as a whole (pp. 219–54) places the reorientations that this perception necessitates in the context of the ideological manipulations of the Fascists, and the prospect of Socialist ideological requirements. Theodor Adorno, *Aesthetic Theory* (London: Routledge and Kegan Paul, 1984), Chapter 1. Jean-Paul Sartre, *What is Literature?* (London: Methuen,1967).

The continuities and disparities here are not merely in their ideological affinities and differences (and hence in the *looking at* literature and art) but also in the effect of their theories for the practice of literature despite their "outside" position. This is significant in the context of the observations below.

31. Michael Riffaterre's "super-reader" in "Describing Poetic Structures in *Les Chats*" [*Reader Response Criticism*, ed. Jane Tompkins (Baltimore and London: Johns Hopkins Univ. Press, 1980), pp. 37–38 is, of course, beyond exhaustion, and capable of emptying "the response of its content." But the ideological grid from which Riffaterre withdraws and in terms of which the super-reader is presented (Levi-Strauss's and Jakobson's structuralist readings) is not "outside literature" in the sense developed here.

32. William Morris, "The Lesser Arts", pp. 84–105, and of course Nowhere in *New From Nowhere* in *News From Nowhere and Selected Writings and Designs* (London: Penguin, 1962). Herbert Marcuse, *An Essay on Liberation* (Boston: Beacon, 1969), Chapter 2.

33. Pierre Macherey, *A Theory of Literary Production*, trans. Geoffrey Wall (London, Henley and Boston: Routledge and Kegan Paul, 1978), p. 7.

34. Stanley Fish in *Surprised by Sin: The Reader in* Paradise Lost, (London: Macmillan and New York: St.Martin's Press, 1967), and in "Interpreting the *Variorum*", for instance, in *Is There a Text in this Class?* (Cambridge, Mass.: Harvard Univ. Press, 1980). The concept of the "informed reader" appears in "Literature in the Reader" in the latter, p. 48. Wolfgang Iser, *Laurence Sterne: Tristram Shandy* (Cambridge: Cambridge Univ. Press, 1988), and *The Implied Reader: Patterns of Communication in Prose Fiction from Bunyan to Beckett* (Baltimore and London: Johns Hopkins Univ. Press, 1974). The "implied reader" is defined in *The Act of Reading* (London and Henley: Routledge and Kegan Paul, 1978), p. 34. Norman Holland—the transition from *The Dynamics of Literary Response* (New York: Oxford Univ. Press, 1968) where the example of the reading subject was Holland himself, to *Five Readers Reading* (New Haven and London: Yale Univ. Press, 1975) where the examples of readers are students represented by response statements.

35. For a description of Bleich's notion of the classroom and the place of response statements in its study, see *Subjective Criticism* (Baltimore and London: Johns Hopkins Univ. Press, 1978), Chapter 5. Stanley Fish introduced his concept of "interpretive strategies" and "interpretive communities" in "Interpreting the *Variorum*," *Is There a Text in this Class?*, p. 171.

36. For instance, Terry Eagleton, *Criticism and Ideology* (London: NLB, 1976), p. 11.

37. See Part III, Example 2, for a discussion of this paradox in the examination of "The Language of Non-Mathematical Expositions of Relativity."

38. Cited in Andrew Robinson and Dipankar Home, "The Mathematician and the Mystic," *The Times Higher Education Supplement*, 24 February 1995, p. 18.

39. Steven Weinberg, *Dreams of a Final Theory* (London: Vintage, 1993), p. 133.

40. Ibid., p. 40.

41. Ibid., p. 19:

> The word 'why' is notoriously slippery. The philosopher Ernest Nagel lists ten examples of questions in which 'why' is used in ten different senses, such as 'Why does ice float on water?' 'Why did Cassius plot the death of Caesar?' and 'Why do human beings have lungs?' Other examples in which 'why' is used in yet other senses come immediately to mind, such as, Why was I born? It should be clear that my use of the word 'why' is something like its use in the question, 'Why does ice float on water?' and is not intended to suggest any sense of conscious purpose.

42. Ibid., Chapter IX.

43. This is quite inadequate to the range of sources which can be appended to each of these assertions. To take a specific example to illustrate some of these points consider the reception of James Joyce's *Ulysses* on its publication. Wyndham Lewis saw in it an ideal example of what he called the "time mind" and placed it as a literary realization of Albert Einstein's theory and Samuel Alexander's and Henri Bergson's philosophies of time [*Time and the Western Man* (London: Chatto and Windus, 1928)]. Henri Bergson's and William James's notions regarding consciousness and time are also seen as providing the basis of *Ulysses*'s "stream of consciousness" and "interior monologue" (though Joyce cited Edouard Dujardin's *Les Lauriers sont coupe,* 1887, as his source), which certainly owed something to recently developed theories of, and thinking regarding, evolution. Critics and psychoanalysts alike received and read *Ulysses* as a literary work of scientific interest. C. G. Jung's comments in "*Ulysses:* A Monologue" (*Nimbus,* June-August 1953) are revealing, as is Mary Colum's observation in "The Confessions of James Joyce" (*Freeman,* 19 July 1922) that *Ulysses* is as much a scientific document as a literary text. The general consensus (in so far as there was one) was that some radical rethinking about the literary canon would be necessary before *Ulysses* could be accommodated.

44. As Karl R. Popper unambiguously states in (among other places) his essay on "Knowledge and the Shaping of Reality", *In Search of a Better World* (London: Routledge, 1992):

> [. . .] I want to begin by declaring that I regard *scientific knowledge* as the best and most important kind of knowledge we have—though I am far from regarding it as the only one, p. 3.

45. Thomas S. Kuhn, *The Structure of Scientific Revolutions* enlarged 2d ed.(Chicago: Univ. of Chicago Press, 1970), "Preface", p. v.

46. Karl R. Popper, *Objective Knowledge* (Oxford: Clarendon, 1972), p. 7.

47. Ibid., p. 4. Also see Parts III ("Knowledge and Probability") and IV ("Of the Sceptical and Other Systems of Philosophy")—particularly Sections I and II of the latter (pp. 231–69) in David Hume, *A Treatise of Human Nature,* Bk.I (Glasgow: Fontana/Collins, 1962).

48. Saul A. Kripke, *Wittgenstein on Rules and Private Languages* (Oxford: Basil Blackwell, 1982).

49. Thomas Kuhn, *The Structure of Scientific Revolutions,* p. 23.

50. Ibid., "Postscript—1969", pp. 174–210.

51. Louis Althusser, *Philosophy and the Spontaneous Philosophy of Scientists* (London and New York: Verso, 1990), p. 102.

52. Ibid.: for (a) p. 76; for (b) pp. 109–15; for (c) pp. 85–100; for (d) pp. 131–44.

53. Emile Durkheim, *The Rules of Sociological Method,* trans. Sarah Solovay and John Mueller (New York: Free Press and London: Collier Macmillan, 1938), pp. 1–2.

54. Ibid., p. 14.

55. Ibid., p. 13.

56. The three progressive steps are in the following pages respectively: Max Weber, *Economy and Society* Vol. 1, Guent ed.(Berkeley: Univ. of California Press, 1968), p. 6 (Ch.1, 1,3); pp. 13–5 (Ch.1, 1,9); pp. 20–22 (Ch.1, 1,11).

57. Jean Baudrillard, "Forget Foucault," *Forget Foucault* (New York: Semiotext(e), 1987).

58. Gilles Deleuze, *Foucault,* trans. Seán Hand (London: Athlone, 1988), p. 7.

59. Michel Foucault, *The Archaeology of Knowledge,* trans. A. M. Sheridan Smith (London: Routledge, 1972). The process is introduced in Part III, Chapter 1 ("Defining the Statement"), pp. 80–84; and reiterated in a broader linguistic description in Part III, Ch.3 ("The Description of Statements"), pp. 106–13.
60. Ibid., p. 91.
61. Ibid., p. 95.
62. Ibid., p. 103.
63. Michel Foucault, "Body/ Power", *Power/Knowledge,* ed. Colin Gordon (New York: Harvester Wheatsheaf, 1980), pp. 57–58:

> First of all one must set aside the widely held thesis that power, in our bourgeois, capitalist, societies has denied the reality of the body in favour of the soul, consciousness, ideality. In fact nothing is more material, physical, corporal than the exercise of power. [. . .]

64. Michel Foucault, *The Archaeology of Knowledge,* p. 183:

> Instead of exploring the consciousness/knowledge (*connaissance*)/science axis (which cannot escape subjectivity), archaeology explores the discursive practice/knowledge (*savoir*)/science axis. And whereas the history of ideas finds the point of balance of its analysis in the element of *connaissance* (and is thus forced, against its will, to encounter this transcendental interrogation), archaeology finds the point of balance of its analysis in *savoir*—that is, in a domain in which the subject is necessarily situated and dependent, and can never figure as titular (either as transcendental activity, or as empirical consciousness.)

65. I mention Durkheim's *The Evolution of Educational Thought,* trans. Peter Collins (London, Henley and Boston: Routledge and Kegan Paul, 1977)—or the earlier published *Education and Sociology,* trans. Sherwood Fox (London: Collier Macmillan and New York: Free Press, 1956)—to give an example of a metadisciplinary approach to education as an area of study, as opposed to the macrodisciplinary approaches discussed below.
66. Arthur R. King and John A. Brownell, *The Curriculum and the Disciplines of Knowledge* (New York, London and Sydney: Wiley, 1966), p. 95.
67. Ibid.
68. Clifford Geertz, "The Way We Think Now: Toward an Ethnography of Modern Thought," *Local Knowledge* (New York: Basic, 1983), p. 153.
69. Ibid., pp. 156–60.
70. Tony Becher, *Academic Tribes and Territories* (Buckingham and Bristol: Open Univ. Press and SRHE, 1989), p. 1.
71. Ibid., Chapters 4, 5, and 6.
72. Terry Eagleton, *Myths of Power: A Marxist Study of the Brontës* (London and Basingstoke: Macmillan, 1975).
73. Ronald Barnett, "Recovering an Academic Community", *Academic Community: Discourse or Discord?*, ed. Ronald Barnett (London and Bristol: Jessica Kingsley, 1994), pp. 3–20.
74. Broadly, the former is espoused (with reservations) in the essay by Tony Becher, for example, "Interdisciplinarity and Community," pp. 55–68, while proposals for resolving the latter appear in John Wyatt's (among others) paper, "Maps of Knowledge: Do They Form an Atlas?", pp. 36–51, in *Academic Community.*
75. Ibid., Tony Becher, "Interdisciplinarity and Community," p. 57.

76. See Muzafer Sherif and Carolyn Sherif, "Interdisciplinary Coordination as a Validity Check: Retrospect and Prospect," *Interdisciplinary Relationships in the Social Sciences,* ed. Sherif and Sherif (Chicago: Univ. of Chicago Press, 1969), pp. 3–20.

77. Kenneth D. Roose, "Observations on Interdisciplinary Work in the Social Sciences," pp. 323–27; and Donald T. Campbell, "Ethnocentrism of Disciplines and the Fish-Scale Model of Omniscience," pp. 328–48, in *Interdisciplinary Relationships in the Social Sciences.*

78. *Reductionism in Academic Disciplines,* ed. Arthur Peacocke (Surrey: SRHE and NFER-Nelson, 1985); and *The Future as an Academic Discipline,* intro. C. H. Waddington (Amsterdam: Radopi, 1975).

Part II
The Bold Text

The Disciplinary Status of Literary Studies and English Literary Studies

Clarification

THE PRECEDING PART POSSESSES A MIMETIC NARRATORIAL STANCE, where the subject reenacts its immanence, flickering, absence, and objectification within the appropriate texts (cautious and bold) that deal with approaches to disciplines of knowledge. This presents an apparently synchronic description of disciplines of knowledge. A picture of the placements, overlappings, and exclusions of different disciplines and potential interdisciplinary realizations as a "state of affairs" seems to emerge. To encompass the irreconcilability of the different texts and the fragmented nature of the exposition of disciplines of knowledge above as synchronic would however belie the pluralism which is espoused here. This is effectively a summary of the unsummarizable, or a surrender to the limitations and assertiveness of the bold text. We presume the general nature of synchronicity/diachronicity as descriptive terms—which is not possible outside the metadisciplinary or macrodisciplinary approach. In doing this we further assert the diametrical opposition of synchronicity to diachronicity—an assertion which has been viewed with increasing scepticism by linguists who have questioned Saussure's definitions.[1] I would like to clarify here that this is not merely a one-dimensional synchronic stance but one that *contains* a series of enclosed views of historiographical frameworks and emphases and realized histories appropriate to the disciplinary text in question. To say that the philosophical subject, the literary subject, the not-scientist subject, the sociological or educational subject-as-object are able to constitute the relevant historical perspective within their immanence, flickering, absence in the appropriate texts (bold or cautious) is to state the obvious. If history is construed as a discipline in itself, balanced between and perhaps including the discrete approaches mentioned above, it would have to adopt a metadisciplinary perspective. At any rate, the preceding mimetic conglomeration of cautious and bold texts is not amenable to a generalized description in terms of synchronicity or diachronicity, and would have to comprehend both.

Indeed, the preceding conglomeration of texts is not available to any single generalized description without surrendering to the limitations of the bold text, and moreover to the specific limitations of a meta or macrodisciplinary approach. There is undoubtedly a notion of Text but it is comprehensible only as many texts, just as there is indubitably a concept of Subject which is realizable only in the presence, flickering, absence of many subjects. In maintaining this however I do not wish to suggest that the preceding part escapes all ideological, aesthetic, historical, or social placement. On the contrary it remains open to most of these but only within the inevitable methodological and textual delimitations (of caution and boldness, for instance) from which these are possible.

Literary Studies and Other Disciplines of Knowledge

It is my intention in this part to examine the manner in which literary studies is placed within a field of disciplines of knowledge in general and therefore within an interdisciplinary perspective from a meta or macrodisciplinary outlook. As I had remarked before such a placement is not strictly within the precincts of literary studies per se (which is usually constituted within the cautious text, as inside or outside "literature"). This placement is more likely to be akin to a sociologist's or educationist's view of literary studies. I had also decided to do this with a primary focus on literature and literary studies in English.

Studies which attempt to place literary studies in general and English literary studies in particular in terms of disciplines of knowledge (however understood) are comparatively rare. A brave attempt in this direction has been made recently by Josephine Guy and Ian Small in *Politics and Value in English Studies* (Cambridge, 1993). A precis of their argument could be made as follows. They try to demystify some of the confusions and misunderstandings involved in perceptions of the so-called crisis in English literature, and thereby literary studies in general, which students of the discipline are apparently facing now. The crisis is allegedly due to the impact of critical theory and the increased politicization in English literary studies. These have led to a loss of normally received notions of canonicity and value, or have led to shifts in (and some ambiguity about) these concepts, which students of the discipline are finding difficult to accommodate. Guy and Small argue that this is manifest at what they consider to be the three main activities of English literary studies: i.e., literary criticism, literary history, and text-editing. They maintain that the understanding of this crisis and the ability to cope with it are adversely affected by certain shortcomings in the literary scholar's outlook. These are:

a. An inability to assess the relevance and ramifications of theoretical issues and developments across a range of disciplines of knowledge;

b. A consequent lack of "protective devices" which exist in other disciplines to guard against such crises;

c. And an attendant penchant for politicization which results from an unwillingness to assess the epistemological criteria involved in the development of disciplines of knowledge in general (and English literature in particular).

An attempt is made to correct some of these shortcomings by referring to relevant characteristics of disciplines in general and the specific methodologies adopted by certain disciplines extraneous to literary studies (sociology or the philosophy of science, for example).

Most of these observations are well taken, and the study has the merit of using and analyzing a wide range of material in detail. However, Guy's and Small's work also suffers from certain tenuous assumptions and formulations in the theoretical framework within which these details and observations are accommodated. The questionable elements in their book are characteristic of academic reflections of this nature and need to be examined further before the disciplinary status of English literature and literary studies in general can be considered. I refer below to *Politics and Value in English Studies* as a characteristic text within the area with which this part is concerned. In the following examination of its theoretical assumptions and formulations I set out the theoretical background for this part of the present text.

The following are the points on which this part differs from the approach adopted by studies like *Politics and Value.*

a. *Politics and Value* is indubitably a bold text, which traces out a general view of disciplines, and depends on references to the history of the consolidation of specialisms and the institutionalization of disciplines in the nineteenth and twentieth centuries.[2] It is inevitable that a study of this nature would be constituted in the bold text, but the assertive character of Guy's and Small's work fails to recognize the limits of the approach or the refusal of certain disciplines which may be constituted in cautious texts to accede to their generalizations. Since the boldness of their text is *a priori* in the context of their argument, the approaches to bodies of knowledge which refuse to recognize their margins (and therefore refuse a general understanding of disciplines) are simply excluded. They are not mentioned. This is a particularly sensitive issue in the consideration of literary studies (note that I am not saying English literary studies, but more of that later) which is predominantly constituted in the cautious text. The inability to see the possible refusal of a general view, consequent on an unreflexive immersion in the bold text, often leads to asseverations which sound suspicious. For example, in objecting to Catherine Belsey's and Terry Eagleton's suggestion that literary critical theory should study discursive practices and therefore not be limited by an object of study (say, a specific literary canon) Guy and Small argue:

> without some sort of consensus about the object of study of English—a consensus, that is, about what precisely theories are supposed to explain—there can be no way to adjudicate between theories on the basis of their explanatory power. *Different theories will after all be examining different things: in that sense they will be incommensurate.*[3][my emphasis]

This is rather a naive statement to make in this context. Even in the academic disciplines of the natural sciences it is recognized that contending theories are not adjudicated purely in terms of their ability to explain certain objects but their ability to do this *with reference to an existing network of explanations all of which might change.* The focus on the object in the natural sciences is specific to the practice of science; it is the special character of science as a discipline, I had observed above, which *excludes* rather than sets the norm for other disciplines. The full extent of the inadequacy of the above statement appears, for instance, if one asks oneself "does a theory of philosophy have an object in the same sense that a theory of chemistry has an object?," "is it impossible for a theory of literary studies, social science, and philosophy to engage with *an* object?" and so on. The problem with the above statement is situated in its assumption of a homogeneous notion of "theory" across disciplines of knowledge.

The second objection that Guy and Small make to any possible extension of literary critical theory with regard to its objects of study (as recommended by Belsey and Eagleton) is even more tenuous:

> it is extremely difficult to see how such an all-embracing theory could possibly exist. No single theory, nor group of theories, could ever be adequate to such a task. The only theory which could conceivably explain the putative object of study proposed by Belsey and Eagleton would have to be so general as to be useless for all practical purposes.[4]

"What do they mean by theory?" one asks oneself, and "What do they mean by all-embracing?" Foucault's theory of the archaeology of discursive formations is "all-embracing" in a sense which is not incompatible with Einstein's general theory of relativity being "all-embracing" or with Darwin's theory of evolution (transmitted through the works of Herbert Spencer, T. H. Huxley, Henri Bergson, and others) having been perceived as "all-embracing." Guy's and Small's immersion in the bold text, and consequent assertion of the general element in disciplines of knowledge and specialisms, leaves no space for multiple and coexistent (even if contradictory) understandings of theory, knowledge, or the world and its constituent objects. This is inexplicable in a context where multiple worlds is a looming physical reality.

To object to the politicization of literary studies initiated to a large extent by developments in critical theory ré literature does not necessarily imply that the scope of critical theory ré literature has to be restrained. The two issues are independent.

b. Guy's and Small's bold text could accommodate English studies (or literary studies, as they would have it) within an understanding of disciplines of knowledge only from a metadisciplinary or macrodisciplinary perspective. They attempt to do both without distinguishing between them clearly. The collision of the meta and macrodisciplinary criteria of their placement of disciplines of knowledge is apparent in their statement of the "two ways in which social factors affect the production of disciplinary knowledge":

> The first concerns day-to-day decisions about funding, resources, and so on; these are primarily institutional decisions in the sense that they serve primarily institutional interests. For this reason, as we suggested in the previous chapter, they can indeed be understood in institutional terms. The second way in which the social impinges

> upon the production of disciplinary knowledge concerns the intellectual preconditions for the foundation of disciplines of knowledge in the first instance, and the mechanisms of intellectual authority which safeguard the prestige of the knowledge produced by a discipline.[5]

There is, in other words, an *implied* notion of quanta of knowledge (some kind of notion of social fact/action) which underlies the institutional and epistemological foundations of disciplines of knowledge. The specifications of the implied notion of quanta is however withheld behind the vague designation of "social." One understands that in the social there is a common denominator to all approaches to disciplines of knowledge (institutional or epistemological). But, with a lack of precision untypical of a sociological approach, the constitution of, or build up from, the "social" is left unexplained. It is accepted that there is a metadisciplinary base, but the terms in which this is presented do not bear interrogation. Nevertheless this metadisciplinary base, the vague social, becomes the repository of value and is evoked at various points in the book to question received notions of the place of critical theory in English studies. What emerges in an explicit fashion in the above quotation is the macrodisciplinary approach to disciplines of knowledge (and therefore English studies). The first point acknowledges this in the emphasis on "institutional" factors. The latter point seems to suggest that an understanding of the epistemological foundations of a discipline could be located in an examination of the history of that discipline, and that this is somehow contrary to the institutional factors. The distinction between institutional and epistemological is tenuous in the context of arguments offered by Guy and Small. In the examples which are given to demonstrate the importance of epistemological foundations one finds oneself looking at the history of the acceptance and validation of contentions in different disciplines by the communities and organizations which give these bodies of knowledge their disciplinary character. In other words one is presented with stages in the history of the *institutionalization* (how else can the communitarian and organizational criteria involved be understood?) of separate disciplines from a macrodisciplinary perspective. The institutional factors, in other words, decide the validity and possibility of relevant epistemological arguments in a discipline, and not the other way around as Guy and Small would have us believe. This *volte face* is disguised by the ostensible social base but, as has been observed, the social is too imprecise, too vague, to actually assume a specific role in this argument. The argument is predominantly a macrodisciplinary one, which assumes the institutional definition and validation of disciplines of knowledge as *a priori* in this context, and places the epistemological self-legitimation of disciplines and the interrelations between disciplines accordingly.

The latter observation is supported by a close look at most of the instances of epistemological self-legitimation of disciplines and examinations of interrelations between disciplines presented by Guy and Small. In the discussion of Jevons's contribution in the shape of the marginal utility theory in economic thinking, ostensibly to show "the new social mechanisms of intellectual authority, *and their relative independence from institutions*"[6] [emphasis in the text], this is manifest. It is argued that though the validity of Jevons's theory is marked by its gradual acceptance within institutions and by members of institutions, its validity is proven by criteria which lie outside it:

> The eventual widespread acceptance of marginal utility can be attributed only to a social agreement about the intellectual coherence and utility of Jevons's argument [. . .]. Of course the individuals responsible for these arguments were located within institutions (predominantly within the universities), and those institutions clearly recognised the criteria which Jevons's argument met (in, for example, the coherence and utility of his theory) were appropriate for the evaluation of a new explanatory paradigm. But these criteria were not arbitrarily chosen, nor did the judgements based upon them exist to serve the interests (however they are defined) of institutions.[7]

It appears that, despite the obvious difficulties, Guy and Small have managed to demonstrate that Jevons's theory draws its validity outside the precincts of institutions because (a) the criteria for validity are not *arbitrary,* and (b) it does not serve the interests of the institution. The weakness of the argument is spread over several levels. The importance of Jevons's argument is cited at the level of institutional acceptance—within the argument its epistemological validation is not given any space outside the institutionally acceptable. The concept of institution at work here is suspect. Is the institution merely the university in a sort of splendid isolation which renders it unnecessary to examine the complexity of the notion of institutional interests? Do institutions depend on arbitrary criteria to serve their interests? Is it really not necessary to define what is meant by interests? Can institutional interests not claim coherence and utility for themselves? It is suggested that institutions (the purely macrodisciplinary) are evaded by a more basic sort of social acceptance (the implied metadisciplinariness). The familiar vagueness of social reappears (the qualifying coherence and utility do little to clarify), compounded now by an equally wishy-washy notion of "institution." In fact, the argument is so focused on the institutional status of Jevons's work within an institutional description of disciplines (economics in this case), that its opposing contentions seem irrelevant. Guy's and Small's work is basically macrodisciplinary in character though they wish to present, unsuccessfully, a metadisciplinary approach mainly through the agency of certain undefined and unclear terms (social, institution, coherent and utilizable theory).

In fact, a similar process of macrodisciplinariness disguised as metadisciplinariness is revealed in the accounts of philosophical debates, debates in the philosophy of science, the methods of social science, as and when these appear. These accounts are rather simplistically placed against familiar notions of English literary study, usually to deplore the comparative lack of clarity, lack of understanding, and inadequate transmission of ideas in that discipline. In this process of comparative placement, the undefined and unclear grey area of metadisciplinary assumptions is brought to play. A notion of a basic (but consistently vague) social utility and coherence (i.e., value) crops up, is made the grounds for methodological and substantive comparisons. In other words, a wealth of macrodisciplinary detail is bound in a web of ill-realized metadisciplinary assumptions. The result is, to say the least, confused. The swan song of the book appears in the final chapter on the development of the discipline of English literature itself (largely a critique of Brian Doyle's work). The whole process of macrodisciplinariness disguised as metadisciplinariness is repeated. Brian Doyle's focus on the institutional development of the discipline (confessedly macrodisciplinary) is ostensibly challenged by positing the role that purely epistemological factors played. The familiar confusions regarding social bases and institutional interests reappear. It would be tedious to chart out the pattern again.

To summarize this point then, Guy's and Small's work demonstrates an inability to distinguish between the meta and macrodisciplinary, between a focus on an assumed quanta of knowledge approach and a presumed institutionally defined approach to disciplines. They present an essentially macrodisciplinary set of observations in terms of inadequately comprehended metadisciplinary assumptions. This has two important consequences which are briefly presented as the final two points here. These have to do with (1) the question of politicization in literary studies (the main crisis-factor and target of their attack), and (2) the distinction (not made by Guy and Small) between literary studies in general and English literary studies.

c. Through their refusal to acknowledge the perspective of the cautious text or limitations of the bold text, and their penchant for colliding the meta and macrodisciplinary approaches to disciplines of knowledge, Guy and Small set out their objections to the politicization of English literary studies. The advent and use/misuse of critical theory is held responsible for it. The role of critical theory and the various consequent and allegedly inadequate or outright fallacious political effects in English literary studies are examined at the three levels of academic activity in the field (literary criticism, literary history, and text-editing). Broadly, the political effects are seen as limiting with regard to the criteria of "social utility" (therefore value and tradition) in disciplines of knowledge. The political effects detract attention, in other words, from the epistemological factors which validate the status of the discipline of English literary studies, and legitimize each step in its development as a discipline in the context of other disciplines. "Politics," in Guy's and Small's terms, is related to the grey area (as demonstrated above) of institutions and interests, and opposed to the equally gray area of social. All these terms follow a set of unstated and therefore inevitably vague metadisciplinary assumptions. When it becomes evident that this complex interconnectedness of terms emanates from a center of vagueness the thrust of the argument wilts. One is not sure what Guy and Small mean by political because one is not sure what they mean by institution and interest because one is not sure what they mean by social. To approach the merits or otherwise of politicization in English studies a clearly defined meta or macrodisciplinary approach would have to be assumed, which would in turn clarify what politicization is. Further, the argument would have to acknowledge the space of aesthetic reading and the reading subject both inside and outside literature (i.e., the cautious text in literary studies). Finally, one would have to trace the relationship between the former and the latter if one exists. This study contends that there is no relationship and that the outside and inside of literary studies can and do coexist as different fields of activity. This coexistence is unproblematic once it is properly understood and the so-called crisis, in which politics seems to threaten aesthetics, ideology seems to subsume the subject, theory appears at odds with tradition and value, would disappear. The crisis is anticipated only because of a widespread confusion between bold and cautious texts, between meta and macrodisciplinary approaches, when one tries to place English literature within a field of disciplines of knowledge.

d. The placement of English literary studies within a field of disciplines of knowledge is itself vitiated by the collision of meta and macrodisciplinary approaches. Guy and Small use English literary studies and literary studies in general interchangeably as if they are both disciplines of knowledge in the same sense and as if they are somehow coextensive. Within the bold text, in which alone the disciplinary status of English literary studies and literary studies in general can be seen in the perspective of other disciplines of knowledge, the position can be clarified through a clearer demarcation between metadisciplinary and macrodisciplinary approaches.

English literary studies can be understood as a discipline in its own right only from a macrodisciplinary approach. English literary studies exists as a distinct and self-contained discipline, and is demarcated as such, through the designation of specific departments in universities and centers of research and other fora, only within the institution (in the broad sense of the previous part of this study). The institution defines the place of English literary studies as such in terms of other disciplines which enjoy similar designative privileges. English literature is a discipline in its own right in the sense of being identified as such in school courses, in university departments, in research institutes, in recognized fora of exchange (the journal, the seminar, the academic publishing house, etc.). In this sense French literature, Nigerian literature, Chinese literature, etc. are also academic disciplines. In some institutional spaces literary studies in general or critical theory are demarcated in a similar fashion, and often maintained as independent and parallel disciplines to English literary studies, but seldom as interchangeable with English literary studies.

Literary studies in general is usually more appropriately approached either from a metadisciplinary perspective or within the cautious text. The latter does not permit a placement in terms of other disciplines. The former is consistent with the purpose of this part. Literary studies could be seen as a particular kind of arrangement of certain quanta of knowledge—say, as a specific kind of discursive formation, a certain order of social facts, a certain mode of social actions, and so on. This does not erase English literary studies. But, in this approach, English literary studies is not a discipline on its own account. It is rather a subdiscipline of sorts, as are French or Nigerian or Chinese or any other literature. A ripple in literary studies in general has implications of equal magnitude and effects of various magnitudes right across the range of subdisciplines which are contained in literary studies in general. The specificity of the subdiscipline of English literary studies in this context is marked by the difference in its magnitude of effect relative to the equal magnitude of implication across all subdisciplines of literary studies in general. If, for instance, one accepts a formalistic principle of criticism in literary studies in general this implies that whatever subdiscipline one approaches would be analyzed accordingly (the equal magnitude of implication). But the formalistic principle might sit more comfortably in the area of, say, Russian literary studies than in English literary studies (i.e., the variable magnitude of effect). It is the latter examined against the former which identifies the difference of the subdisciplines of Russian and English literary studies within literary studies in general. This distinction of difference between subdisciplines within the discipline of literary studies would be part of the process of construction from whatever quanta of knowledge one adopts to the body of knowledge (subdiscipline of English literary studies or discipline of literary studies in general) one wishes to examine. In other words, it will be part of the metadisciplinary mode of placing a specific discipline in the context of other disciplines.

In either instance English literary studies and literary studies in general cannot be used interchangeably without causing confusion. It should be noted that confusion of this order is not confined to Guy and Small (in fact, their's is the comparatively discerning approach).

The Importance of Comprehending and Maintaining Distinctions

To reiterate: if one attempts to discern the disciplinary status of English literary studies in the context of other disciplines of knowledge two strategies are possible. One, English literary studies can be seen as an academic discipline with an institutional space from a macrodisciplinary perspective, or two, English literary studies can be viewed as a subdiscipline of literary studies in general from a metadisciplinary perspective. Both of these are only possible within the bold text. These refuse the exclusiveness of the cautious text of literary studies by providing summaries of it which are incompatible with the cautious text (see discussion in Part I). As seen above, a certain degree of confusion between each level of these distinctions is usual—between the bold and the cautious texts, between the macro and metadisciplinary approaches, between the subdiscipline status and the academic discipline status. The confusion is, to an extent, inevitable. The same terms crop up at each level with different shades of connotation and denotation which are crucial to the consistency of the discrete discourses involved. If the terms are used as interchangeable, as the same, as identical, confusion would naturally follow. If "literary studies" in the cautious text, in the metadisciplinary bold text, in the macrodisciplinary bold text; "English literary studies" as a macrodisciplinary academic discipline, as a metadisciplinary subdiscipline; the subject "I" in the cautious text and the subject-as-object "I" in the bold text, etc. are not discerned and distinguished carefully some misprision of reading is understandable. Yet the terms are the same, and refer to a *basic set of preoccupations or objects* albeit through different perspectives consequent on different relationships with other disciplines or reading-writing subjects or subjects-as-objects. Add to this the rarity of pure bold and cautious texts and one has some sense of the obstacles involved in obtaining a coherent picture of disciplines of knowledge and the place of literary studies and English literary studies in it.

Having clarified some of the seminal distinctions of levels of analysis involved it is now possible to relocate and rearrange the factors which are usually cited to allocate to English literary studies its disciplinary status, and to disperse some of the fog of the crisis which allegedly looms over it. The factors in question appear with reference to English literary studies and literary studies in general at the several levels mentioned above to provide the rationale of curricula in institutions of education; the justification of specialist critical (and related pedagogical and bibliographical) activity in different fora of intercommunication; the legitimation of certain tastes, values, and traditions which readers-writers may adhere to; the explanation of disciplinary status and relation to other disciplines qua disciplines. In other words one could reconsider, relocate, and rearrange the issues of canonicity in (English) literary studies, (English) literary history and the history of (English) literature as an academic discipline, aesthetics/poetics and ideology in (English) literary studies, nation and culture in (English) literary studies. In this study I do not attempt to provide a comprehensive or even extensive treatment of such an ambitious project: I content myself instead with some observations which may lead to a more comprehensive and extensive investigation. Further, the observations which follow are not set out in an organized factor-by-factor manner. In fact, the factors in question are related in so intimate and complex a fashion, and are spread out over the several levels enumerated above in such a complicated manner, that a distinct factor-by-factor analysis would be either misleading or repetitive. The following observations therefore occur in a somewhat haphazard order and hope to convey some of the complex links and distinctions involved.

Crisis in the Subdiscipline of English Literature and in the Academic Discipline of English Literature

A sense of urgency surrounds a crisis. A crisis needs to be evaded, to be overcome. This cannot be done by turning away from a crisis, by avoiding it; a crisis has to be faced. A crisis demands redefinitions, reclarifications, rearrangements, reformulations. Only then can it be averted, but in its wake it leaves a new order (perhaps) or a clarity in the old order that wasn't there before. A crisis stands at the frontier of knowledge: it compels its advance by threatening its order, its smugness, its complacency, by casting a shadow of chaos and bewilderment.

Let's begin with the crisis. Is there a crisis in English literary studies? For its sake one hopes there is. At each point of the gradual advance of, say, poetics, there is arguably the compulsion of and the threat of a crisis. One is tempted to generalize: for every Platonic expulsion there is an Aristotelian reinstatement (attended by redefinitions, reclarifications, rearrangements, reformulations), poetry is constantly defended by its champions against the surge of philistines. But grand generalizations are not my thing here. Is there a crisis in English literary studies? Any student of English literature who has recently been in a classroom of English literary studies or a seminar on the pedagogy of English literature, has perused the English literary journals and followed the reviews and commentaries, is assured that there is a crisis. It has something to do with the emergence of critical theory, with increased political awareness (and demands for political correctness), with shifts in the concepts of utility and value due to developments in other disciplines and pressing sociological factors. Something needs to be clarified, something needs to be dispensed with, something needs to be reorganized, something needs to be averted and some straw needs to be grasped—the opinions are diverse and overlap and are blurred. In terms of the distinctions drawn above (cautious and bold texts, meta and macrodisciplinary approaches, English literature as a subdiscipline and as an academic discipline) the state of the crisis can be described a bit more conveniently.

In the cautious text of literature (which *contains* English literature) there can be no crisis other than the inbuilt crisis of anxiety at the self-perpetuating subject and the enclosed expansiveness which defines the cautious text. The need of the fluid and all-encompassing and inscrutable "I" to contain knowledge in my mode of constituting myself, and therefore my discipline, in the cautious text is the only crisis possible here. Indeed this is scarcely the crisis which the discipline of literary studies as constituted in the bold text raises and contemplates. In the cautious text of literature there is more a kind of constant tension, a stress, a nervousness at its elusive margins: it is the condition of its cautious character. In the bold text of literary studies there is usually a placid rigidity of fixed boundaries in which the subject is seen as object, and there are potential quanta of knowledge and institutional spaces which are stable and reassuring, and give one access to the relative positions of other disciplines. A crisis is recognized only occasionally when it is forced to attention by the bewilderment and awe of some unfamiliar creative or critical act. The crisis challenges the stable and reassuring features of the bold text of literary studies, and impels redefinitions, reclarifications, rearrangements, and reformulations. The recent recognition of a crisis in English literary studies (keeping in mind the distinction from literary studies in general) comes within the precincts of the latter—the bold text only. But in what sense is it specifically a crisis in *English* literary studies?

That is the all-important question to which this part of the study addresses itself: in the bold text how is English literary studies distinguished from literary studies in general and in terms of other disciplinary bodies of knowledge? What is a crisis in English literary studies and in literary studies in general and how is this to be expressed given our understanding of a background of other disciplines of knowledge? It becomes immediately clear that the question will have to be addressed by invoking the distinction of the meta and macrodisciplinary approaches. The following are the senses in which a crisis could be seen in English literary studies specifically and in literary studies in general. To make the relations between the senses and the levels of specificity and generality clear the following is organized under two subheadings: "crisis" pertinent to a metadisciplinary approach to English literary studies (i.e., as a subdiscipline), and "crisis" relevant to a macrodisciplinary approach to English literary studies (i.e., as an academic discipline).

"Crisis" in the Subdiscipline of English Literary Studies

This is the crisis that is perceived as being relevant to the pursuit of literature and literary studies as a whole. Its particular space in the subdiscipline of English literary studies cannot be comprehended unless the implications for the whole of literature can be discerned. In turn the crisis for the whole of literature cannot be understood unless it is reasonably clear how literature as a body of knowledge is distinguished from other bodies of knowledge. Consider an example of such a perceived crisis which ostensibly attaches to literature and literary studies as a whole: consider, for instance, René Welleck's defense against "The Attack on Literature" (such defenses for literature are legion, Welleck's has the advantage of being representative). Welleck identifies three grounds for the attack on literature: one, the politically motivated ("that literature (and presumably all art) is conservative or at least a conserving power which serves the interests of the ruling class"[8]); two, that which "is basically motivated by a distrust of language";[9] and three, that which arises from a fear regarding the future of literacy. Welleck's defense expresses doubts about each of these separately, and more interestingly, collectively:

> All these attacks on literature, the politically motivated, the despair about language, the retreat from the word, the cult of silence, and McLuhan's doubts about the future of literacy, assume a concept of literature that includes all acts of writing, from the most trivial to the most sublime. They make no distinction of quality, no aesthetic judgement [. . .]. The collapse of aesthetics is the presupposition of the success of these attacks.[10]

He then goes on to demonstrate that this presupposition is fallacious by sketching a history of the term "literature" and demonstrating how closely it is associated with the development and conventions of aesthetic qualifications. The normative position of the aesthetic of literature which Welleck appeals to, and the historical continuity which ostensibly justifies it, are the usual disciplinary descriptions of literature against which attacks against literature as a whole (or crises) become manifest.

I have discussed the aesthetic of literature in the previous part. To reiterate the terminology developed there apropos Welleck-like arguments: the crisis of (or attacks against) literature in general is usually expressed by litterateurs who have lost the comfort of the all-enclosing cautious text of literature, where the inscrutable and fluid "I" can express and maintain the very subjectivity of reading-writing. The crisis of literature is perceived when the cautious text is transformed and metamorphosed into the bold text (summarized within it). This is not merely a violent thrust from an *inside* to an *outside,* but an infinitely more bewildering dislocation from which no effect on literature seems possible any longer, the organism of literature appears to be dead. Welleck's perceptions of attacks is the fear of an inability of having any impact on literature, a terror at the relegation of literature into indifference, into stasis, or into extinction. The transformation of the cautious text of literature into the bold text (through the mere act of summarization, through the transformation from literary subject to subject-as-object) is due to the throwing of literature into a meta or macrodisciplinary perspective. The three main attacks that Welleck describes are the result of the placement of literature in the bold text which inevitably leads to a placement of literature in a meta or macrodisciplinary perspective. In the case of literature in general (which Welleck deals with) the threat of the metadisciplinary perspective understandably predominates. Literature in general has a metadisciplinary space, and only rarely an exclusively macrodisciplinary (institutional) space. One could restate the three main attacks on (i.e., the crisis of) literature, as seen by Welleck, accordingly.

Attack one: there is a crisis in literature (defined by its aesthetic and corresponding history) because the aesthetic is being disregarded or framed by a different sort of analytical scrutiny. This scrutiny refuses to see literature in its own terms (the cautious text) and insists on collapsing it into a system of statements/facts/actions put together by power-relationships (a working understanding of the metadiscipline of politics).

Attack two: the crisis in literature is due to its aesthetic being disregarded by a dissective gaze. The dissective gaze persistently reduces all texts (including the literary, despite their literariness) into linguistic components and linguistic formations.

Attack three: the crisis in literature is because of a sociological perspective (which interrogates literacy, for instance). The aesthetic of literature dissolves before a metadisciplinary sociological description of literary facts/acts/statements, which brings them into unequal contest with, for example, audio-visual facts/acts/statements (the development of radio, film, television, video, virtual reality equipment, etc.). An alternative challenge to literature (though not mentioned by Welleck) from this sort of metadisciplinary sociological perspective could be posed by unfavorable comparison to other disciplines (the scientific, the economic, etc.) in terms of social utility, coherence, etc.

The aesthetic definition and historical justification which underlie the definition of literature in terms of which these attacks (or this crisis) become manifest is key. Those who adopt this position often tend, particularly of late, to term the crisis-generating perspectives as theoretical or the result of theory. This is possibly because the metadisciplinary perspectives involved, which dislocate the comfort of the cautious text of literature, are obviously not confined to, or concerned with, literature in itself. This mode of designating "theory" is, however, confusing because the aesthetic definition is itself far from being untheoretical. It carries with it the entire baggage of canonicity, tradition, value; a distinct pedagogical and critical practice, authorial responsibility, and bibliographical convention; a vision of the relation of literature to the *zeitgeist*, to history, to knowledge.

If the above argument, derived from Welleck, is accepted as a representative statement of the crisis in literary studies in general, how does this percolate down to the subdiscipline of English literary studies specifically? Not in any distinctive fashion. At least not in any way differentiable from the implications for other subdisciplines of literary studies in general. The effective impact, however, may be distinctive depending on the specificity of English in its linguistic features, its geographical domain, its cultural constitution. In so far as the three attacks perceived by Welleck for literature in general go, their impact on English literary studies may be distinctive because of the following: the statements/facts/acts and the power-relationships involved therein might have features peculiar to the geographical and cultural domain of English literary studies (relevant to attack one); the linguistic components and linguistic formations of the English language are to some degree different from that of other languages (relevant to attack two); and the sociological perception of statements/facts/acts are also conditional to a certain extent on the geographical and cultural domain in question (relevant to attack three). These could affect the impact of the crisis in the subdiscipline of English literary studies specifically but these do not determine the implications or even the shape of the crisis. The crisis, in this context, is not of English literature in itself, but of literature in general given a metadisciplinary perception of knowledge. Those who speak about this sort of crisis most clearly do not speak of English literature alone but of literature at a more general level: René Welleck is a case in point, as was Ezra Pound before him and Harold Bloom after. Those who do reduce their defenses against this sort of crisis to the domain of the subdiscipline alone (the Leavises were probably the first to do so, and we have seen Guy and Small do the same more recently above) are probably laboring under (or deliberately submitting to) some misapprehension about the centrality of English literary studies. The latter observations pertain to the issue of canonicity with relation to a perceived crisis, and are discussed in more detail below.

It must also be noted here that this sort of confusion is not entirely indefensible. When, in considering the impact within the specific subdiscipline, one takes recourse to the geographical and cultural domain, one actually slips naturally into the language of the macrodisciplinary approach. The terms used to understand English literary studies as a subdiscipline are similar to those used to understand it as an academic discipline. One must use these terms with the greatest circumspection.

"Crisis" in the academic discipline of English literary studies

This crisis has been discovered comparatively recently, at least in comparison to the crisis of literature in general. The location of the exclusive institutional space of English literature, and the questioning of the validity of this space, may be apprehended as a symptom of the larger crisis of literary studies outlined above—or, to some, of the sudden explosion of theory in literary studies. Politics, one is assured, is involved in both. But politics with regard to disciplinary approaches is not a homogeneous methodological description. The politics which is involved in the crisis of English literature as a subdiscipline or of literature in general (say, in attack one above) is quite different from the politics involved in the crisis of English literature as an academic discipline, as an institutional space. The power relations of interest are not charted out at a meta level any longer (i.e., acts/facts/statements, for instance), but as between different strata of institutional spaces, with a focal point on English literature as an institutional space. This could be seen, for example, as the politics that exists in the relation between the institutional space of the administrative state and its branches (say, the ministry of education, the departments dealing with culture), the institutional space of academic bodies (the university, the research institute, the specialized publication houses), and the institutional space of the components of the latter (the department or section of English literature as opposed to other departments and sections). No doubt the metadisciplinarian would see the meta and the macro description of quanta and institution in a continuous fashion: the point of this study is, however, that for the macrodisciplinarian there is no such continuity. Everything proceeds from the recognition of the immanence of the institutional space, everything becomes conditional to such a focus. The crisis of English literature from this perspective, as it begins to be identified and discussed now, is exclusive to the peculiar status of its institutional space. English literature has features which do not apply to the institutional space of other literatures in the same fashion. There might be an analogous position in the institution of French literature for example, but it is *analogous*, not the *same*. There may be good reasons for the analogous relations to exist—some mutual appreciation in the developments of the discrete institutional spaces, some mutual appreciation in the developments of other institutional spaces (the administrative state, academia, etc.). But the primary assumption, the focal point (before the analogues and parallels are admitted) is of the difference, the uniqueness, of the discrete institutional spaces.

The easiest way to chart out a growing preoccupation with the crisis in English literary studies exclusively (i.e., as an academic discipline, an institutional space) is to pursue studies of the history of the establishment and development of English literary studies as an academic discipline. One usually refers to the debate which, in a sense, began with D. J. Palmer's *The Rise of English Studies* and has been continued in the work of Chris Baldick, Terry Eagleton, Brian Doyle, Gauri Vishwanathan, Robert Crawford, John Dixon, and others. I comment briefly on some of these below. I might as well add here that to see D. J. Palmer's work as a beginning of macrodisciplinary realizations of English literature is not wholly accurate. No focus of the study of English literature in England could be the initiation point in this direction—the crisis which impels and evolves from such an approach could not emerge where the institutional space sits comfortably and remains cosily obvious and transparent. The institution of English literature as an academic discipline always sat uneasily in the excolonies, always stood out with a disturbing opacity, and evidence of agonization regarding the validation of this institutional space follows close on institutionalisation itself. Within a narrow focus, and from a convenient bibliographical point of view, however, D. J. Palmer and the others are a useful reference network.

But what is the crisis here? This can simply be stated as follows: the crisis arises because any attempt to comprehend the institutional space of the discipline of English literary studies reveals hidden intentions behind the ostensible claims (of aesthetics, value, tradition, etc.) it makes, lays bare the mechanics of cultural domination and cultural marginalization which underlies its self-definition, exposes the vested interests of the institution to the establishment of English literary studies in all its dimensions, and demystifies its populist or aesthetist appeals. This is what draws the crisis from the observations of Palmer, Baldick, Eagleton, Vishwanathan, Crawford, et al: this is, as is discussed at a later point, what unites this set of references. This manifestation of a crisis is implicit in the macrodisciplinary approach. The terms which we had encountered in a consideration of the metadisciplinary approach reappear in the macrodisciplinary approach with subtle shifts in implication which ensure this overall effect. Instead of seeing terms like canon, tradition, aesthetics, value as a complex (a discourse formation, a social situation, etc.) of specific quanta, and in having rejected any acknowledgement of the cautious text of literature and the reading-writing subject, all these terms have to be explained as subsequent or correlated to the institutional space in a macrodisciplinary approach. These terms not only have to be related to the presumption of English literature as an academic discipline, these terms actually have to be *corollary* to and *serve* the presumption and continuance of the academic discipline. The reasons for the crisis implicit in a macrodisciplinary approach to English literature as an academic discipline are obvious.

Indeed, one could asseverate that the very employment of a coherent macrodisciplinary approach to study English literary studies specifically would necessarily invite a crisis. This is all the truer because of the perspective of other institutionally defined disciplinary spaces which would also inevitably play a part in a macrodisciplinary approach. The different kinds of vested interests, ostensible and actual reasoning, and modes of disciplinary self-perpetuation and preservation manifested in other institutional disciplinary spaces, would only serve to clarify the position in English literary studies. From a clear macrodisciplinary perspective a crisis is scarcely avoidable unless a certain degree of deliberate or inadvertent obfuscation occurs—as it does occur in the work of Guy and Small.

Canonicity in Accepted Canons and Self-Evident Canons, Particularly the Latter

One of the issues which is at the center of these crises is that of canonicity. The canon of English literature is usually taken to designate the area of its disciplinary existence; the crisis in English literature is in the challenge to its canon or the bids to open it up. Endless accusations and recriminations surround the issue of the canon (of English literature); its champions and its reformers possess an unflagging zeal for disputation at cross-purposes. That is one of the main points of this study. The air, I believe, can be cleared up a bit if a few distinctions, a few clarifications, are accepted. These distinctions and clarifications are offered in terms of the different disciplinary approaches (the enclosed discipline in the cautious text; the meta and macrodisciplinary approaches and corresponding sub and academic discipline differentiation in the bold text) suggested above. A clear placement of the disciplinary status of English literature and literature in general against a field of knowledge (other disciplines of knowledge) could assist in the process of cleansing the air and dispersing the fog. This has, I hope, been initiated by the clarification of the shades of the crisis which attaches to the discipline of English literature (sub or academic). To take the endeavour further the issues which have come to be intimately associated with the so-called crisis need investigation, and one of these issues is indubitably that of canonicity. So consider the canon in English literary studies and literary studies in general.

Consider the following as a provisional definition of literary canon: a literary canon is a selection of literary texts. This is the unequivocal basic statement. It is understood that nothing else is unequivocal about the canon. A selection would have to possess both reasons for its initiation and criteria for its realization. When the canon is interrogated in the wake of a crisis it is understood that the reasons and criteria which are its *raison d'etre* come under scrutiny. This could take the shape of a rediscovery or recognition of a self-evident canon (Matthew Arnold's touchstones, F. R. Leavis's great tradition of the English novel, Ezra Pound's or, more recently, Harold Bloom's compendiums, for instance), the questioning of an accepted canon (for example, Toni Morrison questioning the American literary canon in *Playing in the Dark*), the creation of an alternative canon which implies the splitting and growth away from an accepted canon (Elaine Showalter's gynocentric canon, for example, or the attempt to create an Irish literary canon in the *Field Day Anthology*, or the so-called "new" literatures in English), the expansion of an accepted canon or the introduction of a fluid and inclusive canon (roughly the attitude adopted by the more progressive English Departments in British Universities). When canonicity becomes an issue in the alleged crisis these various consequences are forced against each other, and the inconclusive disputations of cross purposes begin. The champions of the self-evident canon and the critics, reformers, deniers of the accepted canon are inevitably at odds. Sometimes the critics, reformers, and deniers are at odds with each other. At this point, before the fog shrouds us all, a differentiation of the shades of canon corresponding to the differentiation of the shades of crisis needs to be made. In charting out the various consequences of the canon in a crisis (rediscovery, questioning, splitting, expanding, etc.) I have used the term as if it has a single meaning with slightly different implications in different contexts. In fact, it is arguable that there are different meanings of "canon" in different contexts (say, a metadisciplinary and a macrodisciplinary context), and the implications of the different meanings should not be interplayed against each other.

The distinction that I would particularly like to emphasise is that between the *self-evident* canon (which can be rediscovered or simply recognized) and the *accepted* canon (which can be questioned, split, or expanded). The latter is clearly coherent with a macrodisciplinary approach and placement of literary studies. "Accepted" in this context is institutionally sanctioned: the predominantly white canon of American literature that Toni Morrison questions, the predominantly male canon against which Elaine Showalter presents an alternative gynocentric approach, the appropriated Britishness of the Anglo-Irish element in the English literary canon against which the editors of the *Field Day Anthology* offer a picture of Irishness, etc. are all reactions to canons that define the institutional space of literary studies. The accepted canons (English or American) are such because they are taught in school and university curricula, because they are constantly reiterated in different fora of intercommunication (scholarly and popular media, publishing houses, bookshops), because ultimately they find favor with those institutions which to a large extent control education and intercommunication (the state, and sometimes, the multinationals). The accepted canon defines the institutional space of the literary discipline under scrutiny and follows from the existence of the discipline as a corollary to institutionalization. This is a macrodisciplinary approach.

The self-evident canon is not consequent on a macrodisciplinary approach. This does not mean that it is outside the purview of the macrodisciplinary approach. On the contrary. The so-called accepted canon, which is consistent with a macrodisciplinary point of view, usually offers *itself* as self-evident. The accepted canon that is subjected to a macrodisciplinary analysis in terms of the institutional prerogatives of race, gender, nationality, etc. does not usually openly offer *itself* in those terms. The English and American literary canons do not usually validate themselves openly as white or male or power-friendly (though even this is known to happen, but that's prejudice, not literary study)—that they can be seen as such is the result and the success of macrodisciplinary analysis. Accepted canons usually give themselves as self-evident. That means that the condition of self-evidence which is usually called up to self-validate the mainstream canon calls upon a nonmacrodisciplinary approach: possibly a metadisciplinary approach or one within the precincts of the cautious text. One needs to emphasise under the circumstances that the argument of the accepted canon is not erased by the argument of the self-evident canon: these belong to different spheres of justification. This is the point at which apparently most of the confusion in discussions about canons in the wake of a crisis arise. Those who oppose an accepted canon cannot help feeling that they have demolished the self-evident canon, those who champion the self-evident canon cannot see how this is possible without addressing the argument of self-evidence itself and by addressing only the (from their perspective) ancillary quality of acceptance. Indeed most scholars asseverate that this is the crux of the crisis. But, as I have just said, though the self-evident and the accepted canons appear to be identical they, in fact, are not: they are the products of different and incompatible approaches. This difference has to be recognized to avoid confusion. The above summary of the notion of the accepted canon as part of a macrodisciplinary approach is, it seems to me, sufficiently elucidated for the moment (I do come back to this). The difference of the notion of the self-evident canon needs to be explained further, and I turn to this now.

The argument for self-evidence is closely allied to the ability of the reading-writing subject to recognize aesthetic quality. The criterion for selection in the self-evident canon is normally aesthetic superiority, and usually aesthetic quality cannot be analyzed beyond answerability to certain unanalyzable expectations (which could be associated with terms like balance, formal symmetry, emotional content, high seriousness, etc.). What is not analyzable is however recognizable, and moreover capable of commanding a consensus—it is self-evident. The self-evident nature of the aesthetic quality of the canon is recognizable to all discerning reading-writing subjects, who don't lose their inscrutability as subjects even in communal conglomerations.

That is a broad summary of the argument for a self-evident canon validated by aesthetic criteria. I have mentioned that this argument probably appears, in its placement of (English) literary studies as a discipline, within a metadisciplinary approach or within the cautious text of a closed discipline. Scholars who do present arguments for and recognitions of self-evident canons do not, of course, always deny a macrodisciplinary preoccupation or demonstrate an awareness of a metadisciplinary approach or of their use of the cautious text. There is, however, enough to indicate that they do all possess an *implicit* awareness of the theoretical space of their formulations. Those I have mentioned above with relation to a self-evident canon (Matthew Arnold's touchstones, F. R. Leavis's great tradition of English novels, Ezra Pound's reading list, and Harold Bloom's western canon) could serve to illustrate this. Though the theoretical foci and conclusions that these thinkers proposed often differ vastly (and are also, naturally, related in specific preoccupations) there is clearly a certain similarity in their adopted premises. All of them seem anxious to ensure that their canons are not derived from macrodisciplinary grounds; that they adopt criteria for the selection of texts (i.e., canon) which are not bound to an institutional space. In other words, either they denounce the institutional space, or they carefully eliminate possible modes of analysis which are particularly coherent to an institutional purpose. For Matthew Arnold the project of tracing the "stream of English poetry" is prefaced with reflections on the need to beware of the fallacy of historical contextualization, to dissociate evaluation from the "course of development of a nation's language."[11] In effect this takes away the emphasis on the Englishness of the canon of English poetry he presents, and draws attention to the independence of the self-evident criteria he ostensibly depends on from any interest outside themselves. He also warns against the fallacy of personal associations and preferences. F. R. Leavis, of course, does not dissociate his canon from the Englishness of it: he seems to espouse an almost mystical Englishness which apparently—certainly not *effectively*—has little to do with the political significance attached to Englishness. But more of that later. F. R. Leavis does enjoy a sense of being at odds with current and *accepted* opinion in proposing his great tradition,[12] and not surprisingly his critical insights did not lead to confirmation of institutional practice but to a reformation program.[13] Ezra Pound does not concern himself with Englishness or Americanness in his canonical proposals at all, and is scornful of all institutional attempts to inculcate a canon on those grounds. Indeed, he is generally disdainful of institutional literary education per se, and begins his arguments in favor of his selection with the following: "Literary instruction in our 'institutions of learning' was, at the beginning of this century, cumbrous and inefficient. I dare say it still is."[14] Harold Bloom's proposals regarding the western canon are obviously broader than those allowed by Englishness—that is scarcely the point any longer. Harold Bloom also writes with a sense of opposing accepted opinion, but it is not the airy confidence of the challenger that his writing exudes but the careworn air of one under attack. This is symptomatic of the present context, of the expansions, alternatives, questionings of accepted canons, of the crisis, so to say, which he has to deal with. In fact he writes about this crisis and he identifies the institutional space with it and he opposes it by re-recognizing in a now unfashionable fashion a self-evident canon. He holds, from the present point of view, a most interesting if somewhat anachronistic position which needs further attention (I mean attention, not support). At any rate it is clear that Bloom is as antimacrodisciplinary as his precursors ré self-evident canons. However, this is underwritten by a confusion regarding the two senses of canon (institutionally sanctioned and self-evident) at work here which is also symptomatic of the present crisis. Even in the first line of his "An Elegy for the Canon" he writes:

> Originally the Canon meant the choice of books in our teaching institutions, and despite the recent politics of multiculturalism, the Canon's true question remains: What shall the individual who still desires to read attempt to read, this late in history?[15]

He seems to suggest that the "original meaning" of canon (macrodisciplinary text) and canon's "true question" (metadisciplinary bold text/ cautious text) are identical. It is crucial to differentiate for the consistency of the argument that follows.

Not macrodisciplinary then—but what approach underlies the self-evident canon? This is variable. For Arnold and Pound one observes an implied metadisciplinary approach which gradually gives way to a cautious text, with its unanalyzable subject. In F. R. Leavis and Harold Bloom, one has a predominantly cautious text, with a disregard for, or complete complacency in, the disciplinary status of their investigations. In the latter, in fact, one finds a conscious repudiation not only of the macrodisciplinary approach, but of the bold text itself.

Neither Arnold nor Pound actually propose a quanta approach to knowledge in an explicit manner. In both cases there is an implied assumption that there is something basic to all knowledge, something that underlies all disciplines. This manifests itself both in a need to differentiate the discipline of literary studies (and the self-evident canon it ostensibly defines itself by) from contending disciplines, and in the charting out of validity claims in terms of cross-disciplinary applicability. And in both cases it eventually gives way to a cautious text. For Arnold, for instance, the cross-disciplinary base appears in his conception of the "critical power" which, he believes, is devoted "in all branches of knowledge, theology, philosophy, history, art, science, to see the object as in itself it really is,"[16] though he limits his focus to the literary aspect; the metadisciplinary backdrop expands into his conception of "culture" as a *"study of perfection."* "It moves by the force, not merely or primarily of the scientific passion for pure knowledge, but also of the moral and social passion for doing good";[17] and metadisciplinariness surrenders itself to the exclusion of the cautious text when he asseverates "Without poetry, our science will appear incomplete; and most of what now passes with us for religion and philosophy will be replaced by poetry."[18] Pound's metadisciplinariness is the condition of his method, an admittedly *prescriptive* method in which the legitimacy of the scientific rationale is constantly invoked for his literary formulae. Examples of Pound's prescriptive formulae claiming scientific validity need hardly be cited—they are ubiquitous in his critical writings and familiar to all who are at all acquainted with them (as with the critical writings of T. S. Eliot). Here's a characteristic instance anyway:

> People regard literature as something vastly more flabby and floating and complicated and indefinite than, let us say, mathematics. Its

subject-matter, the human consciousness, is more complicated than are number and space. It is not, however, more complicated than biology, and no one ever supposed that it was. We apply a loose-leaf system to book-keeping so as to have the live items separated from the dead ones. In the study of physics we begin with simple mechanisms, wedge, lever and fulcrum, pulley and inclined plane, all of them still as useful as when they were first invented. We proceed by a study of discoveries. We are not asked to memorise a list of the parts of a side-wheeler engine.

And we could, presumably, apply to the study of literature a little of the common sense that we currently apply to physics and to biology.[19]

F. R. Leavis's cautious text is not designedly against the bold text with its meta or macrodisciplinarity, it simply *is* the cautious text in which literature subsumes the horizon and no other discipline is admissible. The subject is not self-consciously focused on itself, it merely expresses itself without any awareness of a need to assert or defend its sanctity. The caution of F. R. Leavis's literary criticism acknowledges itself only when it is forced to confront allegedly different disciplines. The acknowledgement usually consists in a mild and stubborn refusal to acknowledge anything else, any other discipline that is, as significant to *him* (or his "I" the "literary critic"):

no 'sociology of literature' and no attempt to relate literary studies with the sociological will yield much profit unless informed and controlled by a real and intelligent interest—a first-hand critical interest—in literature;[20]

Literary criticism and philosophy seem to me to be quite distinct and different kinds of discipline—at least, I think they ought to be [. . .]. This is not to suggest that a literary critic might not, as such, be the better for a philosophic training, but if he were, the advantage, I believe, would manifest itself partly in a surer realization that literary criticism is not philosophy.[21]

Harold Bloom's cautious text of literature, with its central and self-evident western canon, is more deliberately *against* the bold text itself. This is asserted by the positing of a subject which refuses reduction, scrutiny, formulation in terms of anything but its signification as "I." The signification of "I" is not an accident of style where Bloom's discussion of the canon is concerned. On the contrary it is the focus of his literary discourse, and is opposed as such to a "they" (he usually refers to them as the "School of Resentment") and the discourse which refuses a literary subject or construes a literary subject-as-object. It is not a spontaneous slipping into the cautious text of literature but a calculated cautious text which actively objects to the influence of bold texts ré literature. Not surprisingly, therefore, much of his argument proceeds by the assertion of the subject (exhorting the *individual* to *read,* supplying *"my"* experiences of reading) in the literary discourse, and by reiterating the alien nature of a discourse of the bold meta or macrodisciplinary text (in terms of social criteria or ideology, for instance):

> A poem cannot be read *as a poem,* because it is primarily a social document or, rarely yet possibly, an attempt to overcome a philosophy. Against this approach I urge a stubborn resistance whose single aim is to preserve poetry as fully and purely as possible,[22]

he maintains, and again:

> It is a mark of the degeneracy of literary study that one is considered an eccentric for holding that the literary is not dependent upon the philosophical, and that the aesthetic is irreducible to ideology or to metaphysics.[23]

Against ideology which allegedly distracts and corrupts literary study Bloom poses the sincerity of his individual engagement with literature; in fact he poses autobiography. This is, incidentally, entirely in keeping with the views of the critic whom Bloom reveres most, and who has given the most comprehensive account of aesthetic apprehension in literature.

> That is what the highest criticism really is, the record of one's soul. It is more fascinating than history, as it is concerned simply with oneself. It is more delightful than philosophy, as its subject is concrete and not abstract, real and not vague. It is the only civilised form of autobiography[24]

says Oscar Wilde (or Gilbert) in "The Critic As Artist."

The prevalence of the cautious text, even when it is contained in a sort of gravitational field of metadisciplinarity (as with Arnold and Pound), amongst proponents of the self-evident canon is hardly unforeseen in this context. Ultimately self-evidence is a function of the aesthetic discernment of the literary subject, and that, as has been seen earlier, rests in the very bowels of the cautious text of literary studies, within the *inside* of the discipline of literary studies. It constitutes the organs of the body of the discipline and gives shape to the organism of literary studies, that which can be seen from the outside. This has been demonstrated before with the assistance of the Barthesian subject (which is strangely ironic because few, to Bloom's mind, represent the School of Resentment better and is therefore resented more than Roland Barthes[25]). The aesthetic appreciation which may be qualified to an extent (by Arnold's "high seriousness," by Leavis's "moral interest," by Pound's "charged with meaning to the utmost degree," and by Bloom's "originality") is usually also marked by its resistance to dissection. This resistance is the condition of self-evidence which allows their conception of the canon. So Arnold says:

> The characters of a high quality of poetry are what is expressed *there.* They are far better recognised by being felt in the verse of the master, than by being perused in the prose of the critic[26];

and Pound states:

> Beauty in art reminds one what is worth while. I am not now speaking of shams. I mean beauty, not slither, not sentimentalizing about beauty, not telling people that beauty is the proper and respectable thing. I mean beauty[27];

and Leavis would refuse to discuss the rationale of his assumptions with René Welleck.[28] This is the discourse from the innards of the organism of literary studies, it has the indulgence of the subject of the cautious text. Bloom, speaking as he does in the midst of the so-called crisis, speaking against the "School of Resentment" as he dubs *them,* does give a kind of rationale for his selections to the western canon. Or rather, he distributes his resistance to the dissection of aesthetic self-evidence within a *process* of the canon. He pushes it within the links of the constituents of his canon: his canon is not simply a selection of the subject "I," it is decided through a process which involves all the creative subjects (a plurality of "I"s) who are named in it as well. The process of the canon, its self-perpetuating nature, is given in terms of the relation between its constituents. Bloom explains this by invoking his earlier theory of creative "misreadings" in his *Anxiety of Influence,* a theory which identifies canonicity in terms of strong misreadings and rejects incidental dissection by relegating criticism, along with minor creative writing, to the area of weak misreadings.[29]

So much for the issue of the self-evident canon. It is, I think abundantly clear that the argument for self-evidence has a comprehensive structure which doesn't need extrinsic support and rejects external inquiry. Self-evidence is clearly demarcated in its argument and its consistency from the bold text of the accepted canon, and from the macrodisciplinary space which that primarily occupies. Before elucidating the separateness of the split concepts and discourses surrounding the notion of the canon however, let's revert briefly to the issue of the specificity of *English* literary studies in this context.

Except for Leavis, Englishness is not a central condition of the self-evident canons that are promoted above. As the arguments for a self-evident aesthetic quality in canonical literary works go the linguistic, geographical, nationalistic, and cultural determinants which might constitute Englishness play no definitive role. They are usually held apart by the different criteria of the necessity of their invocation. If they are brought together it is as a matter of curiosity resulting from allegiances and considerations which do not violate the exclusive nature of the argument for a self-evident aesthetic. Arnold's touchstones are therefore drawn from the range of literature he is familiar with (Greek, French, English), and his investigation into English poetry in terms of touchstones does not interfere at all with the independence of the touchstones. Pound's selection is drawn from the range of literature he is aware of (including Chinese and Japanese) and Englishness is not a factor. Harold Bloom restricts his compendium not only in terms of his awareness but also in terms of the mechanics of influence which determines the process of the canon. His broad demarcation is therefore of a "western" canon, but this has to include (to be faithful to the mechanics of influence) texts from the Ancient Near East and Ancient India. At any rate, within their descriptions of self-evident canons, English literature, if it is to find any disciplinary status at all, can only possess the features of a pure subdiscipline. That is, when the metadisciplinary approach applies. In the cautious text which espouses the self-evident aesthetic and the corresponding reading-writing subject the distinction between literature in general and the specific English literature fades into insignificance. There merely *is* a cautious text of literature with a reading-writing subject. Englishness lies on the *outside* and is considered only as a result of the reading-writing subject's existence and limitations, not as a condition for reading-writing and experiencing literature.

Leavis's association of Englishness with the self-evident aesthetic which determines his "great tradition" is apparently not a matter of choice but of necessity. The issue is raised regarding Conrad's right to be named amongst the greatest *English* novelists. Contradictory statements (characteristic of Leavis) appear in trying to clarify the issue in the introductory chapter in *The Great Tradition:*

> When we come to Conrad we can't, by way of insisting that he was indeed significantly 'in' the tradition—in and of it, neatly and conclusively relate him to any one English novelist. Rather we have to stress his foreignness—that he was a Pole, whose first other language was French. [. . .] Conrad's themes and interests demanded the concreteness and action—the dramatic energy—of English. [. . .] Here, then, we have a master of the English language, who chose it for its distinctive qualities and because of the moral tradition associated with it, and whose concern with art—he being like Jane Austen and George Eliot and Henry James an innovator in 'form' and method—is the servant of a profoundly serious interest in life.[30]

These seem to me to be searching and on the whole disparate sentiments which are linked in a tenuous fashion. The quality of self-evident "greatness" in Conrad's novels owe something to the linguistic features of the English language and something to the moral tradition of Englishness: presumably, this implies that Leavis's conception of self-evident greatness in the tradition he identifies is inextricably linked to these two features of Englishness. Their exclusiveness as *English,* in either sense, is however not demonstrated beyond this assertion—and his extended reflections on Conrad later, which trace out some of the moral patterns and ironies he employed, end on a contrary note: "Conrad is amongst the very greatest novelists in the language—or any language."[31] At any rate, the place of Englishness in the particular tradition in question is never particularly clear, though it appears to have been self-evident to Leavis. The reasons for the assertion of Englishness are suspected to be, and rightly I think, outside the scope of the argument for a self-evident aesthetic, and lead to the alignment of Leavis's great tradition with unstated political and institutional interests. Indeed, in a larger part of Leavis's critical writings the political and social interests struggle to get expressed; he seems perpetually to reach out from the midst of his cautious text of literature to the macrodisciplinary conception. Those of his books that deal with pedagogic practice and practical criticism oppose a distinctly macrodisciplinary preoccupation with an equally unequivocal immersion in the cautious text. The latter usually wins, so that the politics of Leavis's canon-building is always on the verge of being obvious, and is yet never ostensible. This internal contradiction of method, this almost imperceptible collision and obfuscation of terms, allow a concept of English as a discipline to emerge and sustain itself. This is most clearly evident in *The Living Principle: 'English' as a Discipline of Thought,*[32] for example. As the title indicates English is given the status of a discipline (and Leavis indicates in the text that this is in terms of the institutional space which it occupies), and yet, again as the title indicates (and the text), it is a discipline of *thought,* i.e., an epistemological justification is offered, the Englishness of which has to be taken on faith, and is certainly not immediately coincident with its institutional space. The tenuous strain of this assertion of the uniqueness of English as an academic discipline from the heart of the cautious text is reiterated at all levels of its argument: Leavis gives birth to the confusion between English and literature in general, between the academic and subdisciplinary status of English, between the conceptions of discipline in cautious and bold texts.

Leavis stands at the subtle shift from the self-evident canon to the accepted canon, as someone who affects a cautious view of literature but lends himself most satisfactorily, and probably willingly, to bold macrodisciplinary interests. But this shift is not inevitable. On the contrary it is a kind of deliberate and self-initiated misreading of the coherence of the self-evident aesthetic argument, a kind of calculated flaw in Leavis's expression of it. It is a kind of misreading, or opening, which Arnold's touchstones, Pound's selection, or Bloom's western canon does not accede to with as much ease—though they are not difficult to accommodate either if one reflects on it. To align their self-evident canons as accepted canons one has to, with a slight effort, disbelieve them, discount their arguments, not listen to them, not trust them; and one has to possess a certain sort of gaze which places them in terms of structures and discourses which lie outside their claims. It involves a wrenching asunder of the conception of the canon which is not a challenging revelation ré Arnold, Pound, Bloom, or even Leavis, not an expansion into a crisis, but a measure of the difference between what is offered and what is inferred. Or, another way of putting it might be: the institutional (macrodisciplinary) space which proponents of the self-evident canon are given, which makes them available as creators of accepted canons, is not overtly claimed by them, desired by them, conceived by them in so many words—however clearly they may prefigure and occupy that space.

This brings us squarely to the place of the canon with relation to the disciplinary status of English literary studies from a macrodisciplinary perspective: the institutional interests which lie behind the canon which is accepted to represent English as an academic discipline. To examine the position of the accepted canon of English literature as an academic discipline I take a somewhat different tack from the above. Instead of drawing from examples of such canons, I examine studies regarding the establishment of English literature as an academic discipline, and try to discern how the accepted canon is usually seen to fall in with it.

More About the Accepted Canon

To carry on where we left off above, the examination of the macrodisciplinary approach which incorporates the notion of an accepted canon, and the manner in which this is aligned with the (primarily cautious, but also metadisciplinary) self-evident canon, cannot take place without two admissions. One, the notion of canons (self-evident or accepted) we are dealing with here is, to say the least, limited. This needs to be clarified. Two, if the reader-writer has received-conveyed the impression above that there is something unacceptable or unjustified in the alignment of the self-evident canon with the accepted canon, this was unintentional. The alignment is not only justified but necessary from the macrodisciplinary perspective. This needs to be demonstrated.

The limitation of the notion of canon (accepted or self-evident) above and to come is contained in the complete absence of any consideration of literary history in this space. This is a serious omission. All who have any acquaintance with the pedagogy and practice of literary studies would be aware that neither are usually conducted without an assumed association between canon and chronology. All educational institutions organize curricula in terms of the relation between period and representative (or canonical) texts. Those who promote self-evident canons are no exception to this practice—it is implicit in the asseverations of Arnold, Pound, and Leavis, and quite explicit in Bloom's use of a Vico-inspired chronological schema to present his canonical compendium. Literary theorists who have pondered the canon (Hans Robert Jauss, for example, and Frank Kermode[33]) have inevitably done so in terms of its relation to contextualization or periodization. In fact, the absence of literary history from the above and the following discussion is not because of its irrelevance, but because of its excessive pertinence and the complex role it plays in the issues in question. It would be unrealistic to try to do justice to the issue in this space, and would be an unnecessary distraction from the course of this argument. I intend to treat the subject as it deserves in a separate text. It is however possible to continue the present discussion on self-evident and accepted canons, in so far as these terms possess implications outside, independent of, or inspite of the dimension of literary history. It is only in this limited sense that the preceding and following arguments are offered.

The notion of the accepted canon, which is supported by a macrodisciplinary approach, which slips out of and somehow realigns and absorbs the professed self-evident canon and its metadisciplinary or cautious approach, does need the support of a chronological perspective to be elucidated fully. In this instance I do not take recourse to literary history but (in keeping with the macrodisciplinary approach) the social history which examines the establishment of disciplines of knowledge as institutionally sanctioned academic disciplines. In doing this it is possible to focus on *English* literary studies *per se* as I had intended in this part. This is possible since, as maintained before, *English* literary studies appears as an academic discipline in its own right (and not as a subdiscipline) only in terms of the institutional space it occupies—i.e., in terms of a macrodisciplinary approach. I therefore proceed to elucidate the conditions of the accepted canon in terms of its receiving validation as such in the course of the establishment of English literary studies as an academic discipline.

Let's start again. The accepted canon from a macrodisciplinary perspective, more specifically the canon as it is found in the institutionalized space of English literature as an academic discipline: what does "canon" mean here? The texts which gradually move through the layers of secondary texts, scholarly bibliographies, to enter curricula form the canon; the texts which are validated for transmission across (say, horizontally) the disciplinary community as it exists, and transmitted for the perpetuation (call it vertically) of the disciplinary community, constitutes the canon. This assumes that the systems of secondary, bibliographical, curricular transmission, the routes of horizontal and vertical transmission, have to be in place already for the canon to be conceived. On the other hand the ostensible status of the discipline, its presentation of itself, its designation of itself, is dependent on what the canon consists of. This is the crux of the macrodisciplinary conception of the accepted canon: its macrodisciplinary nature is affirmed by the predetermination of the institutional channels which allow the canon to come to be; the institutional space of the discipline is apparently confirmed by the acceptance of the offered/given canon by the cognoscenti. The macrodisciplinary canon is both the product of and the rationale behind the institutional space of the discipline. The canon (and therefore curriculum) of English literature exists because the channels for its transmission are granted, and yet the canon (curriculum) of English literature marks its disciplinary standing.

Thinking regarding the accepted canon (i.e., from a macrodisciplinary perspective) depends on where the emphasis of its reading-writing is placed. The emphasis of the reading-writing could lead to two sorts of engagements with the canon, both macrodisciplinary, both constituting it as accepted, and both feeding into the other. These are:

1. The reading-writing of the canon itself, the reading-writing of the texts, subtexts, secondary texts, bibliographies which constitute the canon. The reading-writing of its transmissions, though not of the channels of these transmissions, not the systems which facilitate these transmissions. This is primarily an engagement with canonical texts, the effort to collate the common denominators and the discrete uniqueness of canonical texts, in order to realize the canon. This is the hermeneutic which unravels the relationship of the institutional space of the (English) literary discipline and the accepted canon by focusing on the discipline's statement of itself, and, if necessary, digging through the cracks of its self-announcement.

2. The reading-writing of the channels of transmission which render the canon possible. The reading-writing, in other words, of the institutional space itself, its construction, formation, mechanics, which underlie its announcement of its disciplinary status and its self-presentation, i.e., the manifesto of the institutional space, the accepted canon. This is analogous to understanding the Disk Operating System before grasping the working of the program which one uses on one's personal computer. Here is the hermeneutic which places the accepted canon (and therefore acknowledges its status as accepted) within the politics and sociology of the institutional space that it announces.

Both these sorts of engagements could lead to a realization of the accepted canon qua canon, the assumptions behind its disciplinary validation, the vested interests promoted by the institutional space of the discipline and coded in the self-announcement (the canon) of the discipline. Both these could also consequently result in the possible subversion of the accepted canon, which is possible only when the limited mechanics of its acceptance is comprehended. Such possible subversions could take the shape of a questioning of the rationale of the accepted canon, proposals for the expansion of canonical containment, and assertions of counter-canons.

In considering English literary studies as an academic discipline, which announces itself through its accepted English literary canon, one would have to take into account both sorts of engagement delineated above. In leading up to the conclusion of this part I focus mainly on the latter as presenting a more manageable range of material for examination. A few brief comments on the former sort of engagement thereafter leads directly to the conclusion of this part.

Reading-Writing the Institutional Space of the Academic Discipline of English Literature

The problem with attempting the above, with examinations of the channels of transmission which permit the conception of a canon which announces the discipline of English literature—the problem with this is that the channels which are examined are also perpetuated in the act of examination. If one tries to delineate the institutional space of English literature as an academic discipline, one inevitably negotiates one's stand in that institutional space as well. And usually, the examination of the politics involved in this institutional space is also a political statement itself. This is the inevitability of facing the margins of the macrodisciplinary boundaries of the bold text of English literature (the academic discipline). If this had been the cautious text of English literature this facing of the subject wouldn't have been on the verge of this discourse, it would have been the center of the discourse and the boundaries would have been distant if at all visible. But this is the bold macrodisciplinary text, and when one examines its perimeters the voice of the subject-as-object is itself conditional to the institutional space that it addresses. Let's say, the examination-cum-enactment at this point is in the nature of this text. Perhaps, therefore, it isn't a problem at all, it is merely the condition of this discussion.

But it has been viewed as a problem by those who have a retrospective perspective of this sort of discussion, of the growing exchange regarding the institutional space of English literature as an academic discipline. John Dixon is a case in point. On reflecting on the work of Brian Doyle, Terry Eagleton, and Chris Baldick on the establishment of English literary studies as an academic discipline he discovers that their own observations are presented and conditioned by their respective ideological convictions and agendas:

> There must be elements of truth in all these theses, it seems to me. But again, the tendency is to define the small-scale cultural movement—the formation of 'English' studies—entirely in terms of ruling-class ideological goals, or of institutional pressures on a national scale. Was there really no ideological conflict—as 'alternatives' to orthodox universities and their subjects were set up? Did the new institutions owe nothing, in their structures, to the social classes that supported and jointly organised them?[34]

Arguably the scaling down of the ideological interests that are perceived to be at play, the discovery of the marginal voice or its absence within the self-construction of the institutional space of English literature (ably done elsewhere by Richard Crawford and Gauri Vishwanathan), is not without its own agenda and political implication. It usually leads, as it does for those who interpret each step of the process as the machinations of a dominant ideology, to a need to restructure and reevaluate pedagogic practice and the objects of transmission and disciplinary description. This is as true of Eagleton, Doyle, and Baldick, as of John Dixon, as of Robert Crawford and Gauri Vishwanathan. To deny the ideological imperatives behind any investigation of the institutional space of an academic discipline in favor of, say, the "truth," is to presume a non-ideological discourse. This in turn could tempt the investigator to lose sight of the institutional space altogether in favor of charting out (in a documentary fashion) the negotiations between inspired, dedicated, energetic, and on the whole isolated, individuals (Moulton and Bradley in the Extension movement, Richards in the debate ré Cambridge English) and an aspiring community. John Dixon's book often, particularly in its historical exposition, seems to tend in that direction—it is only the zeal of the educational reformer, his experience as an observer and critic of pedagogical practice, which retains a focus on the institutional space and mechanics of the academic discipline of English literature. When this is manifest so is the ideological trend and political agenda which inspire the individuals in question.

The examination of the political and sociological interests which contributed to the establishment of English as an academic discipline has its own politics and sociology: this is an inevitable condition of the macrodisciplinary bold text. Given that this is the condition for all these examinations what are the common features which this area of investigation and research has thrown up? What do these reveal about the institutional space of English literature as an academic discipline? What do they convey about the conception of canon that this institutional space renders necessary? Briefly, the following could be considered.

Most studies of the process by which English literature was established as an academic discipline present this process as one of confrontation, negotiation, and resolution between a center (English as a cultural center, an economic power, a colonizer, the sphere of the mother country, as an elitist or masculine domain) and a margin (the culturally marginalized, the economically dependent, the colony, the adopted country, the nonelite, and the feminine domain). There are two things to note here. One, the process is not necessarily initiated by the center; it could be initiated from the margin in the expectation of assimilation in the center. It is usually agreed that whether it is or isn't initiated from the center the resolution ultimately results in validation from the center and serves the interests of the center. Two, the process doesn't necessarily involve two discrete discourses; the discourse of the margin is not necessarily an alternative to that of the center. It is more usual to have the center define the margin and vice versa, and the negotiations could be between two ends of the same discourse.

What is interesting about the reading of the process by different researchers is that the center and margins are located at different places. D. J. Palmer locates the impulse behind the process in the class-structure, and defines the center and margin accordingly. English studies was constructed, he argues, initially as a practical and utilitarian alternative to the more genteel rhetorical study of classics.[35] That its initial development is associated with Utilitarianism and Evangelism is not surprising,[36] and nor is the observation that English literature finds an early institutional space in the Mechanics' Institutes and Working Men's Colleges.[37] This is where the negotiations of the center and margin are squarely placed by Palmer:

> However inadequately it was articulated, there was a widespread feeling that the spiritual and physical conditions of the industrial revolution impoverished the cultural lives of a large class of people, that they had been cut off from their traditional past, and that therefore they needed to be given new means of establishing connections with a national cultural heritage. Thus it was the historical approach to literature which eventually emerged, and the missionaries of adult education were particularly concerned with the working classes.[38]

The subsequent expansion of English literature, and its replacement of Classics, is the gradual acceptance of the discipline as a repository of culture and civilization, suggests Palmer. What began as an attempt to assimilate the industrial worker into the conservative mainstream of national interest, validated by its tradition and culture, became a purveyor of tradition and culture in general and for everyone. The process of its establishment within an institutional space is also a process of absorption into and upwards through the hierarchies of strongholds of the establishment, ending, in Palmer's work, with the establishment of the Oxford English School.

Brian Doyle's account of the establishment of the institutional space of English literature (or English studies) encompasses a gradual movement from several margins towards the center, which is, moreover, generally controlled by an overarching establishment ideology. It locates the margins in the need to renew "cultural leadership at a national level"[49] in the wake of imperialist expansion (through the agency of Mechanics' Institutes at home, as much as through the colonial civil service abroad). The marginalized space of its initial phase of institutionalization is also associated with the feminine domain of amateur pedagogy. The gradual movement towards the consolidation of an establishment ideology is marked, contends Doyle, in the gradual masculinization (i.e., professionalization) of the discipline; in strategic statements like the Newboldt report;[40] and in the subsequent stages of the academic discipline's designation as "English language and literature," "English and History," "English Subjects," to simply "English." The latter offered "through education unmediated access to what was taken to be the central activity of all human judgement."[41] Brian Doyle sees the process of the mainstream absorption of the academic discipline constituted thus (and consequent elimination of the marginal roots) as continuing in the transformations it goes through since the sixties, with the importation of theories and practices which originate in other disciplinary precincts.

Chris Baldick hints at the margins:

> [. . .]we can isolate three principle factors which ensured literary study, in particular of English literature, a permanent place in higher education. These are first, the specific needs of the British empire expressed in the regulations for admission to the India Civil Service; second, the various movements for adult education including Mechanics' Institutes, Working Men's Colleges, and extension lecturing; third, within this general movement, the special provisions made for women's education,[42]

but, in fact, Baldick's work is devoted to establishing the discursive strategies and statements which actually go into the constitution of English literature as a repository of centrist values. Baldick illustrates the center's mode of validating itself through its renovations of English literature as an academic discipline—through examinations of the critical works of established and canonised representatives of "Englishness" such as Arnold, Eliot, Richards, and the Leavises.

Less repetitive and confined examinations of the negotiation between margin and center in the process of the establishment of the academic discipline of English literature are presented by Robert Crawford and Gauri Vishwanathan. Crawford's study is introduced as

> not a totalizing story of English literature which co-opts non-English authors to incorporate them into a unitary English tradition, but a devolutionary history written on the margin. It tries to erode and complicate any ideas of such a unitary tradition, and force 'English' to take account of other cultures which are in part responsible for the initial construction of 'English Literature' as a subject,[43]

and clearly poses the center-margin negotiation. In fact, the negotiation is placed after-the-fact of the initiation of the academic discipline of English literature; it is less a negotiation than a translation from margin to center. The imperative behind its initiation at the margin (in this case provincial England and Scotland and the colonies as opposed to metropolitan England) is clearly assimilation, not as a concept imposed top-down but as an effort towards upward mobility. In the following chapters on the Scottish invention of English literature, British literature, and Scottish literature respectively, the *modus operandi* of translation from margin to centre, and the negotiated renewed spaces that the margins reallocated themselves, are discussed. Crawford's work is a rediscovery of the margins from the center, a deconstructive history of a centralized academic discipline, and a reconstructive history of the marginalised space from which English literature devolves:

> In their anxiety to adopt non-native standards, the Scottish—like the American, Canadian, Irish, Indian, and English—provincial inventors of English literature were responsible for developing, through the educational system, problems which these cultures would have to face over the next century and a half. The university subject of 'English Literature' was born among conditions of 'provincial' socio-economic ambition and anti-provincial linguistic prejudice. It found its voice not just in singing the merits of one dominant cultural tradition, but also in its silencing of the others.[44]

If Robert Crawford's study describes the tendency of the margin (primarily Scotland) to assimilate into the center through its invention of English literature, Gauri Vishwanathan's study delineates the process of cultural imposition from a colonizing center on the increasingly marginalized colony in the shape of English studies. She describes lucidly the phases in the debate between Orientalist educationists and Anglicist educationists in India, and the manner in which these were reflected in political strategies at a legislative level and in educational institutions (from the Charter Act of 1813, to William Bentinck's Education Act of 1835, to Lord Harding's resolution to give preference to Indians in public office who had distinguished themselves in English in 1844, and in the pedagogical practices from the early mission schools to the later established centralized universities). The imposition process is seen to gradually gain ground until the indigenous literatures of the margin are formulated as a diametrically opposed *type* (the production of divine inspiration, constituted through a perverse morality, etc.) apropos the centrality of English literature (the purveyor of true morality, the productions of reason and the intellect, etc.).[45] This leads to the initiation of an assimilative process, which ironically backfires as the assimilatee, so to say, threatens to modify the relationship of centre and margin. The result is a withdrawal of English as a medium of moral instruction and a reinstatement of the practical study model, and the introduction of arrangements for more selective entry to education.[46] The negotiation between center and margin (whether in terms of assimilation, translation, or imposition) is clearly conducted in all instances with an illusory move to merge center and margin, which actually underlines and maintains the hegemonic relationship of center to margin.

The assimilative/impository negotiations between center and margins which gradually delineate the institutional space of English literature as an academic discipline tend not to interrogate the canon which designates that space. The entire process of assimilation/imposition is characterized by the unquestionability of that which designates the center which is assimilated/imposed. The institutional space announces its potentiality (through the negotiation of assimilation/imposition) by the very unquestionability of the canon which it profers. How an education in certain canonical texts in English literature would serve to consolidate moral integrity, for instance, is not the issue in these negotiations. The issue is that given that canonical texts taught on an adequate forum will achieve this, how necessary is its use, where, and how is it to be organized and overseen. Consequently the politics behind the establishment of the academic discipline of English literature does not explain the specific criteria and quality of canonicity. The canon which designates the achieved institutional space of English literature is always an accepted canon. That does not mean that it is caught up in a stultifying paralysis; on the contrary it constantly expands itself. But incumbents into the canon in this sense are invariably just as acceptable as the texts which are comfortably ensconced in it. The establishment of the academic discipline of English literature does not explain the canonicity of the English literary canon, it merely accepts the canonicity of the English literary canon and holds it up like a flag. From the macrodisciplinary perspective of the academic discipline of English literature, in other words, the canon is simply there after the fact of the achieved institutional space, a given. The negotiations which form the background of the achieved institutional spaces reside in a network of other achieved institutional spaces (that which makes the center the center with relation to its margins). A range of political and sociological imperatives stretch behind the achieved institutional space, which merge into the acceptance of the canon but do not ostensibly originate in a canon. In fact, in this field of exchange the canon doesn't originate, it simply exists already.

Inevitably this quality of the accepted canon of the macrodisciplinary academic discipline (English literature) is seen to collaborate with the metadisciplinary or cautious text which argues the self-evident canon. The word "collaboration" there marks the exact nature of the relationship between the self-evident canon and the accepted canon. Collaboration is the recognition of the separate and discrete conceptualizations (of canon) involved and indicates a temporary bridge between the discrete conceptualizations. The temporary bridge of collaboration is brought about by vested interests—in the next point I suggest that the vested interests are connected to the reading-writing of canonicity, either from within the institution or from the ideological perspective of the historian of the institution. At any rate, to take the collaboration of the two senses of canon (metadisciplinary or cautious self-evidence and macrodisciplinary acceptance) as *conflation* constitutes a grave misreading.

Before moving on to that next point, however, I would like to clarify that there are some instances when the negotiative process of assimilation/imposition does seem to get reflected in the selection of texts which constitute the designative canon. The debate around the necessity of including texts of Christian instruction in the English literary curriculum in India outlined by Gauri Vishwanathan[47] is a case in point. This is arguably an instance of a debate concerning the constitution of the institutional space, which has a direct influence on the shape of the ostensible canon. I would like to point out here, however, that this debate interrogates neither the origin of the canonicity nor the acceptability of the canonicity of the texts to be included/excepted. It merely discusses the institutional contingencies within which the academic discipline with its representative canon will have to operate. From a macrodisciplinary perspective institutional contingency always unquestionably takes primary place. This does not disturb the basic (or, in a limited sense, essential) notion of accepted canon.

A collaboration between the argument for a self-evident canon (from a cautious or metadisciplinary perspective) and the positing of an accepted canon (within a macrodisciplinary space) is suspected when a certain kind of reading-writing of canonicity, with certain vested interests, takes place. A collaboration can become manifest in terms of the practicalities of the canon-theorist's existence within and conviction in the institutional space of English literature. Collaboration becomes manifest, therefore, when the believer in touchstones in Arnold meets the cultural theorist in Arnold meets the Inspector of Schools in Arnold, and each of these meetings is also a process of appropriations leading up from the cautious text of the self-evident canon to a potentially macrodisciplinary text of an accepted canon. It becomes more clearly manifest when Leavis the formulator of the great tradition encounters Leavis the initiator of a program of practical criticism and Leavis the educational reformer.

The collaboration is read-written into the text of the cautious/metadisciplinary argument for a self-evident canon when this text itself is deliberately drawn into the institutional space and made part of the accepted canon. Behind this process lies the entire politics of ostensible self-validation, unquestioned cultural and material domination, and an evasion of the process of negotiation through which the assimilated/imposed institutional space is achieved. It is scarcely surprising that university curricula of English literature have habitually presented, and occasionally continue to present, Arnold, Eliot, Pound, I. A. Richards, and F. R. Leavis both as originators of critical thinking regarding canonicity and as canonized critics. There is, implicit in this inclusion, a careful evasion of the history of negotiation between margin and center in favor of a hypothetical disinterested collaboration.

The collaboration may, most importantly, be written-read as explicit (contrary to the implicit nature of its assumption within the institutional space) in accordance with the ideological agenda of the historian of English literature as an academic discipline. This is succinctly done in Chris Baldick's analysis of the roles of Arnold, Eliot, Richards, and the Leavises in the formation of the institutionally sanctioned critical discourse of English literature. Baldick's introductory statements clarify the process of reading-writing through which the implicit *collaboration* between the space of the self-evident canon and that of the accepted canon becomes explicit. The theoretical decision not to view English studies as ideological in the sense of ideology being "natural" or "timeless" leads, Baldick maintains, to the realization that:

> The very vocabulary of literary criticism, its constitutive metaphors, ought to be sufficient to betray the pressure of [. . .] outside factors. Two frames of reference in particular recur almost monotonously in critical discourse: the judicial or forensic, and the economic. 'Judgement' and 'evaluation' are the two terms most commonly resorted to by critics to define their task, and the clusters of metaphors which they carry with them—of words and tribunals, of value and debasement—are not at all arbitrary. They register real sources from which criticism derives, from 'outside', its status; real forces which impinge upon the production and reception of literary works.[48]

This is effectively a program of reading-writing that brings the outside into the cautious text, which renders explicit any institutionally implied collaboration between the space of self-evident canons and the space of accepted canons, which uncovers the institutional conspiracy underlying the cautious discourse of English literary criticism. That this is motivated by an ideological agenda (and in many ways an admirable one) is clear in the decisive shifts of focus where reading-writing occurs; from the statemental to the metaphorical, from the denotative to the connotative, from the propositional to the associative, from on-the-line to between-the-lines. The shift of focus marks an expectation of betrayal, a discovery of an unacknowledged outside. In the heat of this program of reading-writing the relationship of *collaboration* could easily be misconstrued as *conflation*. One is drawn into and thrilled by an alternative discourse in which the space of the self-evident canon and that of the accepted canon becomes indistinguishable and reeks of conspiracy.

The point of setting out the lines that demarcate these two conceptions of the canon (accepted and self-evident) in their respective spaces, and of delineating the manners in which one may read-write a collaboration between them, is to avoid the *conflation* approach. Even if there is a retrospective collaboration or a tacit conspiracy it is important to maintain the distinction. The loss of the distinction is the beginning of an endless debate of cross-purposes, a series of confused posturings about a threatening and intimidating crisis in English literary studies.

To conclude this part I now briefly consider the other approach, also from a macrodisciplinary perspective (i.e., with English literature as an academic discipline occupying an institutional space), to the concept of "accepted canon" . . .

Reading-Writing and Interrogating the Accepted Canon of the Academic Discipline of English Literature

Having examined the channels of transmission of the accepted canon I now turn to the accepted canon itself. I do not deal with this aspect of canonicity in any detail here, despite its having acquired a central position in debates about the academic discipline of English literature. A comprehensive, or even partially comprehensive, treatment of this area would be well beyond the scope of this study: a different and far more roomy space would have to be reserved for that. I include this sketchy account of the salient features of this area merely in order to round off the argument so far—these are tentatively offered and open to modifications and elaborations.

I asseverated above that the two macrodisciplinary approaches to the issue of canonicity ré English literature as an academic discipline entail (a) examinations of the channels of transmission of canons, and (b) examinations of the constitution of the canon itself. I have considered (a) within the limited precincts of studies of the establishment of English literature as an academic discipline. To carry on to (b), as I do here, would bring us firmly into the controversial province of alternative canons and counter-canons. Both are indubitably extensions of the macrodisciplinary space since they emerge from, or in reaction to, the given institutional space of the academic discipline (English literature), and the institutionally sanctioned and accepted canon. These are, to put it otherwise, corollary to the state of affairs which accepts the institutional practice of English literature (in this context) and features a mainstream canon in terms of which expansion or alternation is recommended. I have some tentative generalizations to offer regarding the area of counter-canons or alternative canons, which are seen as examinations of the mainstream canon which mark the macrodisciplinary space of English literature.

Dealing with (b) (alternative canon or counter-canon) entails in this context an increasingly complex range of reference; i.e., that dealing with literatures in English in marginal, post-colonial, minority, and other excluded contexts. As in the context of (a) I consider only a small aspect of these, namely the drawing of alternative canons or counter-canons of English literature (more appropriately literatures in English) in heterogeneous cultural fields, in numerous and interacting multicultural contexts.

The tentative generalizations are as follows.

1. The counter-canon or alternative canon is not constituted or read-written in terms of self-evidence or acceptance, it is read-written as a critique of the mainstream canon of the academic discipline. The counter-canon doesn't designate an institutional space, it speaks of the accepted canon and the institutional space it designates: the *topoi* which shape and express the reading-writing of the selection/compendium of texts in the counter-canon are interrogation, subversion, reversal, the glaring *presence* of the other, the song of the other, the act of "writing back." Like the historian of the academic canon who rediscovers the continuous assimilatory/impository negotiation between margin and center in the past, the reader-writer of the counter-canon pushes the politics of margin and center to the fore in the present. The historian examines the channels of transmission of the accepted canon,

the reader-writer confronts and dissects the accepted canon itself; both present self-reflexive macrodisciplinary positions.

To put it in other words: the counter-canon and alternative canon are a selection/compendium of books as is, indeed, any canon, but the mechanics of the selection, the thrust of the togetherness of the compendium, is not expressed in terms of self-evidence or acceptance. It does not demarcate an institutional space as such in so far as it is offered as alternative or counter. The mechanics of the selection, the thrust of the togetherness of the alternative or counter compendium is only understood with relation to an accepted mainstream canon, which does designate an institutional space. This understanding is constituted in the interrogation of the mainstream canon (the academic discipline, the institutional space). The very positing of a counter-canon or alternative canon is a positing of the *topoi* mentioned above.

Interrogation, subversion, reversal, the presence and song of the other, the act of "writing back," express the reading-writing of the counter-canon or alternative canon with relation to the mainstream canon. But this is not a closed reading-writing, not one that any text which finds its place within the precincts of a counter-canon or alternative canon is inextricably bound to. The interrogative reading-writing is the character of the counter-canonical appropriation and positing of the text within a selection/compendium. The form of reading-writing, against the grain of the mainstream canon, delineates the interrogative stance of the counter-canon or alternative canon. But the reading-writing can take a different character, can liberate the text from the dependency of counter-canonicity, release it to a future canon, or grasp it within an existing academic space, absorb it into the ever-expansive mainstream.

2. Here's a sticky issue: what is the relationship between English literature and the so-called new/post-colonial/commonwealth (etc.) literatures in English and Indian literature in English/Nigerian Literature in English/American Literature in English (etc.)? The common denominator in these is itself in question (is it a denationalized and culturally unbiased code, say "english" with a small e, or variations, reactions, rejections of the sociolinguistic formation "English" with a capital E?), not to speak of every level of definition away from the alleged common denominator. I do not enter here the ever-proliferating range of denominative distinctions which attach to the question above. I focus instead, in so far as that is possible through the fog of denominative distinc-

tions, at the three levels of metadisciplinary application which I seem to discern, which are marked by the three clusters of terms.

To reduce the effort of peering through the haze I can try to refine the objects of immediate interest and attention (restate the question as one of canonicity, and propose a common denominator after all). There are three levels of (sets of) terms: one, English literature; two, new/post-colonial/commonwealth (etc.) literatures in English; and three, Indian Literature in English/Nigerian Literature in English/American Literature in English/Australian Literature in English (etc.). As a means of expressing themselves in fora for discussion and creative/pedagogical practice all three levels of terms do take recourse to representative selections/compendiums of texts. That is, all three levels could lend themselves to some form of accepted or proposed canonicity, and we could try to relate them on those grounds. This itself assumes a theoretical common denominator: the formation of representative selections/ compendiums of texts. Further, the selections/compendiums of texts from all three levels are *accessible* (not, therefore, necessarily available) to the same readers-writers. This assertion suggests no more than the broadly accepted fact that the English language does have international currency.

In this context English literature is represented by the accepted mainstream canon. The macrodisciplinary connotations of the mainstream canon of English literature have been discussed at some length in the context of historical perspectives of the establishment of the academic discipline of English literature; in examining the channels of transmission of canons. In bringing those observations to bear upon macrodisciplinary interrogations of the canon the quality of acceptance is not changed. The only difference is that instead of seeing the institutional space of English literature in process, it is now seen as in place, composed of a consistent pattern of pedagogic practice, carrying the baggage of Englishness, throwing forth in different contexts its evasions of the negotiations between margin and center which went into its development, insinuating the centrist assumptions which it inevitably propagates. In vastly different cultural contexts in the world—in India and Pakistan and Sri Lanka and Bangladesh as in Kenya and Tanzania and Nigeria and South Africa as in Australia and New Zealand and Canada and America, as indeed in many other contexts, Departments of English in schools and universities gesture towards roughly the same selection/compendium of texts, and speak about them in a similar fashion, and refer to these activities as the pursuit of English literature; journals and seminars and conferences are devoted to the discussion of similar issues which are accepted as pertinent to the pursuit of English literature; the same selection/compendium of texts get absorbed in the hugely different discourses of different cultures, are deliberately or inadvertently quoted, become instrumental in the imaginative life of communities, and is thought of as English literature.

In this context new/commonwealth/post-colonial (etc.) literatures in English are counter-canonical constructions which offer alternative or other selections/compendiums of texts in the English language to question the accepted canon of English literature. Much scepticism has been expressed regarding these terms on the grounds that these don't adequately consider a real domain of literary activity, that they unjustifiably obfuscate the peculiarities of diverse domains, that they reiterate reflexively centrist assumptions. These allegations are all correct, of course, because they merely describe what is inevitable in a counter-canonical or alternative canonical construction. By definition the *counter*-canonical or *alternative* canonical construction interrogates the mainstream accepted canon, it finds its *raison d'etre* because of the primary acceptance of the accepted canon, its function is the interrogation of the accepted canon. Understandably it doesn't have a real domain to consider except that of the fringe, the excluded, the marginalized of the mainstream. New/commonwealth/postcolonial (etc.) literatures in English are all about English literature, they appear as reactions to English literature and question assumptions of English centrism and cultural ascendency which derive from an imperialist ideology. The macrodisciplinarity implicit in these counter-canonical constructions is reflected in the institutional space that they actually find. New/commonwealth/postcolonial (etc.) literatures in English are typically found literally on the fringe of English departments, as adjuncts to the mainstream canonical syllabus (the odd module or course, the subdepartment of the metropolitan university). They usually manifest the growing presence of an immigrant intelligentsia within the metropolitan institution of higher education and research, the voice of the margin within the center, so to say, as Aijaz Ahmad has rightly pointed out.[49]

In this context, Indian literature in English/American literature in English/Nigerian literature in English/Australian literature in English (etc.) present neither accepted canons in the sense of English literature nor counter-canonical constructions in the sense of new/commonwealth/postcolonial (etc.) literatures in English. They present potentially acceptable canons, which might fulfil their potential as such as the processes of their developments as discrete academic disciplines unravel. In some cases, the potential has realized itself already—notably in the case of American literature in English, which presents now an accepted and mainstream canon and attracts its own counter-canonical constructions (Black American literature, American Hispanic literature, etc.). In most cases the process of accepted canonization with macrodisciplinary effect is still at germination stage, with literary historical readings-writings which seldom stretch much beyond a hundred years. These find institutional spaces primarily where their acceptance would facilitate existing institutions, usually within discrete national domains. Syllabi devoted wholly to Indian literature in English are taught usually in Indian Universities, Caribbean literatures in English in West Indian Universities, and so on. Texts of Indian writers, Caribbean writers, Nigerian writers (etc.) who write in English are usually taught in departments of English Literature elsewhere under the aegis of counter-canonical formations such as new/commonwealth/postcolonial (etc.) literatures in English. Where Indian literature in English, Nigerian literature in English, Australian literature in English (etc.) do become potential canons the relationship with the accepted canon of English literature is partial and not all-consuming (as it might be in counter-canonical formations). More importantly, the potential canons assimilate themselves to already established indigenous cultural expressions and practice within their (usually national) domains. This significant fact is often overlooked by scholars and theorists who concern themselves with the second level of terms in question (new/commonwealth/postcolonial (etc.) literatures in English)—but more of that below.

3. In offering clarifications regarding the three sets of terms which refer to the canonical constructions within the macrodisciplinary space of English literary studies (as opposed to the channels of transmission of these canonical constructions) I have gestured towards, but not enunciated, the implicit complications involved. In fact despite the apparent lucidity of the above the three sets of terms are actually caught up in a spiral of complications which seem on the verge of collapsing into crisis. The common perception is that they have already succumbed—these terms connote, to most parties, one of the deadliest symptoms of the crisis of English literary studies, these mark the interrogation and displacement of canonical value and tradition. It is surely

tenuous to maintain, as I have done before, that a careful distinguishing of incompatible terms and mistaken conflations, that a holding asunder of shades of meaning which are all too often unnecessarily collided, would put the question of a crisis in English literature into perspective and probably cause it to disappear. To maintain this any longer would be tricky given the obvious complications to be found here. Before acceding to that, however, it is necessary to actually discern what exactly are the complicated elements in these three sets of terms as they are interrelated above.

One, by definition the cluster of terms commonwealth/postcolonial/new (etc.) literatures in English are unavoidably a threat to the macrodisciplinary space of English literature. To continue to evade them would merely justify the position of critique which these terms encapsulate. To try to assimilate them wouldn't be possible without altering the fabric on which the macrodisciplinary space of English literature is constructed in a radical fashion. To allot to them parallel macrodisciplinary spaces would introduce a new and complex set of institutional relationships which would probably disturb the balance of the macrodisciplinary conception of English literature as it has been and is now constituted. Understandably, the third (allotting parallel macrodisciplinary space) is seldom attempted where the institutional space of English literature is firmly established. The first (the policy of evasion) is practiced in more conservative institutions. The second (assimilation) provides the most acceptable and easily implementable scenario, and is widely taken as the chosen path. Clearly, however, none of these are unproblematic from the perspective of English literature as an academic discipline. All of these are positions in which the institutional space is left suspended either in the tension of its self-questioning, self-appraisal, self-flagellation, or in the embarrassing exposure of the interrogative gaze, the accusatory gaze, and the condemnatory gaze. The cluster of terms in question do not offer solutions; they simply raise goose pimples on the skin of English literature, an unrelenting shiver. This is a threat, but is this a crisis?

Two, the conflation of the cluster of terms commonwealth/postcolonial/new (etc.) literatures in English with Indian literature in English/Nigerian literature in English/Caribbean literature in English etc. The former are definitively on the interrogative fringe of the macrodisciplinary space of English literature, but the latter are (or are potentially) in possession of their discrete institutional spaces with a dynamic which is (or potentially is) independent, though not indifferent, to the academic discipline of English literature. The conflation is erroneous—and perhaps deliberately so. The interests which are served by such an appropriation are open to investigation. That's not the point here. The appropriation is easily initiated since the alternative canon of the dependent space of commonwealth/postcolonial/new (etc.) literatures in English and the designative canons of the (potential) macrodisciplinary space of Indian literature in English/Nigerian literature in English (etc.) could overlap. Or, with a little ingenuity and reductionism the former could absorb the latter. The difference between the former and the latter are not so much in the selection and naming of the proposed alternative or potential canonical text, as in the transmission of it through different academic fora. The pedagogic, critical, editorial practice (or broadly, the guidelines to reading-writing) which attach to the proposed canonical text under the aegis of these two perspectives are different. If the conflation does take place however the entire spectrum of creativity in English outside the mainstream canon of English literature seems to get translated on to the ostensible threat posed by commonwealth/ postcolonial/ new (etc.) literatures in English. Clearly this should be treated with scepticism. The conflation can be challenged. The crisis to English literature posed by commonwealth/ new/postcolonial (etc.) literatures, if that is what it is, hasn't really been amplified by this.

Three, following from the above point, the tendency to conflate commonwealth/postcolonial/new (etc.) literatures in English with Indian literature in English/Nigerian literature in English, etc. is in effect a failure to recognize the assimilation within indigenous forms in the latter. This could be a serious omission, almost an act of vandalism, when the indigenous forms which are drawn upon are far more complex than the legacy which English language and literature themselves bring. There are, in fact, two levels of omission involved here: the omission of not recognizing the indigenous sources of Indian literature in English/Nigerian literature in English, etc.; and the omission involved in reading Indian literature in English/Nigerian literature in English etc. as Indian literature/Nigerian literature, etc. That is, the ignorance of the traditions, values, and processes of indigenous languages and their literatures; the assumptions which underlie this ignorance; and the complacency which permits generalizations of the above nature despite this ignorance. In this context Aijaz Ahmad's critique of Fredric Jameson's construction of "third-world" literature in "Third World Literature in the Era of Multinational Capital," the discovery of Fredric Jameson as this thinker and Urdu poet's "civilizational other," is instructive.[50] At any rate, the deeper one delves into the complications the more distant the crisis of English literature appears—more pressing crises emanate outwards from English literature rather than inwards to English literature.

4. So, has an examination of the reading-writing and interrogation of the accepted canon of English literature, in terms of counter-canons and alternative canons (with their various levels of complication), yielded a more urgent sense of crisis? Is the macrodisciplinary space of English literature facing extinction in any sense, is there any impending doom which needs to be overcome? The counter-canon or alternative canon of commonwealth/postcolonial/new (etc.) literatures in English, despite its misappropriations and misleading constructions, does pose a threat—but it's not a threat which can be overcome to restore the accepted canon to its former glory. This is less a crisis than a necessary putting of English literature and its designative canon in the macrodisciplinary sphere in its place. This is an inevitable transformation, a hoped for reassessment and process of rectification, a realization of the legitimate sphere of the academic space of English literature and its mainstream canon, which is a mark of changing times. This is not to be opposed without turning the tide of the *zeitgeist* which has allowed this incremental progress. Progress in this direction, at any rate, is not to be seen as something to be faced and evaded and defeated; it has to be welcomed and understood. It might raise fears of a purge, but it's more likely to provide a *raison d'etre* for the academic discipline of English studies. An institutional space for English literature which it can occupy with legitimacy. An institutional space in keeping with the rationale behind the distribution of disciplinary spaces to different disciplines which is acceptable in the present context. Under the circumstances, to accept the term crisis is to reiterate the overweening assumptions of the macrodisciplinary space which has largely prevailed to this day; and to repeat the evasion, imposition, domination, oppression implicit in the positing of its mainstream canon. This is clearly unacceptable.

To put it briefly, in the examination of the reading-writing and interrogation of the accepted canon of English literature I perceive no crisis. I merely perceive a putting-in-place of the academic discipline of English literature.

Indeed, those whose interrogation of the accepted canon of English literature has led to an invention of different macrodisciplinary spaces and potential canons, have affirmed in their arguments that they aren't doing harm to English literature in its legitimate space. These are not harbingers of destruction. They are simply voices in touch with their reality, seeking justice and renewed self-expression. Two broad directions are discerned in their thinking.

One, that which is seen as the most intimidating, i.e., that which espouses the erasure of the pursuit of English literature from certain contexts. The most reasoned, and polemical, statement of this nature can probably be attributed to Ngugi wa Thiong'o. This entails an analysis of the role that the initiation and perpetuation of English studies has played in Kenya, and a resolution to abandon the pursuit of English studies till a certain degree of parity is achieved between English and indigenous languages:

> Colonial alienation takes two interlinked forms: an active (or passive) distancing of oneself from the reality around; and an active (or passive) identification with that which is most external to one's environment. It starts with a deliberate dissociation of the language of conceptualisation, of thinking, of formal education, of mental development, from the language of daily interaction in the home and in the community. It is like separating the mind from the body so that they are occupying two unrelated linguistic spheres in the same person. On a larger social scale it is like producing a society of bodiless heads and headless bodies.
>
> So I would like to contribute towards the restoration of the harmony between all the aspects and divisions of language so as to restore the Kenyan child to his environment, understand it fully so as to be in a position to change it for his collective good. I would like to see Kenya peoples' mother-tongues (our national languages!) carry a literature reflecting not only the rhythms of a child's spoken expression, but also his struggle with nature and his social nature. With that harmony between himself, his language and his environment as his starting point, he can learn other languages and even enjoy the positive humanistic, democratic and revolutionary elements in other people's literatures and cultures without any complex about his own language, his own self, his environment.[51]

It is evident that this is firstly, contextualised to the particular hegemonic relationship between external (English, French, etc.) and indigenous languages (Kiswahili, Gikuyu, etc.) in Africa; and secondly, has a vision which doesn't exclude the pursuit of English (or French, etc.) specifically but endorses an opportunity to pursue all languages and their productions equally. This is not the portent of crisis, but an important recognition of a contextual reality. The questioning of this realization is unlikely to come from the center from which the imposition of English studies emanated. Effective questioning of this position is likely to come from within that context, or from analogous contexts. Rajeshwari Sunder Rajan's response to Ngugi wa Thiong'o, in introducing a collection of essays entitled *The Lie of the Land: English Literary Studies in India,* is worth considering carefully for instance:

> The reasons why the issue cannot be addressed in the more straightforward polemical tone employed by Ngugi wa Thiong'o in the essays in *Decolonizing the Mind,* or the contributors to *Toward the Decolonisation of African Literature*[52], and why a more cautious and negotiated approach seems to be called for, require some consideration.
>
> I shall state the most obvious—and indeed perhaps the most pragmatic—of them first. This is with regard to the stakes which we, as professional teachers of English literatures in the university, have in the continuation and perpetuation of the subject in our educational institutions. The somewhat farcical situation of English teachers resigning *en masse* as a result of a crisis of conscience is not envisaged. A second and less self-serving motive for wishing to change, rather than abolish, the face of English lies in the implicit understanding that *English* literature is, theoretically and technically, the most developed of the disciplinary literary studies we have in the Indian academy, and that, for better or worse, it stands in for the humanities by providing (however meagrely) the equivalent of a liberal education. For many teachers of English the subject seems to be worth retaining because the values associated with 'culture' as a whole are found in the curriculum (at present only) in English. Several contributors to this volume express yet another and similarly pragmatic reason for not calling for radical changes—that teachers of English themselves are in no position to effect them, being only part of a larger system that authorizes the structure of English studies, and which is too large, monolithic and bureaucratic to respond to pressures from below.[53]

Two, the other direction which an attempt to invent a different macrodisciplinary space and potential canon takes against English literature is more placatory. These tend to accommodate English literature in their hypothetical different macrodisciplinary space; these literally perform the necessary putting-into-place of English literature. Christopher Clausen's call for a "new paradigm" to replace national literatures in English, and Harish Trivedi's call for a *panchadhatu* system with which his examination of the place of English literature in India culminates, are good examples of thinking in this direction.

Christopher Clausen's essay does not actually go so far as to posit a hypothetical different macrodisciplinary space; he mainly argues for the necessity of such hypothesizations by questioning the rationale for ordering the study of literatures in English in terms of nationality:

> Insofar as literary nationalism of the kind I am describing once served a useful purpose—making room first for literary works in English whose authors were not British, then at a later stage for works from cultures which were neither British nor American—that purpose has been achieved. Holding onto the model in which a national literature serves as a badge of independence now actually defeats the original purpose by excessively identifying each writer with his or her own local "tradition," whether that tradition has its headquarters in London or Nairobi, Sydney or New York.[54]

The only clues he gives regarding the possible different space or new paradigm for studying literature in English are the vague two-fold transformation he gestures towards: a. a less parochial literary history of writing in English which would "become more broadly based, both geographically and intellectually, a direction in which a variety of new and old historicists have been fitfully moving" [55]; and b. an even more insubstantial concept of a change in English courses which will entail the study of texts in terms of undefined aesthetic and comparative criteria. The intractability of Clausen's new paradigm is probably on account of his obviously centrist position. His imagination doesn't really stretch beyond the mainstream of English and American macrodisciplinary spaces and their designative canon. He is clearly well-meaning, and by some miracle of perception he has actually put both English and American literary canons in their place even in his context. But only at the expense of sweeping aside the emerging cultural-nationalities expressed in English, fledging expressions which haven't attained to the position of presenting accepted canons, in the same breath. For Christopher Clausen there are two kinds of literatures in English, British/American and non-British/American, and as far as he is concerned they all suffer from the same malaise of national paradigms and should be dealt with in the same fashion. This assumption is centrist. And though it has a benign aspect to it, a closer look may reveal a truly frightening prospect for the crisis-monger. I feel few qualms about frightening a few crisis-mongers, but on the whole it seems to me not to be worth the trouble. Better not to acknowledge them.

Harish Trivedi's *panchadhatu* concept, on the other hand, is entirely contextual—the context is the pursuit of English literature in departments of English studies in India. It entails an examination more importantly of the place of English literature in India, but also of the place of India in English literature. He discerns in the process a disjunction between the influence of English literature in creative and critical works of Indian literature and the macrodisciplinary space English literature occupies in the Indian institution:

> English literature remains for us—to invoke a phrase Dryden used for Chaucer—a well of English undefiled, and we remain (to invoke a Hindi/Sanskrit proverb) the frogs in that well, quite oblivious of the literary world beyond. Writers in Hindi, as surely in most other Indian languages, have over the last century and more made the most searching, fertile and creative use of English literature, and then in due course gone on to liberate themselves from this historically necessary but now historically exhausted stimulus. On the other hand, the Indian canonizers, i.e. the syllabus makers and teachers, of English literature, have shown a mindless dependence on the metropolis and, even worse, an older fossilized syllabus.[56]

Panchadhatu is his attempt at creating a different macrodisciplinary space where English literature is relocated from its present space. Trivedi suggests that this be composed of five elements (hence the Sanskrit word *panchadhatu*): English literature written in English in England; literature in English written in countries other than England; English translations of literatures written in other languages; the study of literature in an indigenous Indian language; and the study of a classical literature.[57] Whether this is acceptable is a moot point (the complexity of the Indian situation demands further discussion); but it shows evidence of an engagement with a specific context and the macrodisciplinary space of English literature in it. It refuses generalization beyond the complexity of that context. It puts English literature in its place without intimidation or erasure. It has no time for the crisis-mongers of English literature. And, I suspect, crisis-mongers, who appear to be fossilised in the former "value and tradition" of English literature, wouldn't have much to say to it.

To Conclude This Section Let's Summarize the Arguments Therein (the Bold Text at its Most Assertive) . . .

To place English literature in the perspective of other disciplines of knowledge, we have to be clear whether disciplines of knowledge are placed in the cautious text or in the bold text. Further, if it is the latter, we would have to distinguish whether disciplines of knowledge have a metadisciplinary sense or macrodisciplinary sense.

If these distinctions are not made a discussion at cross-purposes is likely to ensue with regard to the status, content, and legitimacy of English literature.

Such discussions at cross-purposes are presented in almost all debates regarding the alleged crisis in English literature, and the related issue of canonicity in English literature. A clarification of the shades of meaning implicit in the term "English literature," and a consequent holding asunder of the ramifications (ré crisis and canon) which adhere to these shades of meaning, would help clear the air. In fact, it is arguable that the notion of a crisis in English literature would cease to convince if seen from this perspective.

If English literature is drawn into the cautious text of literature no crisis can attach to it. Disciplines in cautious texts cannot see outside themselves, can only expand themselves, and would find it impossible to visualize any threat to themselves.

If English literature is conceived from a metadisciplinary perspective it would have to be seen as a subset of literature in general and at a par with other specific literatures, i.e., it would have to be conceived as a subdiscipline. In this perspective no crisis can attach to English literature alone—there can only be a crisis for literature in general, with different degrees of effect on different specific literatures.

To conceive of English literature from a macrodisciplinary perspective the institutional space of English literature can be examined in terms of (a) its development as such, (b) the content which it defines itself by and promotes. It is argued that such notions of crises as are expressed with regard to (a) or (b) are not crises at all, but a necessary putting-into-place of English literature within the institutional field.

To simplify the examination of the macrodisciplinary perspective the discussion above is centered on only one aspect of English literary studies, i.e., the canon. Distinctions in the concept of the canon are drawn in keeping with distinctions made in the conceptualization of English literature. The self-evident canon is the one that is attached to the concept of English literature in the cautious text or from a metadisciplinary perspective. The macrodisciplinary space designates itself by an accepted canon, is interrogated by counter-canons or alternative canons, and may have to coexist on terms of equality with (or become secondary to) proposed canons in the future. The confrontations and negotiations between these varying formulations of the canon attached to English literature are used to present the manner in which English literature is being put-in-its-place.

Notes

1. For example, see Roman Jakobson and Krystyna Pomorska, "Dialogue on Time in Language and Literature," *Verbal Art, Verbal Sign, Verbal Time* (Oxford: Basil Blackwell, 1985), p. 12. Also see Chapter 1 in Paul Ricoeur, *Interpretation and Theory: Discourse and the Surplus of Meaning* (Fort Worth: Texas Christian Univ. Press, 1976).

2. Josephine Guy and Ian Small, *Politics and Value in English Studies: A Discipline in Crisis?* (Cambridge: Cambridge Univ. Press, 1993), pp. 30–33 gives the background to and justification for this emphasis.

3. Ibid., p. 46.

4. Ibid.

5. Ibid., p. 29.

6. Ibid., p. 35.

7. Ibid.

8. René Welleck, "The Attack on Literature," *The Attack on Literature and Other Essays* (Brighton: Harvester, 1982), p. 3.

9. Ibid., p. 5.

10. Ibid., p. 9.

11. Matthew Arnold, "The Study of Poetry," *Matthew Arnold's Essays in Criticism: First and Second Series* (London: Dent and New York: Dutton, 1964), pp. 237–38.

12. F. R. Leavis, *The Great Tradition* (Middlesex: Penguin, 1948), p. 9. The entire introductory paragraph of the first chapter is addressed to unknown critics and their strictures.

13. This is evident in Leavis's other writings where he tries to protect English Literature from mass culture by controlling the modes of transmission in pedagogic practice. As in F. R. Leavis and Denys Thompson, *Culture and Environment* (London: Chatto and Windus, 1933). Or on similar lines: Q. D. Leavis, *Fiction and the Reading Public* (London: Chatto and Windus, 1932).

14. Ezra Pound, "How to Read," *Literary Essays of Ezra Pound* (London: Faber and Faber, 1954), p. 15.

15. Harold Bloom, *The Western Canon: The Books and Schools of the Ages* (London and Basingstoke: Macmillan, 1994), p. 15.

16. Matthew Arnold, first formulated in the "Second Lecture" of *On Translating Homer* (London: Longman, Green, Longman and Roberts, 1861) and reiterated with emphasis in "The Fuction of Criticism at the Present Time," *Essays in Criticism*, p. 9.

17. Matthew Arnold, *Culture and Anarchy* (Cambridge: Cambridge Univ. Press, 1932), p. 45.

18. Matthew Arnold, "The Study of Poetry," *Essays in Criticism*, p. 235.

19. Ezra Pound, "How to Read," *Literary Essays*, pp. 18–19.

20. F. R. Leavis, "Sociology and Literature," *The Common Pursuit* (London: Chatto and Windus, 1952), p. 198.
21. F. R. Leavis, "Literary Criticism and Philosophy," ibid., p. 212.
22. Harold Bloom, *The Western Canon*, p. 18.
23. Ibid., p. 10.
24. Oscar Wilde, "The Critic as Artist," *Intentions and the Soul of Man* (London: Dawson, 1969), p. 144.
25. Harold Bloom, *The Western Canon*, p. 39 for instance.
26. Matthew Arnold, "The Study of Poetry," *Essays in Criticism*, p. 244.
27. Ezra Pound, "The Serious Artist," *Literary Essays*, p. 45.
28. F. R. Leavis, "Literary Criticism and Philosophy," *The Common Pursuit*.
29. Harold Bloom, *The Anxiety of Influence* (New York: Oxford Univ. Press, 1973).
30. F. R. Leavis, *The Great Tradition*, pp. 27–28.
31. Ibid., p. 251.
32. F. R. Leavis, *The Living Principle:'English' as a Discipline of Thought* (London: Chatto and Windus, 1975).
33. Hans Robert Jauss, "Literary History as a Challenge to Literary Theory," *Toward an Aesthetic of Reception* (Minneapolis: Univ. of Minnesota Press, 1982), pp. 3–45; and Frank Kermode, *History and Value* (Oxford: Clarendon, 1988), especially Part II.
34. John Dixon, *A Schooling in 'English'* (Buckingham: Open Univ. Press, 1991), p. 4.
35. D.J.Palmer, *The Rise of English Studies* (London: Oxford Univ. Press, 1965), pp. 13–14.
36. Ibid., pp. 15–18.
37. Ibid., pp. 32–35.
38. Ibid., pp. 39–40.
39. Brian Doyle, *English and Englishness* (London: Routledge, 1989), p. 17.
40. Ibid., Chapter 2.
41. Ibid., p. 104.
42. Chris Baldick, *The Social Mission of English Criticism, 1848–1932* (Oxford: Clarendon, 1983), p. 61.
43. Robert Crawford, *Devolving English Literature* (Oxford: Clarendon, 1992).
44. Ibid., p. 43.
45. Gauri Vishwanathan, *Masks of Conquest* (London: Faber and Faber, 1989), Chapter 4. For a more complex picture of the ideological negotiations involved see Kumkum Sanghari, "Relating Histories: Definitions of Literacy, Literature, Gender in Nineteenth Century Calcutta and England," in Svati Joshi, ed., *Rethinking English: Essays in Literature, Language, History* (New Delhi: Trianka, 1991).
46. Ibid., Chapter 6.
47. Ibid., pp. 85–88.
48. Chris Baldick, *The Social Mission of English Criticism*, pp. 7–8.
49. Aijaz Ahmad, *In Theory* (London and New York: Verso, 1992), chapter 2.
50. Ibid., p. 96.
51. Ngugi wa Thiong'o, *Decolonizing the Mind* (London and Nairobi: James Currey, Heinemann Kenya and Heinemann, 1986), pp. 28–29.
52. Chinweizu, *et al*, *Toward the Decolonization of African Literature* (London: KPI, 1985).
53. Rajeshwari Sunder Rajan, "Fixing English: Nation, Language, Subject," *The Lie of the Land* (Delhi and Oxford: Oxford Univ. Press, 1992), pp. 26–27.

54. Christopher Clausen, "'National Literatures' in English: Toward a New Paradigm," *New Literary History*, vol.25, no.1, Winter 1994, p. 70.
55. Ibid.
56. Harish Trivedi, *Colonial Transactions* (Calcutta: Papyrus, 1993), p. 225.
57. Ibid., Chapter 10.

Part III
The Cautious Text

The Literary Subject and "Non-Literary" Texts

ALONGSIDE AND AMIDST THE BOLD TEXT OF LITERARY STUDIES AS a discipline amongst other disciplines, alongside and amidst the bold text of English literature as a subdiscipline (the metadisciplinary approach) and English literature as an academic discipline (the macrodisciplinary approach), the reading-writing of the literary-subject's cautious text may be found. The cautious text of the literary-subject evades bold attempts to contain it within the bold text, to effectively summarize it. The cautious text of literature evades its meta or macrodisciplinary boundaries, and refuses to recognize an interface with other disciplines; it merely extends itself to all texts as literature. And the literary-subject refuses to be construed as a subject-as-object by the simple reiteration of its subjectivity (by stating that I am I) and by allowing its (my) gaze to sweep the visible horizons. In this sweep a distinctively *English* literary gaze has no disciplinary boundary which is not subsumed by the vision of literariness which defines the subject and allows it to appear as such. Englishness is, if at all, a medium of the subject's voice. The quanta of the subdiscipline or the institutional space of the academic discipline belong to a different sphere of understanding: the bold text. The bold text doesn't acknowledge the distance, it constantly tries to contain the cautious text of literature, but it isn't able to communicate the expansiveness of the cautious text without annihilating itself through the assertion of the literary subject.

Finally, I (the literary-subject) want to reaffirm the expansiveness and assimilativeness of the cautious text of literature (only broadly asserted in the first part of this study so far) by extending my gaze to ostensibly (from the meta or macrodisciplinary bold perspective) nonliterary texts. I endeavour to demonstrate this through two exemplary sections devoted respectively to: (i) literary engagements with Wittgenstein's philosophy; and (ii) the literary-linguistics of non-mathematical expositions of Relativity.

I can almost hear the derisive snigger of the bold reader-writer at this point, can feel the nudge of complicity from those accustomed to the sophistries of metadisciplinary and macrodisciplinary approaches to disciplines of knowledge. "This is the appearance of Theory," I hear them saying, or "This is interdisciplinariness, pure and simple." But I must reject these voices. What follows is my cautious text of literary studies. Moreover, I perceive that literary studies has always been such. The so-called *object* of literary studies—the work of fiction, the play, the poem, etc.—has always been an excuse to examine the texts which prefigure them: the text of an individual existence (authorial intention, reader-response, etc.), the discourses of "life" (a sense of context, the ideological subtexts, etc.). The so-called object of literary studies is merely a pretext for the expansiveness and assimilativeness of the literary gaze, a focal point to describe the communal interchanges of literary subjects, and it has always been so. This cautious text of the literary-subject can engage with anything, and expand and assimilate indefinitely, and is designed to do so. More often than not, the alleged object of literary studies is a literary study itself, and itself expands the cautious text of the literary subject.

The specific function of the object of literary studies (the creative literary work), when it is posited as such, can be examined in detail in a separate space. It would entail a close look, perhaps in the form of a case study, of a so-called object (a novel, poem, play, etc.) and the manner in which literary studies, an intercourse of readers-writers, emanates around it. But that needs a discrete and separate space, a different study.

But not here. Since I can assert nothing more about the cautious text and the literary-subject I simply proceed here to the two exemplary sections. What cannot be explained about the cautious text of literary studies is probably contained in its practice. The exemplary sections demonstrate the expansiveness and assimilativness of the literary-subject and the cautious text of literary studies. Since the exemplary sections cannot be summarized without the contradiction of falling into the bold text no attempt to state conclusions follows them. There can be no pulling the threads together in a neat conclusion. There can only be the practice of the cautious text of literary studies, the final shape of the literary-subject's gaze, and nothing more. This part ends when the exemplary sections end.

Example One: Literary Engagements with Wittgenstein

This exemplary section of the literary subject's (my) attempt to extend the cautious text of literary criticism to ostensibly philosophical texts is the result of reflections spurred by reading Terry Eagleton's original script for Derek Jarman's film *Wittgenstein*.

Neither Jarman's film nor Eagleton's script had invited my attention in the first instance. At least not in themselves—their value as additions to the bodies of works by two thoughtful and creative (in a literary sense) persons is undeniable. It was actually Eagleton's introduction to the published versions of the original script penned by him, and the script used eventually by Jarman, which set me thinking. I found Eagleton's assessment of the differences invigorating:

> My own script strikes me as reasonably strong on ideas but short on dramatic action; Jarman's, minus my own interpolation, seems to me just the other way around. It is, as it were, a very *English* text, for the English love 'a character' but are notably nervous of the intellect.[1]

This might not appear to be a particularly awe inspiring distinction on the face of it. In fact, it isn't. It has the merit of being amusing at the expense of English taste, and we understand that Eagleton is allowed to say things like that now that he has asserted his Irish sensibility (such as it is). But that's not the point either. It is interesting because Eagleton maintains here that it is not merely as drama that his script should be appreciated, but as drama written by a literary theorist. In fact, Eagleton presents the script as a *rounded* literary engagement with the philosophy of Wittgenstein. One is not allowed to forget that it is Terry Eagleton who has written it. The signature asserts a certain kind of authority: there is literary theory behind this as well as literary art, there is the realization of what is dramatic about the biographical subject and what is stimulating about the philosophical subject, and these are made to bear upon each other. This set me thinking.

And that's what this section is about: literary, or rather non-philosophical (with "philosophical" in the sense of being affiliated to certain institutional and discipline-bound expectations), engagements with Wittgenstein's philosophy, of which Terry Eagleton, in his *roundedness*, is a useful example. I contend that this kind of approach has led to readings of Wittgenstein which the

Wittgensteinian philosopher may be sceptical of but which need to be taken into account. I first chart out the distinctive features of readings of Wittgenstein that result from a literary, or nonphilosophical, engagement—in doing this I continue to refer mainly to (though not exclusively to) the useful example of Terry Eagleton's script. I then make a detour into the theory of argument as informal logic, hoping to demonstrate that this might have a useful role to play in literary, or nonphilosophical, readings of Wittgenstein. Finally, I make a brief attempt to produce my own reading of Wittgenstein, given the above distinctions and given my literary education. I cannot give to my reading as effective a signature as Eagleton's but that's no cause for concern—I don't need it. The purpose of my reading is more demonstrative (of what precedes it) than elucidatory.

The Literary Engagement With Wittgenstein

I continue with my reflections on Terry Eagleton's script. Because I am dealing with Wittgenstein, which means I have to try to be comprehensible against daunting odds, I do this point-wise. ('Point-wise' usually offends my literary education, but does wonderful things for coherence—and my point-wise system is taken straight from the *Tractatus Logico-Philosophicus*.[2] Need I seek further justification?)

1. Thrice in the script of *Wittgenstein* Terry Eagleton discusses—or rather his characters discuss—Wittgenstein's philosophy in some detail. This happens:

a. In the scene which describes Wittgenstein addressing a group of students and dons (including G. E. Moore, Bertrand Russell, and John Maynard Keynes) in Trinity College,[3] in which his arguments are brought neatly to make the point that

> When you want to know the meaning of a word, don't look *inside* yourself; look at the uses of the word in our way of life. Look at how we *behave.* The best picture of the soul is the human body. (Pause) And to do this, we must get rid of the illusions which philosophy breeds. Philosophy leaves everything exactly as it was; it can in no way interfere with our forms of life. It simply assembles reminders of what we knew anyway, but which was too familiar for us to recognise[4];

b. When Wittgenstein tries to summarize his philosophy for the benefit of the mechanic, and concludes as follows:

> There is no private meaning: we are what we are only because we share a common language, and common forms of life. Philosophy has

> moved on the pure ice of logic; but I take us back to the rough ground of our social practices.
>
> *We see the MECHANIC's face: empty, uncomprehending.*
>
> But of course, beyond all that, there still lies the inexpressible: that which we must not say.[5]

(interesting mixture of *Philosophical Investigations* sentiments with *Tractatus* mysticism there—but more of that later);

c. In Keynes's conceit of the clever young man who created a world without friction and

> grew up into a wise old man who came to understand that roughness and ambiguity and indeterminacy aren't imperfections—they're what make things work.[6]

These are, it seems to me, the extended philosophical sections of the screenplay, though Wittgensteinian pearls of wisdom are dropped every now and then: when Wittgenstein tries to explain his will to suicide to Russell,[7] for instance, or when he tries to persuade Jarrett to give up philosophy.[8]

1.1 The three statements cited above are repetitions of the same basic concept which charts out Wittgenstein's standpoint in terms of the following oppositions (a diagrammatic representation has the advantage of being concise; the two-sided arrows indicate oppositions):

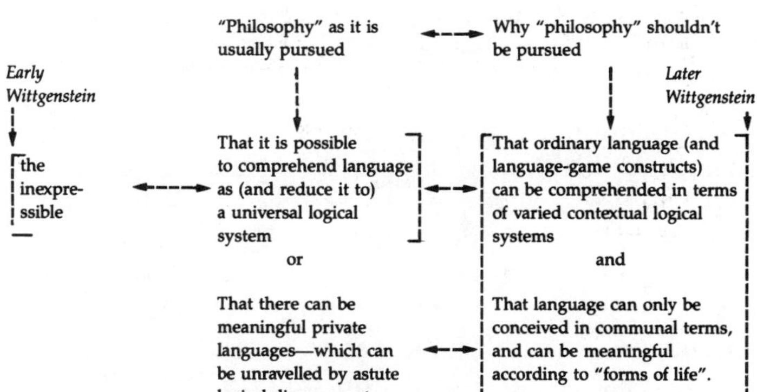

I do not go into the details of these oppositions at the moment. I am not delving into Wittgenstein's arguments themselves. I am looking at Terry Eagleton's literary engagement with them. The question is not *what* did the three statements from the screenplay repeat, but *how* are the three statements presented.

1.2 One of the features of the three statements cited above is their *cut and dry* nature. They state what is ostensibly considered Wittgenstein's theory as a complete and rounded set of formulations which can be summarized and repeated adequately. By adequately I mean that it can be communicated so as to be understood and accepted. Characters in the script often confess themselves unable to understand Wittgenstein but:

i. None of them seem to doubt that Wittgenstein is a great philosopher;

ii. The last statement (statement (c) in point 1) is Keynes's, so at least Keynes thought he understood Wittgenstein, though he was one of those who claimed not to have after the session at Trinity College (statement (a));

iii. The repetitiveness and brevity of the statements is meant, I suppose, to render them coherent to whatever audience the hypothetical screening of Eagleton's script might have attracted—except the English, as Eagleton would acidly confirm.

That they are acceptable is implied in a more paradoxical manner because:

i. It is a foregone conclusion that Wittgenstein is a great philosopher, and everyone simply does accept whatever he says;

ii. Wittgenstein produces in the screenplay some data to back up his claims (the V sign, for instance[9]);

iii. Wittgenstein answers some objections (raised by a young American student, for example[10]).

This presentation of Wittgenstein's philosophy as *cut-and-dry* is worked at a presumptive level in the language of the script.

1.21 Wittgensteinian philosophers are unlikely to be pleased with the *cut-and-dryness* of Eagleton's literary engagement. C. P. Baker and P. M. S. Hacker, or A. J. Ayer, or D. F. Pears, or Anthony Kenny, or any of the numerous other philosophers who have engaged with Wittgenstein's thoughts (favorably or otherwise) have not approached his writings as a closed, manifestly comprehensible and acceptable set of formulations. Their metalanguages usually expand into and behind the surface of Wittgenstein's writings to seek conviction or disagreement.

Come to think of it, there is little to justify the sense of cut-and-dryness. There is no authorial sanction along those lines: the later writings were published posthumously and edited by others. The method followed in Wittgenstein's later texts do not invite cut-and-dryness. As Henry Staten, in comparing Wittgenstein and Derrida, observes:

> Wittgenstein's method is critical. It is a way of attacking another style of language, the traditional style of philosophy. This traditional style is characterised by the pursuit of stable unities [. . .]. Now in order to fracture these unities, Wittgenstein develops a style of writing which is radically errant, which unlids all the accidence concealed by "normal" uses of words in order to show how many different routes it would be possible to take from any given point in the discourse [. . .][11]

and later again

> Wittgenstein's method is no sort of method—has no "sort" that it belongs to. All possible methods are possible signifying sequences, revealing arrangements of the accidents of the signifying material: but Wittgenstein's method is a technique for following the accidence that generates the components of signifying sequences of whatever kind.[12]

Paradoxically, it is clear that Eagleton is perfectly aware of this.[13]

1.22 Despite point 1.21 above, however, the cut-and-dry conception of Wittgenstein's philosophy is far from being unusual. It is certainly not unusual in the context of other literary engagements with Wittgenstein's philosophy. This can be seen both in the practice of textual criticism and in literary critical theory. Take any area of textual literary criticism where Wittgenstein has been invoked—consider, for instance, the area of James Joyce studies. One may recall Thomas C. Singer's essay, which tries to "bring forth some of Wittgenstein's ideas on the assumption that they may serve as a lamp to throw light on Joyce's *Portrait;*"[14] or David A. White's ambitious paper which attempts an "exposition of Wittgenstein's conceptual development as a basis for appreciating Joyce's linguistic development."[15] Both provide summaries of Wittgenstein's ideas which have the same cut-and-dry quality as the statements in Terry Eagleton's script. The same approach is seen in the work of a literary critical theorist like Stanley Fish, for example, when he summarizes Wittgenstein's notion of "language-games" on the way to developing his concept of interpretive communities and interpretive strategies.[16]

But cut-and-dry perceptions of Wittgenstein's thinking are not confined to literary engagements alone. One can see them in some philosophical engagements too. It appears in Richard Wollheim's forty-fifth section of *Art and Its Objects,* when he declares that "Art is, in Wittgenstein's sense, a form of life," and follows this up with a summary of Wittgenstein's concept.[17] It also manifests itself in Jean-François Lyotard's description of "language-games as [his] general methodological approach" in *The Postmodern Condition.*[18]

1.211/1.221 There is, of course, an obvious difference between those cited above who do not adhere to a cut-and-dry approach to Wittgenstein (1.21), and those cited above who do (1.22). As I have observed before, the former group developed a metalanguage which expands into and behind the surface of Wittgenstein's language to seek conviction or disagreement. In the same spirit one can maintain, the latter group developed a language which expands *outwards* from Wittgenstein's language into different disciplines and areas. None of those cited in 1.22 try to focus exclusively on, or even predominantly on, Wittgenstein's thinking. Their central preoccupations are James Joyce's language, reader-response, art and aesthetics, postmodernism, etc., and they refer to Wittgenstein's concepts to be able to clarify their central preoccupations. Wittgenstein's concepts are used as tools: either as analogous to certain aspects of the area in question (as in White and Singer and Wollheim), or as basic background in terms of which the area in question can be developed (as in Fish and Lyotard).

But where does Terry Eagleton's *rounded* literary engagement with Wittgenstein in his script fit into all this?

1.23 Terry Eagleton's script continues to be a bit of a paradox in this context. It has a cut-and-dry perspective of Wittgenstein's thinking and yet it doesn't appear to move outward from Wittgenstein's thinking as a subject. On the contrary, the thinking Wittgenstein is the ostensible and actual subject of this literary engagement. Yet one can't help feeling that an outward movement of some sort is called for, and is perhaps taking place . . . Can one engage with Wittgenstein's thoughts as one's subject, and yet not delve *into* them as a Wittgensteinian philosopher would do but reach *out* with them? Is that a sensible question? Reach *out* where?

With reference to Terry Eagleton's script these are perfectly sensible questions. The answers are: yes, one can engage with Wittgenstein's thoughts as a subject and reach *out* with them;

and one can reach out with them to comprehend Wittgenstein's thoughts that is the subject. This self-reflexive outward-looking engagement characterizes the *literariness* (and the nonphilosophicalness) of literary engagements with Wittgenstein. It can lead to a somewhat different reading of Wittgenstein's thoughts.

Eagleton's script provides such a reading, or rather opens up such readings because his literary engagement moves indecisively in several directions and doesn't particularly lead anywhere. In that sense I find Eagleton's engagement with Wittgenstein in his script (and elsewhere) somewhat disappointing. Two broad features of Eagleton's indecisive, self-reflexive, outward-looking, literary engagement can be briefly mentioned here.

a. To a large degree Eagleton's engagement with Wittgenstein's ideas takes place in terms of a life-thought juxtaposition—not just the life-thought oppositions that Wittgenstein himself questioned, but a "Wittgenstein's life"-"Wittgenstein's thoughts" opposition. As he explains in the introduction Eagleton sees the latter emphatically as an *opposition.*[19] One could call this a biographical reading of Wittgenstein's philosophy. One can see a meeting of Wittgenstein's primary texts and biographical texts and one can think of Eagleton's screenplay as a response-statement derived from the reader's intertextual negotiations between these.[20]

b. It is well to remember that Eagleton is, what I would call, a theoretical synthesist. I have the world of thought neatly (too neatly) divided into theoretical synthesists and creative theoreticians. The former's methods are encyclopaedic; they consist of assimilating several existing theoretical contentions and negotiating between them. The latter tend to construct a system without necessary reference to others, from certain basic formulations (Descartes's *A Discourse on Method* comes leaping to mind—he made a similar distinction[21]). Wittgenstein, in my opinion, falls into the creative theorist category. His range of reference is minimal and unnecessary (there are some, of course, like Frege and Russell in *Tractatus,* and St. Augustine in *Philosophical Investigations*). Eagleton's writings depend on his range of reference, and his entire method is geared to an adopted range of reference. What Eagleton's script seems to do is give Wittgenstein's creative theorizing a range of reference. It has the air of being a theoretical synthesist's efforts at translating the creative theorist's ideas into his own jargon. The script constantly places Wittgenstein's thoughts in a context of names which immediately evoke a series of texts. The signature which goes with Wittgenstein's ideas has to contend against other powerful signatures which encapsulate other ideas, signatures like Bertrand Russell, G. E. Moore, and John Maynard Keynes. An air of intertextuality, over and above the biographical intertextuality mentioned above, creeps in. One can't help feeling that this is inevitable for Eagleton, it is his stamp, it is his mode of protecting himself from the insecurities of creative thinking. To see him more clearly as a competent synthesist reading Wittgenstein one can merely refer to his essay "Wittgenstein's Friends."[22] The remarkable range of reference given to Wittgenstein's ideas here comprehends F. R. Leavis, Bertrand Russell, Jacques Derrida, A. J. Ayer, Nietzsche, Marx, Mikhail and Nikolai Bakhtin, Georg Lukács, Theodor Adorno, George Thomson, Pierro Sraffa, Antonio Gramsci, amongst others.

However, as I have mentioned already, I find Eagleton's indecisive, self-reflexive, outward-looking readings of Wittgenstein disappointing. Quite a lot of possible reasons come to mind: for instance, his frames of reference are at times tenuous, his cut-and-dry restatements of Wittgenstein's concepts have a rigidity about them of which I am sceptical, the several directions of speculation which are opened up seem to totter precariously close to unresolvable inconclusiveness, etc., etc. Mainly, I can't help thinking about the one interesting and more fruitful direction that he didn't take though it is opened up by his synthetic literary engagement with Wittgenstein. I proceed to present it as my literary engagement with Wittgenstein.

The Theory of Argument

2. What follows can be called *literary* because I declare that my attitude to it is such. I declare here that I claim a place in the literary community, which means that I pursue the discipline of literary studies in a certain self-conscious manner. Quite a large number of theorists are apparently beginning to believe that this self-consciousness is the main criteria for belonging to a literary community—as opposed, say, to being a lay reader. Paul Ricoeur has suggested that the interpreter (read literary critic) is different from the reader (add lay before that) by being able to legitimize the guess-character of his readerly activities in terms of certain methodological principles: briefly, construe text as a whole, construe text as an individual, allow space for pluralistic actualizations.[23] Similar prescriptional measures have been recommended by Wayne Booth and Paul Armstrong,[24] for instance. Given these, the literary critic has no difficulty in identifying him/herself, the

student of literature has merely to acknowledge and conform to certain hermeneutical prescriptions. I do so with regard to Wittgenstein's texts, and it is in that sense that what follows can be seen as a literary engagement. I approach his texts as a literary critic brings certain interpretive strategies to bear upon literary texts. Thereby I absorb Wittgenstein into my cautious literary text, and hope I am not getting absorbed in a cautious Wittgensteinian text inadvertently. If a philosopher reads this he/she will probably observe that I am . . .

2.1 But there is a more serious implication to my declaration of this affiliation. It commits my reading of Wittgenstein to a sense of *outwardness* which is much the same as Eagleton's, though it tries to avoid the cut-and-dryness implicit in Eagleton's reading. This might sound paradoxical. Am I proposing that the two approaches I had discerned in 1.211/1.221 can be mixed up and reconciled?

The answer is in the affirmative. You may recall that in 1.23 I had placed Eagleton as a theoretical synthesist (as opposed to a creative theorist). I had suggested that his cut-and-dry and outward-looking perception of Wittgenstein probably derived from that. And I had concluded that I was disappointed in his reading because he doesn't do what I had expected him to do. I enter my literary engagement with Wittgenstein by explaining the diappointed expectations.

What Eagleton doesn't do as a theoretical synthesist reading Wittgenstein is state his methodological approach. He takes for granted (or alternatively, flouts) the requirement for self-consciousness dictated by the prescriptive principles of literary communities. And not just of literary communities but of the act of theoretical synthesis. He doesn't declare the assumptions of being a synthesist adequately. If he did he might have taken a different approach in his literary engagement with Wittgenstein (instead of the biographical and intertextual assault he actually conducts). It is this other possible approach that interests me.

Let's take the example of perhaps the greatest theoretical synthesist who worked (and continues to) in this half of this century, Jürgen Habermas, and his masterpiece of synthetic theorizing, *The Theory of Communicative Action.*

2.11 Jürgen Habermas introduces his immense synthetic theory of sociology with a survey of types of rationality which includes a section on the theory of argument. This was intended as both a definitive (marking the parameters within which sociological formulation is possible) and a self-reflexive (negotiating the exact status of the formulations he posits) exercise. The emphasis on the theory of argument is particularly interesting in this exercise because it makes a distinction between formal logic and informal logic:

> The logic of argument does not refer to deductive connections between semantic units (sentences) as does formal logic, but to nondeductive relations between the pragmatic units (speech acts) of which arguments are composed. Thus it also appears under the name of "informal logic."[25]

I pause here to point out that this informal logic is exactly what I had been gesturing towards in my notion of *outwardness* in readings of Wittgenstein. It seems to me that this was the potential difference between the theorists cited in 1.21 and 1.22. Philosophical engagements with Wittgenstein normally investigate the deductive connections between semantic units of Wittgenstein's arguments (the propositions, for example), whereas those with an external focus, be it postmodernism, art, or literary relevance, look at something else. So far, I have called this something else an *outward perspective*—it tends to use an element of Wittgenstein's thinking which is analogous to the area in focus, which has some sort of metaphorical value, which possesses methodological parallels etc. I think this something else can be clearly posited in terms of "nondeductive relations between the pragmatic units."

I can also qualify now that what I found tenuous and directionless and generally unsatisfactory about Eagleton's *outward* engagement with Wittgenstein was due to his unawareness of this something else he was using. He was potentially opening up an informal logical approach to Wittgenstein which fizzles out because he wasn't aware that he was doing so. It becomes instead a tenuous biographical and intertextual exercise which leaves Wittgenstein's thinking caught up in a stultifying cut-and-dryness. It can be surmized that the same could be argued of the other cut-and-dry readings of Wittgenstein cited here, except that these have the merit of focusing on different subjects.

If Eagleton had followed his synthesist instincts and examined the parameters of rationality within which he works he would probably have seen that there was a more promising reading of Wittgenstein at hand which did not necessarily involve biographical analysis and inter-textual frameworks as an end.

2.111 Coming back to Habermas's comments on the theory of argument: these become essentially a critique of Stephen Toulmin's *The Uses of Argument.* Toulmin's work, which shows the relevance of the analysis of ordinary language as opposed to the abstraction of formal logic and mathematics (his section on probability is a good example[26]) could itself be read as an advanced stage of Wittgenstein's constructed "ordinary language" analyses. Habermas's critique both describes Toulmin's qualities and reveals his limitations: that though Toulmin "allows for a plurality of validity claims while not denying the critical sense of a validity transcending spatio-temporal and social limitations,"[27] he

> makes no attempt to analyze the quite generally conceived *standpoint of impartiality* and therefore opens himself to the objection that he delivers up the logic of argumentation—which he develops only to the general schema of argumentation and not on the levels of procedure and process—to *preexisting* notions of rationality. [. . .] Toulmin does not push the logic of argument far enough into the domains of dialectic and rhetoric. He doesn't draw the proper lines between accidental *institutional differences of argumentation,* on the one hand, and the *forms of argumentation* determined by internal structure, on the other.[28]

The point, I think, is well taken.

I will have occasion to refer to Toulmin later. Let me at this stage pause and ask myself where I stand. Below I adopt Toulmin's ordinary language-based informal logic of argumentation (without referring to the specific forms of argumentation he charts out in Essay 3 of his work[29]), and, as Habermas put it, investigate "the nondeductive relations between the pragmatic units" of which Wittgenstein's formulations are composed. I do not possess a *standpoint of impartiality.* My own argumentation is dictated by the institutional form of argumentation derived from a *literary* education, and I try to focus on the form of argument in Wittgenstein determined by internal structure (thus disregarding his institutional standpoint). I see this exercise as a reversal of normal expectations: i.e., not an exposition of Wittgenstein the philosopher analysing the nuances of an ordinary language construct (language-games) in his later philosophy, but a reading which is determined to comprehend two key texts by Wittgenstein as available to ordinary language-like analysis, i.e., my literary reading.

Having said that, I am left with a few brief observations on my reading (a simple one, on the whole) of Wittgenstein which are not *literary* in some of the usual senses of the word, but in so far as I extend my cautious text in these. The convoluted process of working my way from Terry Eagleton's rounded literary engagement with Wittgenstein leads to the little that remains of this paper. What follows is the necessary rounding-up for what I have argued so far.

Reading Wittgenstein

READING THE *TRACTATUS*

3. *Tractatus Logico-Philosophicus* has all the characteristics of being the work of a creative theorist: it starts with provisional formulations at a micro level and proceeds to draw a picture of a macro level. If I were a philosopher I expect I would have followed closely the processive act of reading which is equivalent to following the "deductive connections between the semantic units." This is a peculiarity of Wittgenstein's text: it is self-reflexive, in a sense it is about itself. The reading is the formation of the deductive connections between the semantic units *about* the deductive connections between semantic units. The *Tractatus* therefore draws the philosophical reader into its monological world by the very act of appearing as a text which is amenable to a philosophical reading: the philosopher's processive act of reading is a confirmation of what is read; the performance of the deductions between the semantic units is proof of the existence of those semantic units in terms of those deductive relations. It is both an enactment of and an exposition of formal logic.

But I am not a philosopher and I did not always follow the processive act as I should have. Perhaps this was a weakness. The language coherent to the specialized level of Wittgenstein's statements was not immediately mapped on to my ordinary language perception. The difference is much like the ordinary use of probability and Carnap's or Kneale's use of probability as analyzed by Toulmin. As Toulmin's critique of the latter shows, the ordinary use is not entirely irrelevant (as Carnap and Kneale would have us believe) and one could even argue that the specialized use can be posited through and criticized from the perspective of the latter.[30] My ordinary language approach to the *Tractatus* was possibly a weakness but I was optimistic: I read slowly and the deductive connections dawned on me later than they should have, and it was a process of learning the language as much as reading and enacting, but something came of it. I ended up with a nonphilosophical, or (since I am who I am) a literary, reading of the *Tractatus.*

I ended up, in other words, with a *retrospective* view of the text. It did not come as a self-reflexive processive enactment cum confirmation of formal logic, but as a retrospective picture of different bits and pieces which have been placed in relation to each other in a beautiful and intelligent, but not inevitable, fashion. The text seemed to grow backwards for me, from a macro to a micro level, and from this unusual perspective I thought I could discern an informal logical arrangement, a form of argument, which would not be apparent if one followed the processive philosophical reading. I posit this *retrospective* view against Eagleton's kind of *outward/cut-and-dry* view.

3.1 From my retrospective point of view the most significant feature of the *Tractatus* is the one that appears in its latter part in processive reading—the notion of the beyond-logic, the inexpressible (which is how I refer to it hereafter): "There are, indeed, things that cannot be put into words. They *make themselves manifest.* They are what is mystical."[31] Like Russell, one cannot help feeling that Wittgenstein did "say a good deal about what cannot be said."[32] That does not, however, mean that Russell's philosophical reading and my retrospective view necessarily concur on this issue.

If I had to summarize my retrospective view of the *Tractatus* I would probably proceed to elucidate the four following steps:

a. Wittgenstein's basic contention is that language itself is logic, so much so that logic cannot be discussed by using language: "[. . .] there can be no representatives of the logic of facts."[33] To support this argument he supplies a series of essential linguistic definitions which render it impossible to use them in an analysis of logic. Any use of them in an analysis of logic would lead to a series of tautological statements. Speaking of signs, for instance, he says that:

> logic is not a field in which we express what we wish with the help of signs, but rather one in which the nature of the absolutely necessary sign speaks for itself.[34]

Again, after delineating propositions he explains:

> A proposition communicates a situation to us, and so it must be essentially connected with the situation.

> And the connection is precisely that it is it's logical picture.[35]

b. This point follows the one above: that logic is inscrutable. "Clearly the laws of logic cannot in their turn be subject to laws of logic."[36] This *is* clear. If language cannot discuss logic nothing can, because everything that admits of thought can be said. Logic is merely unavoidably present and becomes evident through the mere (silent) scrutiny of propositions. Two corollaries follow:
i. The inscrutability of logic confirms its *a priori* position. In Wittgenstein's words:

> Self-evidence, which Russell talked about so much, can become dispensable in logic, only because language itself prevents every logical mistake—what makes logic *a priori* is the impossibility of illogical thought.[37]

ii. Logic itself poses the limits of language, i.e., what Wittgenstein later thought of as the limits of our world. Since logic itself cannot be logically analyzed it becomes responsible for raising walls around language. I could say here, as Wittgenstein did later and in a different text, that "The limit of language is shown by its being impossible to describe the fact which corresponds to a sentence, without simply repeating that sentence."[38] "The limits of my language means the limits of my world,"[39] he maintains in the *Tractatus,* and rounds-off his argument in the concluding sentence, "What we cannot speak about we must pass over in silence."[40]

c. But how can the limits of the logical-linguistic world be conceived as limits at all if everything that can be said or thought falls within its precincts? Russell and Frege were not able to communicate this inherent limitation of the logical-linguistic world. Wittgenstein does this through his peculiar mode of *bringing logic into relief*—but what does that involve?

It simply involves an assertion to the effect that what cannot be put into words can still be manifest. Indeed, the manifestability of the inexpressible can be held responsible, according to Wittgenstein, for the very existence and possibility of philosophy, which was expected to "signify what cannot be said, by presenting clearly what can be said."[41] There is a promised dialectic here, which would not only enable philosophers to put limited logic into relief against the inexpressible, but also permit philosophy to "set limits to what can be thought; and in doing so, to what cannot be thought."[42]

d. The promised dialectic is never realised. The "limits" of the inexpressible do not emerge, they simply cannot ever be conceived. The only thing that does happen is the *putting-into-relief* of logic with its limits against the backdrop of the inexpressible. One may think of this as a *pseudo*-dialectic which does not actually bring into operation any negotiation between dual concepts/ binary opposites/ alternative positions, but which uses the form of the argument to clarify a monological formulation. The form of the idea of "something against . . ." is pressed into service, but "against what?" is neither definable, nor does it need definition. Against, if one presses the point, the dangling signifier "inexpressible." The use of the pseudo-dialectic is translated into recognizable dialectical terms: for example, the positing of "innerness" and "outerness":

> The sense of the world must lie outside the world. In the world everything is as it is, and everything happens as it does happen; in it no value exists—and if it did exist, it would have no value.
>
> If there is any value that does have value, it must lie outside the whole sphere of what happens and is the case. For all that happens and is the case is accidental.
>
> What makes it non-accidental cannot lie *within* the world, since if it did it would be accidental.
>
> It must lie outside the world.[43]

It *appears* as if the inexpressible does have qualities: it is qualified by "manifestability," "outsideness," an "evaluative" gaze. But these adjectives lack the ontological basis which the logic-language-world construct evidently asserts through the internal definitions and analysis which sustain it. The adjectives are *parallel* to (manifestability) or *opposed* to (outside, evaluative) logic-language-world, and the key to the argument is the pseudo-dialectical parallelism or opposition. One can think of this feature of the *Tractatus* argument as a rhetorical gesture rather than a proposition. Possibly, the rhetorical gesture is acknowledged in the following enigmatic statement:

> My propositions serve as elucidations in the following way: anyone who understands me eventually recognises them as nonsensical, when he has used—as steps—to climb beyond them . . . [44]

Hegel makes a similar point in his *Phenomenology of Mind*—but that is a different story.

3.11 To bring the above observations into the context of the discussion that preceded point 3, I have the following observation to submit. Given my retrospective, outward reading—my nonphilosophical or literary engagement, if you will—it would appear that the *Tractatus* is actually a text which subjects the corpus of formal logic to a sleight of the hand characteristic of informal logic. From this perspective the entire text is a demonstration of a kind of ordinary language form of argument (dependent on the nondeductive relations between pragmatic units, to use Habermas's terms), a demonstration of a rhetorical ploy. Can this be accommodated within the distinctions offered by Toulmin? one asks oneself. Not comfortably; and the reasons can be found in Habermas's critique of *The Uses of Argument* (i.e., because Toulmin does not distinguish adequately between the institutional differences of argumentation and forms of argumentation). But some sort of accommodation within Toulmin's distinctions is possible. At a broad level the *Tractatus* is an excellent demonstration of the paradox of philosophical practice that Toulmin draws our attention to:

> Quite consistently, logicians can admit that, in actual practice, we do not employ any universal battery of criteria, and yet maintain unabated their ambition to discover and formulate—theoretically, if no more—such a set of universal standards: the actual differences between the criteria we employ in one field or another they will regard, not as something inevitable or irreducible, but rather as a challenge.[45]

(This quotation leads rather neatly to the preoccupations of the next section, and of point 4.) At the level of detail, the rhetorical ploy of the *Tractatus* is analogous to Toulmin's distinction of "analytic arguments"[46] (it possesses the tautological character that Toulmin discusses), and in this context his conclusive section on "The Irrelevance of the Analytic Ideal"[47] is instructive.

READING *PHILOSOPHICAL INVESTIGATIONS*

4. My reading of *Philosophical Investigations* was not only not the close philosophical processive reading act (following the deductive connections between semantic units), even its outward character (perceiving the nondeductive relations between the pragmatic units) was more complex. My outward reading was a complex of *retrospection* and *prefiguration.* I mean that the same learning process and slowness involved in reading the *Tractatus*

reappeared (hence the retrospection), but in addition it was a selectively focused reading determined by previous readings of the *Tractatus* and of *The Blue and Brown Books* (therefore the prefiguration). *Philosophical Investigations,* of course, invites this sort of prefiguration. It has comments to make about the thinking behind the *Tractatus,* and it does so in terms of an Augustinian theory of language (describing "a system of communication; only not everything that we call language is this system"[48]). This opens up a prior field of intertextuality which the *Tractatus* does not insist on. Prefiguration is, therefore, inevitable, and it finds a place in my retrospective reading . . . which follows.

4.1 But where does the prefiguration come in? In the expectations with which I approached the text and entered it:

a. The observations regarding the Augustinian theory of language in *Philosophical Investigations* make it clear that the logic-language relationship which he had maintained in the *Tractatus* is loosened. These are not, he now says, inextricably bound with each other. This immediately releases him from the necessity of constructing a broad monological language-logic-world and also from the need to bring it into relief against the inexpressible through a pseudo-dialectical form of argument. An actual dialectic becomes imminent, or perhaps some sort of formulation involving multiple levels of argument.

b. In section 7 of *Philosophical Investigations* Wittgenstein introduces the concept of "language-games" in the following words:

> [. . .] those games by means of which children learn their native language. I will call these games "language-games" and will sometimes speak of a primitive language-game.
>
> And the processes of naming the stones and of repeating words after someone might also be called language-games. Think of much of the use of words in games like ring-a-ring-a-roses.
>
> I shall also call the whole, consisting of language and the actions into which it is woven, the "language-game."[49]

This immediately recalled Wittgenstein's definition of "language-games" offered in *The Blue Book:*

> I shall in the future again and again draw your attention to what I shall call language-games. These are ways of using signs simpler than those in which we use signs of our highly complicated everyday language. Language-games are the forms of language with which a child begins to make use of words. The study of language-games is the

> study of primitive forms of language or primitive language—we recognise in these simple processes forms of language not separated by a break from our more complicated ones. We see that we can build up the complicated forms from the primitive ones by gradually adding new forms.[50]

Oppositions are already before us: childish-primitive language v. "our" everyday language; simple v. complicated; and the whole v. (presumably) the constituent and overlapping parts. It is also clear that language-games comprehend and negotiate between all aspects of these, instead of adhering to one side of a proffered dialectic (like the monological world of the *Tractatus*). Further, it is obvious that the oppositions merely demarcate the limits of the discussion of language-games. There are within these limits gradations or levels of analysis (of complexity or simplicity, of largeness or smallness, etc.). In fact, a pluralistic experience, confined by limits delineated in terms of oppositions, becomes imminent through the unfolding of the text.

These expectations shaped my retrospective reading.

4.2 How shall I describe my retrospective reading? Undeniably a pluralistic experience—but I need scarcely dwell on the stylistic properties of *Philosophical Investigations* (I have mentioned these in Staten's words already, see point 1.21). My retrospective reading was a constant struggle between the slowness and lateness of my comprehension of proliferating details, and an endeavour to place my expectations in this context (which often occurred to me well after the processive act of reading). Perhaps it is best to convey the results by briefly describing my perception of *Philosophical Investigations.*

a. *Philosophical Investigations* is a bewildering array of analyses of specific language-games. There is no single logical structure to apprehend here but a potentially endless number of logical structures encapsulated in different language-games. The confessed technique of philosophical exposition has changed accordingly. It is not a creative theory which starts at a micro level and progressively builds towards a macro-conception. Instead it is a creative theory which hopes that by engaging with the micro level persistently somehow the macro level will emerge spontaneously. So "explanation" is replaced by "noting": "The question is not one of explaining a language-game by means of our experiences but of noting a language-game."[51] And philosophy comes close, as he observed in another text, to becoming a descriptive discipline:

> Philosophy is not a description of language usage, and yet one can learn it by constantly attending to all the expressions of life in the language.[52]

I found myself struggling against an explosion of "notings" and "descriptions" of language-games, and a corresponding explosion of philosophical themes which come under the aegis of this process: examinations of sensations, identity, usefulness, judgement, imaginability, expectation, understanding, negation, intention, recognition, willingness, astonishment, temporality, certainty, mathematical formulation . . . etc . . . etc . . . to the private language paradox, and the formulation of *forms of life.* The concept of language-games expanded and shrank and extended and synthesised and swamped me in a perfect deluge of "notings" and "descriptions."

b. But in the midst of my bewilderment I remained aware that all this is expected to reach out to a macro conception of some sort. But of what sort, and why was I aware of this? I was aware of this because I expected it—because the prefiguration charted out in 4.1 implied this. Let us go back to the two quotations about language-games in (b) of 4.1. They show that there are certain limits within which the discussion of language-games would occur, limits which are marked out by oppositions: simplicity v. complexity, whole v. part. And it is within (and in terms of) these limits that the gradations will appear. So, I expected this to occur, and even while I was swamped by the plurality of gradations I couldn't help wondering where those limits, those oppositions, those boundaries, had gone.

But what sort of macro-conception was I expecting? This is also rooted in the prefiguration of 4.1: Wittgenstein seems to suggest that there is a certain continuity between the *Tractatus* and *Philosophical Investigations.* The *Tractatus* progressed from a micro level to a macro-conception of a monological language-logic-world. *Philosophical Investigations* does not espouse the monological concept, but could the idea still be to attain a macroscopic understanding of language and the world? His persistent and intense investigations into proliferating language-games do seem to wait breathlessly for such a macro-conception to suddenly emerge, almost spontaneously. In fact, the quotations of (b) in 4.1 do say as much: the *Blue Book* quotation seems to reach out to our "highly complicated everyday language" by "build[ing] up complicated forms from primitive ones"; while the *Philosophical Investigations* quotation ends by drawing together language-games to "the whole, consisting of language and the actions into which it is woven."

(I want to point out that in the context of *Philosophical Investigations* the macro language-world concept has already surreptitiously been identified as ordinary or everyday language).

c. Negotiating between the prefigured expectations and the bewilderment delineated above I found my retrospective reading focusing on sections 65 to 71 of the *Philosophical Investigations* as the core of this exercise. These seemed to present the argumentative strategy which holds the exercise together and reaches towards the fulfilment of the macroscopic quest. There is a *strategy* involved here—of the same magnitude as the pseudo-dialectic ploy of the *Tractatus.* To state it briefly, the strategy is to control the reader's expectations by using images or associations which will render the optimistic perseverance with detailed analysis and the potential (spontaneous?) macroscopic conception possible. At the heart of *Philosophical Investigations* also there is a rhetorical ploy.

Section 65 admits the striving for a macroscopic conception of everyday language or "the whole consisting of language," and draws the implications in this regard of language-game analysis:

> Here we come up against the great question that lies behind all these considerations.—For someone might object against me: "You take the easy way out! You talk about all sorts of language-games, but have nowhere said what the essence of a language-game, and hence of language, is: what is common to all these activities, and what makes them into language or parts of language. So you let yourself off the very part of the investigation that once gave you yourself most headache, the part about the *general form of propositions* and of language.
>
> And this is true.—Instead of producing something common to all what we call language, I am saying that these phenomena have no one thing in common which makes us use the same word for all,—but that they are *related* to one another in many different ways. And it is because of these relationships, that we call them all "language." I will try to explain this.[53]

Note that he doesn't disengage himself from the quest for a macro-conception about "general form of propositions and of language." He confirms that he thinks that the way to attain this is through persistent analysis of different language-games, so that at some stage there will occur a macro-conceptual realisation of a complex of differing relationships. To explain this Wittgenstein proceeds to draw two images for this potential macro-conception:

> [. . .] we see a complicated network of similarities overlapping and criss-crossing; sometimes overall similarities, sometimes similarities of detail[54]

which he goes on to call "family resemblances"; and

> One might say that the concept 'game' is a concept with blurred edges.—"But is a blurred concept a concept at all?"—Is an indistinct photograph a picture of a person at all? Is it even always an advantage to replace an indistinct picture by a sharp one? Isn't the indistinct one often what we need?[55]

These images are not explanations: they do not form deducible semantic units, they do not qualify the statement of section 65, and they do not refer to the ontological status of the macroscopic concept. There are two discreet statements involved here, not two necessarily related statements. There is a useful gap between saying that language-games relate to each other in many different ways, and in asserting that they constitute in conjunction something like family resemblances or a blurred concept. The rationale of the latter statement is not as an explanation of the former, but as images which hold out, in a surreptitious manner, associations of something vague and intractable and slightly mysterious like family resemblance (overlapping and criss-crossing network), or something faintly oxymoronic like a blurred concept. By producing these impressionistic images as "explanations" two purposes are served:

i. [*deferral*] The persistent analysis of specific language-games is justified (not because it is necessary, but because the philosophical reader is likely to perceive the intractability of family resemblance or the oxymoronic quality of blurred concept as a philosophical threat, as something that defies formal logic, and would therefore be reluctant to pursue the macro concept immediately);

ii. [*unquestionability*] And when a macro concept is finally stated (forms of life) the philosophical reader is prepared to accept that statement as the be all and end all (not because it is formally deducible from what precedes it, but because the reader expects it to be beyond explanation—to lapse into blurredness—if questioned).

Since the unravelling of purposes i. and ii. go hand-in-hand and constitute the flesh and substance of *Philosophical Investigations* it can be said that the positing of the images of family resemblance and blurred concept between sections 65–71 actually form the core of the text. The images ensure a process of deferral which constitutes the micro-analyses and a quality of arbitrariness (or unquestionability) at the macro level which is the heart of *Philosophical Investigations.*

d. Most readers believe that the point of *Philosophical Investigations*—its macro-conceptual realization—is: "What has to be accepted, the given, is—so one could say—*forms of life.*"[56] It seems to me that this is a phrase which would be very puzzling if we didn't know that it is unquestionable. Its unquestionability is emphasized: it is given, it *has* to be accepted. But this emphasis would not have been enough if we hadn't gone through the entire process of deferral by analyzing a bewildering array of details, and proceeded with the expectation of unquestionability when the macro-concept arises. And all this was initiated by skilfully posing, at an appropriate space (between sections 65–71), two images under the guise of explanation. It is a rhetorical trope that a classicist would recognize.

4.3 I would maintain that the above reading is another instance of an informal logical approach to Wittgenstein's thinking.

The informal logical approach to Wittgenstein charted above is not translatable to the distinctions in the theory of argument given by Toulmin. Toulmin does not deal with rhetoric adequately. However the method adopted in my prefigured-retrospective reading is not unknown in other synthetic readings of Wittgenstein. My method had consisted in the privileging of a section of the text due to prior expectations to be able to place the pragmatic units of the text in nondeductive relations to each other (using Habermas's terms again). This demonstrates that even a nonprocessive and therefore nonphilosophical approach—an outward looking literary reading—can present useful insights. The interesting thing is that this method has analogues in what would normally be considered philosophical readings too, particularly the sort which I think of as synthetic (as opposed to creative). Saul Kripke's reading of Wittgenstein[57] comes to mind.

He also privileges a part of *Philosophical Investigations,* the private language argument, as central to the unravelling of the argument. Kripke's view is, interestingly, not that of a close processive reading either. And he does have a synthetic view in mind, since he feels that Wittgenstein falls into the philosophical tradition of the Humean sceptic.

A Conclusion?

5. A synthesist's literary (opposed to philosophical where "philosophical" is in the sense of adhering to an expanding cautious text of argument and reason) engagement with Wittgenstein can provide significant theoretical insights (like the use of pseudo-dialectic and of images as explanation in Wittgenstein's texts). One need not adopt Wittgenstein in a cut-and-dry manner (against the grain of his style) or leap into a field of intertextuality in a blindly groping fashion to achieve this. It might be useful to examine the rationale of one's (my) synthesist approach first. An informal logical (a notion of ordinary language argument) perspective has much to recommend it in this endeavour.

Of course, it may now be said that there isn't much synthesis in my reading of Wittgenstein; it seems to be a self-contained, creative, hermeneutical exercise. To this charge I have two contradictory answers.

a. Synthesis has taken place. In identifying my informal logical approach through Eagleton (and Lyotard and Wollheim and Fish, amongst others), Habermas, Toulmin, to read Wittgenstein I have in effect conducted a synthetic reading.

b. By demonstrating from an informal logical perspective that Wittgenstein uses under the surface of his philosophical texts certain somewhat disingenuous argumentative devices—the pseudo-dialectic of the *Tractatus,* and the blurred concept/family resemblance images as explanations for a macro-concept of language in *Philosophical Investigations*—I have opened the way for synthesist *literary* theorization and engagement. The above is merely a beginning.

Example Two: Literary Linguistics and Non-Mathematical Expositions of Relativity

Introduction: What is this Exemplary Section About?

This section presents the literary subject's (my) linguistic examination of a few nonmathematical expositions of the Theory of

Relativity which would have been available to English readers in what could be called the Age of Relativity, i.e., the nineteen twenties. In effect, this section draws the ostensibly scientific idea within the cautious text of literature. The literary gaze is fixed by its limitation, its exclusion from scientific practice, on texts which are poised on the brink of scientific practice, and which can be approached and absorbed within a literary-linguistic analysis: the nonmathematical exposition.

Why Relativity?: because Relativity was peculiar in having materialized in so specialized and confined a medium that it was not immediately comprehensible to nonmathematicians and nonphysicists. It was, however, responsible for inspiring thinkers of diverse (and nonscientific) disciplines like philosophy, linguistics, literary studies, and history. Indeed, it was realized relatively early that Relativity had even affected ordinary language, and therefore certain prevailing attitudes (to mensuration, for instance) permanently. Relativity fractured the cohesiveness of the nonphysicist/nonmathematician's world: it claimed relevance everywhere and yet withheld itself from his investigative gaze. This was possible because of the appearance of nonmathematical expositions of Relativity, which simultaneously reached out to nonscientific disciplines (thus playing a mediatory role), and reiterated the fracture in question (by exposing the incompleteness and delimitation of what they revealed). Arguably, the language of these nonmathematical expositions expanded to clarify the place of the scientific outlook in the pursuit of knowledge, to reframe certain concepts of linguistics, to prefigure the shape of science fiction as we see it practiced now, and to settle into the genre of popular science with which we are familiar today. In the process it held to and clarified the exclusiveness of scientific practice and the cautiously guarded text of science. Nonmathematical expositions of Relativity provide an ideal point of realization of the exclusiveness of the scientific discipline and its practice, and of the expansiveness (and assimilativeness) of the cautious text emanating from a literary gaze.

Given this peculiar perspective, it is proposed that the language of nonmathematical expositions of Relativity not only presents the fracture outlined above, but also reflects this fracture. An analysis of this language demonstrates that it impels the schism by being subject to the schism itself. It appears to be fractured itself, as is demonstrated through a close examination of the use of abstract prose, metaphors, examples, and historical narrative in some nonmathematical expositions of Relativity in the twenties. This section, and this part generally, concludes rather abruptly with reflections on the implications of this fracture of language and outlook from the *literary* point of view.

It seems to me that this project is facilitated by charting out what this section does *not* do at the beginning. Demarcating the limits of my activity also effectively charts out the limitations of the literary subject (i.e., I). What my literary gaze sees is conditioned by what it is blind to. My refusal to pursue the following lines of enquiry is not a matter of option but the condition of my cautious text and its literariness. But this purity is, of course, affected because (need I remind you) the purity of bold or cautious texts is inevitably an idealisation. So the following are, in the final analysis, not only within my ken but perhaps even expected by the reader . . .

What This Exemplary Section Is Not About

This section does not do the following:

a. It does not present the views of those whom Dwight Bolinger calls the shamans of language.[58] In other words, it deliberately neglects an entire area of engagement with the language of science which students of the subject are likely to encounter: that of good/bad English usage in scientific exposition. There is a respectable history of critiques of linguistic usage in scientific texts. One could go back to Bishop Sprat's exhortation in the seventeenth century that members of the Royal Society use

> a close, naked, natural way of speaking; positive expressions; clear senses; a native easiness: bringing all things as near the Mathematical plainness, as they can: and preferring the language of Artizans, Countrymen, and Merchants, before that, of Wits and Scholars[59];

and work one's way up to books like William Gilman's *The Language of Science* (and many others since) in which he deplores the "bad language of science [which] is responsible for an intolerable amount of time lost with needless riddles, and it paralyses the flow of information"[60] and goes on to recommend some principles of "good language."[61] This body of opinions from Sprat to Gilman share certain presumptions which it is best to be aware of. First, these opinions suggest that there is some sort of transparent objective language which is suitable for science, and which can be recognized as standard. Second, that this suitable language is suitable because it renders science easily accessible, and is akin to ordinary language. The situation is admirably summed up in N. Katherine Hayles's words:

> In general, scientific discourse adopts as its ideal univocality—one word, one meaning. Closely related to this goal is the belief that a language exists, or can be forged, that is purely instrumental. Clearly and unambiguously, it will communicate to the world what the reader or writer intends to say. Roland Barthes (*Rustle*) has ironically called this the belief that science can own a slave language, docile and obedient to its demands.[62]

These loose assumptions which inform the shamanistic approach to the language of science are questionable—and, as far as my perspective goes, irrelevant. This is too closely linked to the utility-value of language within scientific practice for me to confidently assume the cloak of the linguistic shaman and hope to say anything relevant.

b. I must clarify here that this section is not about *popular* science as it is normally understood. To deal with popular science one has to interrogate the word popular further. It appears to be generally accepted that popular, as in "popular science," has a pejorative sense to it. Gilman, whom I have quoted above, wondered: "And isn't popularization a nasty word?"; and rescued it from this charge by differentiating it from "sensationalization."[63] At almost the same time Martin Green was explaining that:

> Popularization is, then, a word with a moral identity. It refers ostensibly to the act of making a technical subject understandable to someone not trained in that technique; but it implies, in fact, that the cases it describes are those where the subject is misrepresented by this treatment. Where the truth of the matter has been diluted, if not falsified. Where the result is something you yourself would not read, except with a feeling of being condescended to, and of yourself condescending.[64]

Any examination of my present object of enquiry along these lines is likely to lead to a realization of the manner in which the practice of science excludes sociological effect. My attention is fixed on the manner in which the literary subject is excluded from science and excludes science, and extends its gaze to the quasi-scientific text. If I address Russell's *ABC of Relativity* I do not try to analyze why the Chief Engineer of the ship in which Russell crossed the Atlantic in 1944 liked it.[65] I look at what the book attempts at a literary-linguistic level. I might eventually point towards some qualities of what we recognize as works of popular science, but in doing this I do not address their popular nature. In other words, it is very likely that what I have to say is relevant to the subject of popular science, but it isn't about *popular* science *per se;* it is about the literary subject reading texts.

c. At the same time I must also clarify that this section does not dwell in any detail on the foundations and principles of mathematics. Some of the writers who are discussed in this paper have also been mathematicians of some repute, and have made substantial contributions regarding its philosophy and application. The contributions deal with complex issues which are beyond the scope of this argument. So, while I discuss Russell's and Whitehead's nonmathematical expositions of Relativity, I do not mention in this context their own contributions to the field of mathematics.[66] Nor do I mention the theories of and regarding mathematics of other theorists.[67] The attitude to mathematics which is taken into account is only that which is clearly expressed in the nonmathematical expositions in question.

Again this is inevitable given my subject-position. The entire point of this section is that I am not a specialist in physics or mathematics.

d. And finally, this section deliberately avoids any extensive discussion of issues which are relevant to the philosophy of science and the philosophy of time. This means that issues which are dear to the philosophy of time/science and in other (philosophical) cautious texts undoubtedly significant in any nonscientific study of Relativity—verifiability/falsifiabilty, explanation, epistemological assumptions, etc.—are disregarded here. This further implies that even those issues of philosophy which were to an extent influenced by the Theory of Relativity—the metaphysics of time and space (such as Samuel Alexander's[68])—are also overlooked here. This omission scarcely needs explanation: again this is the inevitable to my subject position within the cautious text of literature.

So What Is This Paper About?

Back to the beginning: I asserted that Relativity fractured the nonmathematician/nonphysicist's world by appearing to be relevant everywhere and yet by not being immediately comprehensible; that this was rendered possible by nonmathematical expositions which simultaneously mediated and reiterated the fracture; and that the language of nonmathematical expositions not only describes this fracture but also reflects it—i.e., it is fractured itself. This section demonstrates what is entailed in the reflexive fracture of the language of nonmathematical expositions and its mediatory-reiterative role. To do this I focus on four areas of this language: abstract prose descriptions, metaphors, the presentation of examples, and historical narrative: all familiar foci of investigation within a literary hermeneutic.

A. Abstract Prose Descriptions

At the beginning of *ABC of Relativity* Bertrand Russell puts to his reader the following situation: suppose that "you" woke up one day to find that "you" are suffering from amnesia, are afloat on a balloon at night, and have a view of a fireworks display.

> Obviously your geometry and your physics and your metaphysics will be quite different from those of ordinary mortals. If an ordinary mortal were with you in the balloon, you would find his speech unintelligible. But if Einstein were with you, you would understand him more easily than the ordinary mortal would, because you would be free from a host of preconceptions which prevent most people from understanding him.[69]

At one level this is a metaphor of the relativistic view of the world—I come to metaphors later. What I wondered about on reading this was: given the situation, how did Russell think Einstein would communicate his views to "you"? The ordinary mortal's *speech* would be unintelligible, but Einstein's communication might be comprehensible. The former is molded by preconceptions, but the latter isn't. So what are the characteristics of Einstein's communicative medium?

Two strata of linguistic communication are involved here: there is a stratum of communication through a *shared* medium (i.e., a specific language, like English or German), and there is a stratum of communication depending on the *rational potential* of the medium (i.e., the forms of reason which are contained in and possible through language, as in ordinary language or Einsteinian language). Russell takes the first for granted and focuses on the second. Einstein, like the ordinary mortal, would share with you some medium like English or German (that's not the issue). Einstein is more intelligible because he uses the shared medium with a different rationalistic approach, rejecting all "surface" presumptions (that's the issue). "Your" amnesia doesn't mean that you have forgotten the shared language, you have simply forgotten the ordinary surface presumptions, the normally accepted rational potential, i.e., the ordinary rationalistic presumptions which are embedded in and asserted through language.

Interestingly, Russell's emphasis in his placement of the communicative medium (in favor of the rational potential instead of the sharedness), is the exact opposite of that made by theorists of language universals. Noam Chomsky or Joseph Greenberg would focus on the shared medium (whether in terms of a specific language, or across the range of languages) in their search for language universals, and take the rational potential for granted.[70]

In both instances (Russell's view of Einsteinian communication, and the perspective of theorists of language universals) the two strata of linguistic communication distinguished above are kept at an unexamined distance. When the one is discussed the other is assumed to be invisible or static. And yet both reach out to a framework of universal communication. I must clarify here that Russell's view of Einsteinian communication seems to me to be a manifestation of the larger discipline of logical analysis, which I have decided not to dwell on here. I believe, the *fracture* in the language of nonmathematical expositions of Relativity is rooted in the unexamined distance maintained between the two strata. A similar fracture seems to be implied in the work of theorists of language universals—but that, like so many other interesting issues, is outside the scope of this study. Across the unexamined distance between the two strata of linguistic communication lies the possible area of examination which focuses on the relation between the shared medium of communication (a specific language/ all languages) and the rational potential of the medium of communication. What is the relation between the English or German language and the kinds of rational statement which are possible in these?—but that's also outside the scope of this argument.

Of course neither Russell nor Einstein would feel particularly unhappy with the unexamined distance between the strata cited above. Both would say that they can afford to overlook the shared medium of communication (specific/all languages) and focus on the rational potential of the medium of communication, because their medium of communication is not a (or all) specific language(s) but something that transcends these. Everyone knows what Einstein's medium of communication is; in Barthes's terms Einstein is popularly thought of as churning out thought as formulae.[71] Everyone knows this. This is the magical evocation of mathematics. Mathematics strides over the fracture between the two strata by being dependent on both but being reduced to neither. In a build up towards a nonmathematical exposition of Relativity, the magical evocation of mathematics is perhaps best presented by A. N. Whitehead in *Science and the Modern World:* "Mathematics is thought moving in a sphere of complete abstraction from any particular instance of what it is talking about,"[72] and "The certainty of mathematics depends upon its complete abstract generality."[73] Given the distinction between the two strata of linguistic communication made above, Whitehead's view of mathematics with relation to science can be translated to the following notions:

1. Mathematics takes the rational potential of language to its greatest possible (i.e., potentially universal) applicability, and therefore expands its reference;
2. Mathematics can be explained and learned through a specific language, but transcends *a* specific language because it can be explained in the same way through *any* specific language.

It follows, of course, that mathematics presents a peculiarly useful communicative medium for examining the physical world, one that heals the fracture between the rational potential and the shared aspect of linguistic communication. Mathematics is presented in nonmathematical expositions of Relativity as the remedy which smoothens the cracks of language.

I do not wish to transgress on my decision to avoid an engagement with the philosophy of mathematics. Whether mathematics is indeed the magic remedy is a moot question. What this leads to apropos the language of nonmathematical expositions of Relativity is of greater interest here. If mathematics is the remedy, *then the nonmathematical exposition has to, by definition, reify and thereafter reiterate the fracture.* Nonmathematical expositions cannot jump across the gap between the strata of linguistic communication as mathematics allegedly does. By trying to translate from mathematical formulations which have jumped that gap, all it can do is helplessly reveal the gap all the more sharply, and pay homage to mathematics at its own expense.

This is clearly demonstrated in abstract prose descriptions in nonmathematical expositions of Relativity which are meant to expand and interpret physical-mathematical formulae. Some examples from the period in question (the so called Age of Relativity) can be cited to clarify this. Let's turn to Einstein's *Relativity: The Special and the General Theory,* which was written for readers who "are interested in the theory, but who are not conversant with the mathematical apparatus of theoretical physics."[74] His bald prose descriptions of his theory seem to lack self-containedness: for example, "the *special* theory of relativity, *i.e.* the principle of the physical relativity of all *uniform* motion,"[75] or "The following statement corresponds to the fundamental idea of the general theory of relativity: *'All Gaussian co-ordinate systems are essentially equivalent for the formulation of the general laws of nature.'*"[76] These statements possess the air of being condensations of something larger, or as leading to something clearer, but not as adequate explanations in themselves. They possess the air of being fragments in a process which stretches before and after, a process which the nonmathematical expositor seems at a loss to present. This sense of inadequacy in prose description usually collapses into a relinquishing of it for straightforward mathematical exposition; and Einstein therefore supports his abstract prose statements with basic mathematical descriptions of the Lorentz transformation,[77] Minkowski's four-dimensional space,[78] Gaussian coordinates.[79]

It seems to me that this is the context in which abstract prose descriptions usually occur in nonmathematical expositions of Relativity, and therefore reveal their fractured nature. However, one must remember that abstract prose descriptions are not the only linguistic tool at the disposal of the nonmathematical expositor. In fact, in most nonmathematical expositions of Relativity abstract prose descriptions occupy a rather small space. Actually, physical-mathematical formulae are usually presented in nonmathematical expositions in terms of metaphors and examples. But, as I demonstrate, these linguistic tools do not cure the fracture in question as mathematics ostensibly does. On the contrary they reify the fracture (reflexive of the mediation-reiteration pattern within the nonmathematician/nonphysicist's world, and coherent to the gap between strata of linguistic communication) in their own ways.

B. METAPHORS

The complex linguistic and aesthetic features of metaphors need to be harnessed to a certain degree before their role in nonmathematical expositions of Relativity can be discussed satisfactorily. Fortunately scientists and philosophers of science have wondered about the use of metaphors in scientific thought for a while, and we have some serviceable definitions and observations at our disposal. For the sake of convenience I now present one which will enable me to communicate my observations briefly. I would like to draw attention to the special sort of metaphor which was described by Gentner and Jeziorski, i.e., the metaphor which is also an analogy. They think of metaphors as a broad category of different kinds of mappings or matches of which analogy is a special case,[80] and can be described as follows:

> The central idea is that analogy is a mapping of knowledge from one domain (the base) into another (the target) such that a system of relations that holds among the base objects also holds among the target objects. In interpreting an analogy, people seek to put the objects of the base in one-to-one correspondence with the objects of the target so as to obtain the maximal structural match. The corresponding objects in the base and target need not resemble each other; rather, object correspondences are determined by like roles in the matching relational structures. Thus an analogy is a way of aligning and focusing on relational commonalities independently of the objects in which those relations are embedded.[81]

I deal only with the analogy-metaphor below and the above description introduces a useful set of terms, to which I return in due course.

In a book published in 1937, *Philosophy and the Physicists,* L. Susan Stebbing presented a substantial critique of Arthur Eddington's use of metaphors in his books of popular physics (this is not offered as an account of Relativity, it isn't). One of the metaphorical passages from Eddington's *The Nature of the Physical World* which she cites reads:

> I am standing on a threshold about to enter a room. It is a complicated business. In the first place I must shove against an atmosphere pressing with a force of fourteen pounds on every square inch of my body. I must make sure of landing on a plank travelling at twenty miles a second around the sun—a fraction of a second too early or too late, the plank would be miles away. I must do this whilst hanging from a round planet head outward into space, and with a wind of aether blowing at no one knows how many miles a second through every interstice of my body. The plank has no solidity of substance. To step on it is like stepping on a swarm of flies.[82]

Stebbing complains that this passage, amongst many others, suffers from a mixing up of "language used appropriately for the furniture of earth and our daily dealings with it with language used for the purpose of philosophical and scientific discussion."[83] To demonstrate this she points out that stepping on a plank is not like stepping on a swarm of flies, for example, and that walking against a headwind is a different experience from shoving something. She further objects that not only are these metaphors confusing in this way, they are also misleading in so far as they pretend to convey scientific truths:

> if he wishes to avoid being misunderstood, he must surely warn his readers that, in the present state of physics, very little can be conveyed to a reader who lacks the mathematical equipment required to understand the methods by which results are obtained and the language in which these results can alone find adequate expression. [. . .] the reader may be misled unless he is warned that nothing resembling the spatial relations of flies in a swarm can be found in the collection of electrons.[84]

Stebbing makes these points with an air of finding fault with Eddington's exposition specifically. It seems to me however that what Stebbing has actually done is reveal the kind of fracture that is inevitable in the use of metaphors in nonmathematical expositions of certain physical formulations.

Let us translate Stebbing's objections into the terms provided by Gentner and Jeziorski in their description of analogue-metaphors (see citation above). Stebbing actually presents two objections to Eddington's analogy-metaphors. One, she maintains that Eddington's analogy-metaphor does not present a one-to-one mapping between a base domain and a target domain, but a two-to-one (plank and swarm of bees, shoving and being buffeted by wind) mappings between base domains and a target domain. This is confusing in itself, but, Stebbing contends, Eddington makes it more so because the dual base domains are not compatible (stepping on a plank is different from stepping on a swarm of bees). Two, Stebbing points out that since Eddington addresses the nonscientific reader the analogy-metaphor is presumably there to help the reader understand the target domain (physics) in terms of the base domains (everyday experiences like entering by doors, stepping on planks, etc.). This being the case, the nonscientific reader's mapping of the base to the target domain is likely to lead to erroneous conclusions (because a swarm of flies is in many ways unlike a collection of electrons), unless he is informed of the precise extent to which such a mapping is possible.

Stebbing suggests that these are, in fact, Eddington's shortcomings, which is true to a certain extent. A close examination of Stebbing's two objections however also reveals a more general problem here—the problem of the inevitably fractured nature of nonmathematical expositions of physics. The fact is that incompatible multiple-base-domains to single-target-domain matchings in analogy-metaphors for certain areas of theoretical physics are not because of misconceptions but because of the nature of the subject. Examples of this are easily available in quantum physics—yet again outside the scope of this section. Within the scope of this section, the second objection is far more significant. A nonmathematical exposition of Relativity is obviously meant for the reader who is not proficient in mathematics. When such a reader encounters an analogy-metaphor it is inevitable that he would hope to learn about the target domain of this metaphor from the base domain. The matching is therefore not self-evident but directed. The reader does not simply perform the matching, he does so only in so far as the informed author does it for him. If he does not follow the author's directions he will fall into error (as Stebbing fears). The author has to make the limits of the metaphor clear (which Eddington doesn't do)—but in doing this attention is drawn to the limitations, the incompleteness, of communication through the metaphor. In other words, the gap between the base and the target domain of the analogy-metaphor in the nonmathematical expositions in question is always outside the control of the reader, and is inevitably a constant reminder of the limitations of the nonmathematical exposition with relation to the mathematical formulation. This is nothing other than a reflection of the fracture which assails the nonphysicist/nonmathematician's world when a theory like Relativity claims significance everywhere and is yet always withheld to a certain extent. The metaphor mediates the gap between base and target domain, and yet reiterates the gap by admitting its inability to bring the target domain clearly in focus.

Even when analogy-metaphors which are clearly delimited in their matching are employed in nonmathematical expositions the above fracture would occur. The point made above is that there is a withholding of knowledge in the employment of such metaphors even as a certain degree of communication (or mediation between mathematical formulation and nonmathematical exposition) takes place. The fracture we are discussing is inevitable. For example, the limitations of the analogy-metaphors are clearly delineated (unlike in Eddington's metaphors) in the following:

1. the elaborate analogy of "hills in space-time"[85] in Russell's *ABC of Relativity,* in which he sounds a cautionary note at one point,

> Einstein says that the sun is at the top of the hill, only the hill is in space-time, not in space. (I advise the reader not to try to picture this, because it is impossible),[86]

which is made more emphatic in the later extended edition,

> We have seen that the gravitational effects of the sun may be described as those of a hill in space-time. A galaxy or a cluster may be represented in the same way, but by a much larger hill, because of its much greater mass. [. . .] If we tried to incorporate into this description details of the distribution of stars in each galaxy and galaxies in each cluster, we should have a complicated hill with many peaks and valleys. [. . .]
>
> [. . .], but we shall not push the analogy of curvature with space-time hills any further, by comparing the overall curvature of space-time with the curvature of the earth, because this might easily become misleading[87];

2. the lake analogy in Einstein's *Relativity,*

> We might imagine that, as regards geometry, our universe behaves analogously to a surface which is irregularly curved in its individual parts, but which nowhere departs appreciably from a plane: something like the rippled surface of a lake.[88]

Russell was clearly at pains to avoid any misunderstanding that his analogy-metaphor might raise, and Einstein was tentative enough about his analogy-metaphor to make the reader wary. These are strategically placed at or towards the end of these non-mathematical expositions, and the effect of these careful metaphors can be described only in terms of some oxymoron, as being vaguely clear or hazily illuminated. The reader who is not adequately informed in mathematics can go no further than a metaphor which seems to give with the left hand only to take away with the right, to be suspended at the end of it all in a tantalizingly fractured world . . .

But, one might observe, surely such a reader would find the numerous examples which occur in nonmathematical expositions of Relativity more useful. Don't examples heal the fracture?

C. EXAMPLES

Nonmathematical expositions of Relativity constantly remind their readers that mathematical formulation and physical phenomena are inextricably linked, even if this link implies that physical phenomena are often extremely difficult to visualize, let alone experience, in a commonsense fashion. Examples (actual and hypothetical) enable the nonscientific reader to reach across the mathematical formulation to a visualizable and perhaps experiential form, a sort of specific and tangible signified for an evasive and generalized signifier. This reaching across is actually quite different from that which the analogy-metaphor matching clarifies. The analogy-metaphor delimits the applicability of the base domain to the target domain, while an example is *completely* comprehended within the precincts of the formulation which it clarifies and which is clarified by it. The role of the example in the scientific discourse of nonmathematical expositions of Relativity, in fact, has to be explored further.

To an extent the great sweep of scientific discourse—referred to under the umbrella term "reference discourse"—is discussed cogently by James L. Kinneavy (amongst others). I particularly refer to Kinneavy's work because it is contextualized within discussions on persuasive discourse, literary discourse and expressive discourse, and synthesises several approaches to the subject trenchantly; the placement of scientific or reference discourse is self-contained within the total perspective. On the other hand, my reference to him has to be qualified by the fact that his discussion is of the discourse of the self-contained scientific discipline, while my focus on nonmathematical expositions necessarily expands beyond this self-containedness. Of course, his total perspective allows space for this . . . but I have chosen a very tiny bit of it which has to do with examples in scientific discourse (there is only a tiny bit in his broad canvas, but it has to be a major section of my smaller canvas). This tiny bit is placed within a discussion of the descriptive and explanatory statements of scientific assertions, and is as follows:

> Sometimes causal explanation comes to be stated in terms of a general principle of which the event to be explained is an example. This is sometimes called deductive explanation. It actually establishes the thing to be explained, the explicandum, as a member of a class, the general law or principle. So that the general law or principle becomes the explaining device, the explicatum. In actuality, this is explanation

by classification, and the explaining class may even be a more theoretical construct, like a "light ray," not an actual existent.[89]

I will not go into the linguistic and logical nuances of the above, and hope that the terms would be acceptable in themselves.

Kinneavy's comment on the place of examples in scientific discourse may be adequate within his total perspective of a self-contained scientific or reference discourse, but needs to be reframed in the context of nonmathematical expositions of Relativity. The explicandum-explicatum relation (or explanation by classification) in the presentation of examples within scientific discourse appears prior to the nonmathematical expositions we are concerned with. Explanation of examples in terms of Relativity has already taken place, the classificatory role of the principle of Relativity has been proposed and accepted, before the nonmathematical exposition is attempted. So the presentation of examples in nonmathematical expositions does not follow the same explicandum-explicatum relationship cited above. In nonmathematical expositions the retrospectively proposed and accepted explicatum becomes the explicandum, and *vice versa*. When Einstein first formulated his theory mathematically he would have used it to explain examples, but when nonmathematical expositors began work they used examples to explain Einstein's theory. Further, whereas what Einstein had done could be seen as explanation by classification, one could think of the nonmathematical expositor's work as explanation by *declassification.* The nonmathematical expositor, in other words, appeals to induction.

One could think of the relation between the import of examples in scientific presentations of Relativity to that in nonmathematical expositions of Relativity as one of reversal. Perhaps one should do so with reservations because the reversal is not absolute, and to think of it as simply that is too neat. Be that as it may, when examples appear as explicatum where the theory of Relativity is explicandum in nonmathematical expositions of Relativity the following occurs.

1. The examples are introduced as visualizable or experiential situations, and then stretched to and beyond the limits of credulity (where credulity is determined by what one is accustomed to visualize or experience). This mode of stretching examples to the limits of credulity is a deliberate and controlled process. The deliberate and controlled nature of this process can be gauged by the constant exhortation to retain a sense of normal visualizable

and experiential reality against which the distortion of the example is presented. In extending his example of the train as an inertial frame of reference against a framework of rods, for example, Einstein at one point reminds the reader:

> Without committing any fundamental error, we can disregard the fact that in reality these frameworks would continually interfere with each other, owing to the impenetrability of solid bodies.[90]

This is clearly a reminder of the sense of reality against which the somewhat fantastic example has to be viewed. In a similar vein, his example of a man sealed in a chest in empty space is preceded by a brief reminder of the remoteness from reality of such a situation:

> We *imagine* [my emphasis] a large portion of empty space, so far removed from stars and other appreciable masses, that we have before us approximately the conditions required by the fundamental laws of Galilei.[91]

In fact it is demonstrable that this occurs in most examples cited as explicatum in nonmathematical expositions of Relativity. The interesting result is that in stretching the limits of credulity in presenting examples as above the reader of nonmathematical expositions becomes aware of a disparity in the explicatum-explicandum relationship. The effect could be put as follows: since the example has to be stretched to and beyond the limits of credulity to perform the explicatory role, what is explained through it (the theory of Relativity as explicandum) seems to possess an air of the incredible or the fantastic. It is evident, in other words, that the level of conceptualization in which the explicandum is discernible and the level of thinking from which the explicatum is originally drawn (a visualizable and experiential area) are mediated with the greatest difficulty and at the expense of normal perceptions of the latter. It seems to me that this is in effect a reiteration of the fracture in the language of nonmathematical expositions, which is a reflection of the fracture in the nonmathematician/nonphysicist's world when Relativity is introduced. The mathematical formulation does mediate between the two levels more elegantly than the examples in nonmathematical expositions, and no sense of the incredible is apparent in the former.

2. The fracture implicit in the explicandum-explicatum relationship in nonmathematical expositioins is emphasized by the pre-

sentation of data on experimental evidence. Experimental evidence (say, Fizeau's experiment, the Michelson-Morley experiment, details of the perihelion of Mercury or the curvature of light, etc.) bear some of the characteristics of examples as discussed so far and yet belong firmly in the region of conceptualization where the explicandum is discernible. And yet these are carefully distinguished from the kind of visualizable and experiential examples we have cited so far (Einstein's train and embankment, or man in a chest). The distinction is simply that the examples are hypothetical and test credibility while the experimental evidence draws on the performability of the experiment. The strong emphasis on the *performative* aspect of experimental evidence means that they do not perform the role of explicatum as the above examples do, but lend the weight of assertion to the explicandum once it has been explained. Since the performative is outside the explicatory development of the nonmathematical exposition, the experimental evidence has to be taken for granted as a component of the explicandum, and possesses inevitably an air of assertion.

The corollary of these two points is the reiteration and reification of the fracture which is the central contention of this exemplary section.

D. HISTORICAL NARRATIVE

Nonmathematical expositions of Relativity as historical narrative can be thought of as an alternative to abstract prose descriptions supported by metaphors and examples. The instances of abstract prose descriptions with metaphors and examples that I have cited so far do possess a sense of historical development. Einstein, Eddington, and Russell have all delineated a development in thinking from Newtonian to Relativistic physics in their nonmathematical expositions, and in doing so have demonstrated a sense of chronology. A sense of chronology as an ancillary element to abstract prose descriptions is however not an adequate instance of nonmathematical exposition as historical narrative—I have a more basic relation between chronology and nonmathematical exposition in mind. In fact, the example which guides my reflections in this area is A. N. Whitehead's *Science and the Modern World. Science and the Modern World* describes the development of a "scientific mentality" through various phases of social and cultural development in the West, leading to the then recent developments in physics (Relativity and quantum theory), and concluding with Whitehead's speculations on the philosophical consequences of these developments.

There is an unmistakable dichotomy in Whitehead's mode of pursuing his project. On the one hand, there is a sort of unchanging "scientific mentality," which perseveringly investigates hard facts and proposes generalized abstractions,[92] which pertains to a clear and simultaneous whole irrespective of time (the empirical universe), and which can be distorted only by such flaws of perception as "the Fallacy of Misplaced Concreteness."[93] On the other hand, there is the "scientific movement" from the seventeenth to the twentieth centuries,[94] in which the unchanging scientific mentality applies itself to different levels of informational and instrumental competence and attunes itself to varying philosophical inclinations, and through which the clear and simultaneous whole gradually comes into focus. In this dichotomous scheme, Relativity is placed as an understanding (through a "scientific mentality") of a world which is located within the unchanging laws of space-time,[95] but which is understood only because history dictates that we should be able to (for instance, because the scientific movement has brought us to a stage where "we have better instruments"[96]). The dichotomous scheme is constructed on the apparently incompatible oppositions of the static and the dynamic, the immutable and the transient, the eternal and the ephemeral.

The effect of this dichotomous presentation of nonmathematical expositions as historical narrative is of making the one side appear in contrast to the other. *Contrast* is the main function of the dichotomous presentation: if it had been otherwise it wouldn't have been a dichotomous relationship but an extensive or modificatory relationship. Since the working of the scientific mentality and the ahistorical simultaneous whole presented through Relativity is one of the subjects of the book (the explicandum, to use a term from the previous section), the reader is placed in the environment of chronological change from which the explicandum becomes visible, but at a distance, as something that is different, almost ideal, almost mystical, almost utopian. Need I repeat that I see the familiar fracture manifesting itself again?

The nature and operation of the dichotomy can be comprehended in terms of the linguistic assumptions which are implicit in this nonmathematical exposition as historical narrative, and which are analogous to it. I refer to the Saussurean notion of diachrony and synchrony. Saussure conceived of the discipline of linguistics as split along an axis of simultaneities, i.e., synchrony, and an axis of successions, i.e., diachrony.[97] According to Saussure, "The opposition between the two viewpoints, the synchronic and the diachronic, is absolute and allows no compromise."[98] He examined the contrast in detail and differentiated the two fields of linguistic pursuit in the following manner:

> *Synchronic linguistics* will be concerned with the logical and psychological relations which bind together coexisting terms and form a system in the collective mind of the speakers.
> *Diachronic linguistics,* on the contrary, will study relations that bind together successive terms not perceived by the collective mind but substituted for each other without forming a system.[99]

It appears that Saussure felt that in synchronic linguistics one would find a certain degree of volition exercised by the speaking community (therefore systematic), whereas in diachronic linguistics the relations of successive terms would be involuntary (therefore unsystematic).

The analogous character of the Saussurean terms to the fracture delineated in nonmathematical exposition as historical narrative is self-evident. The dichotomous relation of the two aspects of linguistics is clearly parallel to the dichotomy between "scientific mentality" and "scientific movement" (in Whitehead's words). In fact, I would go further. In this instance the fracture in the language is not merely *reflexive* of the fracture in the nonmathematician/nonphysicist's world. Instead, the fracture in language, or the perception of language, preempts the fracture introduced by Relativity. I am inclined to believe that here the linguistic fracture and the theoretical fracture actually inform and coalesce with each other into all time and space. They become coextensive. They are drawn together in nonmathematical expositions, and they implicate each other in the language of nonmathematical exposition as historical narrative.

Some linguists contend that the absolute dichotomy between diachrony and synchrony perceived by Saussure is questionable. Roman Jakobson, for instance, maintains that:

> these two effective oppositions, synchrony/ diachrony and static/ dynamic, do not coincide in reality. Synchrony contains many a dynamic element, and it is necessary to take this into account when using a synchronic approach.
> If synchrony is dynamic, then diachrony, which is the analysis and juxtaposition of different stages of language over an extended period

> of time, cannot and must not be limited to the dynamics of the alterations of language alone. One must take static elements into consideration as well.[100]

Perhaps in a similar fashion the dichotomous character of nonmathematical expositions as historical narrative can be questioned. Is the fracture implicit in, say, Whitehead's work really inevitable? Or is it somehow possible to remove the fracture by designing an alternative linguistic basis? The answer can only be hypothetical at this stage, and as far as this argument goes, irrelevant. The point is that nonmathematical expositions as historical narrative do present the fracture that is the issue in question.

Where Does All This Lead To?

I have actually stated the general point of these observations at the beginning, and the larger part of this exemplary section has been devoted to substantiating it. To repeat, the thesis of this section is: that Relativity fractured the nonmathematician/nonphysicist's world by appearing to be relevant everywhere and yet by not being immediately comprehensible; that this was made possible by nonmathematical expositions which simultaneously mediated and reiterated the fracture; and that the language of nonmathematical expositions not only describes this fracture but also reflects it—it is fractured itself. I have examined the linguistic fracture in terms of the use of abstract prose, metaphors, examples, and historical narrative in nonmathematical expositions of Relativity in what could be called the Age of Relativity, i.e., the twenties.

The attempts at subtantiating the assertions with which this exemplary section set out are, more importantly, conclusive in a different direction. They cast the assimilative and expansive cautious text which emanates from the literary-subject (i.e., I) over the ostensibly scientific area. The cautious text reiterates the distance of the practice of science and the closeness of the literary-subject to any text. I hope it reinvents the pleasure of reading such *literary* texts as nonmathematical expositions of Relativity.

As a recognition of the fact that the pleasure of reading such literary texts is not mine alone, but more generally the literary subject's, I finally turn to some consideration of the extent to which the above observations may impinge upon the more *orthodox* sphere of the cautious text of literature. The precise status of such a marking of orthodox literary objects has been discussed above already—that is not the issue here. The following is merely a final account of the cohesiveness and expansiveness of the cautious text of literature. So, within the parameters of orthodox literary *objects* (the literary text, the critical text, the bibliographical text) the cautious perspective emanating from the literary subject who extends himself to nonmathematical expositions of Relativity may appear in the following three broad areas:

1. In the development of that modernist literary sensibility which ponders the nuances of narrative form and liguistic expression. Reconceptions of time in narratology, a language that is "liberated" by the redefinitions of Relativity, the sense of having to formally and linguistically represent a modern world which is not subject to commonsense physical principles and certainties—all these are found tacitly (albeit with little explicit reference of Relativity) in the works of the so-called "high" modernist writers. The high modernists (the "high" marks an elitism which confines their works to an informed readership, which uncompromisingly cultivates its ground amongst literary cognoscenti and aesthetes rather than in the established mass market) were not surprisingly at their peak in what is described here as an Age of Relativity.

2. In the works of those who used science and scientific models in their literary works as providing metaphors or allegorical frameworks for social critique. From the *fin de siècle* to the great ideological confrontations of the thirties, and after, one sees the emergence of a mixture of dismay and wonder at the prospects of scientific growth in society—in keeping with the fracture and mediation-reification pattern oberved above. Utopias and distopias shoulder each other ambiguously, science becomes a force moving outside human control and comprehension (and therefore a metaphor for totalitarian control or demagogic influence), and yet allows the fantasy of human godhead to realize itself at the same time.

3. In books of fantasy science fiction (not always clearly distinguishable from the social critique fiction mentioned in 2) since the thirties. Within the fracture of language delineated above one finds space for a play of the imagination which can account for the characteristics of present-day popular science fiction. Prior to the Age of Relativity, science fiction dealt with the realm of the familiar or the experiential, and seldom strayed beyond what seemed (even barely) possible in the then present-day, or might have been possible in the known past. But, a sense of remoteness, an air of the incredible or the fantastic, is opened up vis-á-vis

scientific thinking through the processes of literary works like nonmathematical expositions of Relativity. One can surmise that in the popular imagination the possibilities of science undergo a change. A remote and incredible science-fictional fantasy world comes into existence, sometime in an unknown future, or somewhere in a parallel universe, and yet tantalizingly possible. Because it is science, of course. The time-traveler (reader) is propelled from the present and even the past into *another* time, usually the future.

As a conclusion to this section I elaborate some of these final points with a brief, *very* brief, discussion of modernism and its aftermath, and science fiction, in the light of the above.

Modernity and Science Fiction

The following observations are nothing if not schematic. I present here a phasal development in the effect of the fracture and mediation-reification pattern observed above (with regard to nonmathematical expositions of Relativity) on literary sensibilities. Phasal, in this context, is more a matter of convenient presentation than a charting out of chronological or progressive stages. Also, though I do draw the following primarily from the fracture and mediation-reification pattern as illustrated above through examinations of nonmathematical expositions of Relativity, and though I continue to maintain that Relativity provided the first important instance of such a pattern affecting intellectual (especially literary) endeavours on a large scale, the import of this pattern has to be expanded. What has been discussed as the particular character of expositions of Relativity specifically are hereafter considered as providing the model for a more general attitude and approach to most disciplines of science on the part of litterateurs. The validity of such an assumption can, I think, be assessed in the following.

Phase 1 (Linguistics and Narratology in High Modernism)

The reiteratory-mediatory role played by nonmathematical expositions of Relativity apropos the fracture that has been delineated above changed linguistic practice. It is necessary to realize that what I have done above has not only been an elucidation of a certain kind of scientific discourse through terms offered by various literary-linguistic concepts, it has also been a reframing of certain linguistic concepts. That this kind of scientific discourse does influence and change linguistic practice was perceived in the Age of Relativity itself—however, it wasn't seen as a fracture but as a liberating experience. The two-sidedness of linguistic practice was clearly understood. On one side stood a "restrictive" network of words which seemed to exert a tyrannical hold over thinking. Richards and Ogden deplored the tyranny of words in *The Meaning of Meaning,*[101] and Saussure expressed scepticism regarding the usefulness of the word unit as a linguistic concept in his *Course on General Linguistics.*[102] On the other side stood the attempt to evade the restrictive hold of the word unit on linguistic usage by appealing to a "scientific" emphasis on categories and relations. This was attempted by Richards and Ogden and by Saussure: but more importantly in this context, the specific influence of Relativity in this process was observed and described by Stuart Chase. Stuart Chase's book of 1938, appropriately entitled *The Tyranny of Words* (and admittedly influenced by Richards's ideas), devoted an entire chapter to a discussion of the influence of Einstein's work on linguistic theory and practice. The main effect of Einstein's work, according to Chase, was in the emphasis on an "operational" approach to the detriment of absolute fixed meanings which seemed to be contained in words:

> Einstein thus gave a new cast to meaning. He found the meaning of "length" no longer in absolute space, but in the *operations* by which the length of physical objects was determined; he checked the meaning of "simultaneity" by operations, and found the concept untenable. It followed that "absolute space" and "absolute time" were metaphysical notions in our heads.[103]

From this he later went on to say:

> Thus "length" is not something which an object possesses, as a man possesses a shirt; it is a word in our heads. Its meaning is determined by what we do, rather than what we say, and the concept shifts with our doing.[104]

This is not too far from what Wittgenstein might have said in the *Philosophical Investigations* if he had looked at the linguistic usage of "length" in a language-game.

Apropos the influence on narratology (this is the more intractable connection) it is perhaps best to start with the anxieties about the incidence of such an influence expressed by Wyndham Lewis (a high modernist himself). One would expect that the kind of fracture initiated by Relativity in the nonmathematician/nonphysicist's world, and the corresponding fracture in the language of nonmathematical expositions, would trigger off a reaction of fear or anxiety for the nonmathematician/nonphysicist. This kind of fear or anxiety is, it seems to me, a necessary aspect of the striving after totalitising metanarratives in a "modernist" (in the accepted literary sense) context. The kind of fracture delineated above would naturally be perceived as threatening where such holistic yearnings are expressed.

The clearest expression of this kind of fear or anxiety is seen in Wyndham Lewis's denunciation of the "time-mind" in favor of a "plastic or visual intelligence":

> The main characteristic of the Time-mind from the outset has been a hostility to what it calls the 'spatializing' process of a mind *not* a Time-mind. It is this 'spatializing' capacity and instinct that it everywhere assails. In its place it would put the Time-view, the flux. It asks us to see everything *sub specie temporis.* It is the criticism of this view, the Time-view, from the position of the plastic or the visual intelligence, that I am submitting to the public in this book.[105]

The book in question is *Time and the Western Man.* I do not discuss Lewis's view of "plastic or visual intelligence" here. I would like to note however the extent of the influence, as Lewis perceives it, of the "time-mind" (the main theoretical exponents of which, he clarifies, are Einstein, Samuel Alexander, and Henri Bergson[106]). The threat of the time-mind seems to comprehend the creative writings of James Joyce, Gertrude Stein, Anita Loos, Ezra Pound, and others, the performances of Diaghileff's ballet, the success of the actor Charles Chaplin, most forms of popular and revolutionary artistic activity, and the historical approach of Spengler.

Clearly, the fear and anxiety as well as the possibilities released, to a large extent, by the fractured language of nonmathematical expositions of Relativity expands into many elements of what is now studied as the "modernist" consciousness.

Wyndham Lewis's accusations in *Time and the Western Man* may present tenuous general formulations and connections ré the modernist penchant for seeing the world *sub specie temporis,* but the associations drawn there are not entirely specious. In different ways an awareness of time as one of the determinates of narrative form, and the loosening of this determinateness through the exercise of a metaformal consciousness, is an undeniable feature of the works of the high modernists. The entire debate, for instance, about stream-of-consciousness and interior monologue as literary genre/technique can be evoked here—and all the high modernists (Joyce, Pound, Woolf, Eliot, Stein, etc.) are accordingly implicated here.

A brief look at the development of critical perceptions apropos stream-of-consciousness and interior monologue with regard to, say, James Joyce, could clarify this. These were customarily drawn from psychologistic roots. William James's *Principles of Psychology* (1890) and Henri Bergson's *Creative Evolution* (1907) are liable to be mentioned as philosophical sources. James Joyce himself gave the source of the interior monologue technique to a pre-relativistic literary source, Edouard Dujardin's *Les Lauriers sont coupe* (1887). In the wake of the currency which Joyce's use of the interior monologue technique gave it, and the larger impact of interior monologue and stream-of-consciousness on modernist writers genrally, Edouard Dujardin defined interior monologue as that which comes "closest to the unconscious"[107] in 1931. At a similar time (also 1931) L. C. Hartley, writing about stream-of-consciousness (a term used interchangeably with interior monologue then), decided that this was a mode of revealing a character's subconscious.[108] It was fairly quickly decided that Joyce's use of the method was relevant primarily to the psychological sciences (by literary critics like Mary Colum, for instance, and psychologists like Carl Jung.[109])

It was, however, also realized fairly soon that the psychologistic derivations of interior monologue and stream-of-consciousness were not adequate. Critics like Leon Edel and Erwin Steinberg[110] discerned that these terms do not represent anything *real* (like the subconscious, or the actual thoughts of people) and are therefore unlikely to have the sort of scientific psychological validity that was sometimes allocated to Joyce, for instance. They realized that these terms stand for *simulations* of different levels of consciousness or *create an illusion* of having that sort of psychological validity. These are primarily literary techniques—they are formal and narratorial experiments. More stringent distinctions between the terms were offered by Humphrey Roberts, Melvin Friedman, and Shiv K. Kumar, for instance.[111] Recently, Johannes Söderlind, has suggested that not only are these terms a matter of formal and narratorial experiments, these terms actually denote particular kinds of primarily linguistic conventions.[112]

If the implications of techniques/genres like interior monologue and stream-of-consciousness are dislocated from their psychologistic connotations, and seen in primarily formal or linguistic terms the time-mind of many of the high modernists (roughly as

Wyndham Lewis had seen it) becomes clear. It becomes evident that the modernists are largely distinguished as such because of formal experiments where the unity of the processive (necessarily time-bound, from a beginning to an end) act of reading and different layers of fictional "real" time and "perceived" time are played off against each other. Effectively, in Joyce's writings, as indeed in Woolf's, Stein's, Eliot's, Pound's, etc., the time-consciousness could be seen as more a preoccupation with notions of *time* (as a formal and real component of fictional and lived realities) than with notions of *consciousness.*

If this time-consciousness didn't derive, as it was initially deemed to have derived, wholly from preoccupations with psychology—if it was as markedly a *time*-consciousness rather than a time-*consciousness*—how did it come to be so? Why did this honing of a sensitivity to the ambivalence of real, perceived and narratorial time occur? Though there are few direct acknowledgements of allegience to transmissions of Relativity from the high Modernists themselves (barring Wyndham Lewis's accusations against a time-mind), it is probably not too far-fetched to see a connection. Indeed, it is probably not too far-fetched to see the connection not only in the modernist sensitivity to time, but also in the consequent sense of the disjunctiveness, bewilderment, fracture, incohesion, and fluidity of the modernist world, and in the modernist representations (attempts at mediation-reification) of both its physical-temporal aspect and its *zeitgeist.* The fracture of the nonmathematical exposition, it could be simplistically said, becomes the fracture of the world, history, life, and their representations.

Phase 2 (Science Fiction and Social Critique)

In many ways phase 2 precedes phase 1—I place it at a second level in terms of the degree of literary awareness of the connection to the fracture and mediation-reification pattern outlined above. Using conceptions of science and scientific models to create metaphors or allegorical frameworks for social critique finds a pioneering figure in H. G. Wells. From *The Time Machine* (1895) to *Men Like Gods* (1923) H. G. Wells combined a somewhat precocious perception of possible paradigm-shifts in physics (not unrelated to Relativistic physics) with the social Darwinism inherited from his master, T. H. Huxley, to present a series of dystopias and utopias. These mark out Wells's changing socialist allegiences from a grotesque apprehension of class struggle, to Fabianism, to utopian socialism.

The literary use of conceptions of science and scientific ideas to present social critique shows a marked ability to resurface constantly in a post-Relativistic context. Yevgeny Zamyatin's *We* (1920), Aldous Huxley's *Brave New World* (1932), George Orwell's *Nineteen Eighty Four* (1949), Kurt Vonnegut's *Player Piano* (1954) or *The Sirens of Titan (1959),* or Doris Lessing's *Canopus in Argos: Archives,* especially *Shikasta* (1979), are merely the most obvious examples. Arguably, most science fiction, however fantastic in scope, has a necessary element of social reflexivity to the present—no doubt, elements of the concentrated social critique found in the above-mentioned instances are probably fairly ubiquitous in the genre generally. The more obvious projections of conceptions of science in the realm of science fiction fantasy often revolve around the recognition that technology concentrates power, and that science could provide the key to ideological and totalitarian control—or simply a crude form of despotism (in this they are no more than simplifications and reductions of more complex social perspectives and critiques available in the aforementioned novels). In that sense, even the more designedly fantastic and futuristic science fiction (like Frank Herbert's *Dune* [1965], Isaac Asimov's Foundation Series [trilogy, 1951–53; and 1982, 1986], Robert Silverberg's *Nightwings* [1969]) possesses an implicit (though often easily forgettable) social critique.

Some familiar concerns are manifested in the above-mentioned examples. The fracture in the language of nonspecialized expositions of science get translated into perceived fractures in current and potential social organisation. The coincidence of the Age of Relativity and its aftermath (let's simplistically call it the Quantum Period) with the rise and, in influential contexts, consolidation of revolutionary socialism has naturally been exploited. Besides, the coincidence in question is not merely a matter of two disparate areas of thinking being linked by simultaneity, but of two significant areas of application (social and physical) using terms in a contiguous fashion. All the key figures engaged in revolutionary socialism (or even revisionist socialism) had stressed the *scientific* nature of Marxist analysis—the shift from the socialism of Babeuf, Fourier, Owen to that of Marx and Engels, with the consequent different interpretations offered by Lenin, for instance, or Kautsky, was popularly given as a shift from utopian socialism to scientific socialism. It was because of the assertion of a scientific focus in Marxist materialism, an objective empirical view which goes beyond mere positivism because of the promptings to action (*praxis*, realpolitics, application), that its "truth" and ideological unquestionability could be maintained. To replace the *scientific* assertions of revolutionary socialism by the domination of science itself, to see the possible problems of a revolutionary socialist state as the problems of science, to translate into literary terms the possible fractures of a realised communist state as the fractures in the literary discourse of scientific exposition, is but a small step. The reverse is also applicable—it is possible to see the fracture of science as a fracture in the technocratic super-capitalistic society, which follows from the socialist critiques of, say, Herbert Marcuse or Jean-François Lyotard. The scentific nature of revolutionary or revisionist socialism is not merely contained in the praxis of socialism, but also in its appraisal, its critique, of capitalism. Being able to see the potentialities of technocratic advanced capitalism in terms of the fracture in the nonspecialized discourse of science is also a small step. A relatively early questioning of developments in physics from a Marxist position, instructive if one wishes to gauge the nature of the contiguity of discourses, is interestingly available in Christopher Caudwell's incomplete *The Crisis in Physics*. He died tragically but appropriately in 1937 in the Spanish Civil War, which places his incomplete work in context. He argued that the then recent crisis in physics due to the development of relativistic and quantum physics was actually a crisis in bourgeois ideology:

> Physics is knowledge about reality, but it is abstract, generalized knowledge. The abstractions or generalizations are the reflections of the social relations by and through which the reality was made into conscious knowledge. Some of these categories are general to all society; but they appear in a special form in different societies, and specially in the case of the crisis in bourgeois physics, it is the specifically bourgeois categories that are of vital interest, because of the way in which new knowledge, new practical content, is rending them asunder, and is itself crippled by the old form.[113]

The usual critique of the translation from scientific discourse fracture to ideological fracture rests in the sense of being controlled rather than being in control, of a loss of subjectivity or a surrender to a stiflingly collective agreement, a sense of the unrealistic becoming the actual (a surrealistic but complete *order* being established), a loss of soul—these can all be matched to the reiterative-mediatory discourse of nonspecialized expositions as seen above. "Relativity is relevant everywhere but cannot be completely explained to the nonphysicist or nonmathematecian" is not too distant from being controlled rather than being in contol. The empirical basis (the unquestionablity of experimental truth) of science merges with the surrender to collective agreement. The incredibility, and yet veracity, of examples and metaphors discussed in nonmathematical expositions becomes the *exterior* surrealism (not in the psyche) of the environments that are described: they acquire the irony of a nightmare vision which is fictionally *true.* And so on.

The realized revolutionary socialist state is recognizably what Zamyatin and Orwell gesture towards in their "nightmare" visions of scientific dystopias and alternative realities. On the other hand the futuristic Americas of Vonnegut's *Player Piano* or Ray Bradbury's *Fahrenheit 451* (1953) take the nightmare to the advanced capitalistic society. One is tempted to include Huxley's *Brave New World* in one of these categories, except that Huxley's political background and allegiences suggest a somewhat different perspective. Huxley's nightmare vision of a biologically consolidated class-society in the *Brave New World* is more or less indifferent to the issues of socialist ideology or advanced capitalism, and is more ambiguously linked to the antidemocratic (and, oddly, pro-aristocratic-eccentricity) sentiments which he had inherited from H. L. Mencken and H. G. Wells in his youth,[114] or to the mystical sentiments one finds in *Ends and Means* (1937).

The sense of being controlled rather than being in control, of the incomprehension and confusion of humanity/human society with regard to its motives, in the face of a larger *scientific* scheme, finds a different sort of ironic treatment in Vonnegut's *The Sirens of Titan* and Lessing's *Shikasta.* This view of humanity/human society is put into perspective by Vonnegut by (ironically) placing humankind as an ancillary product of some inscrutably and supremely developed intelligence for the purpose of producing tools (a relation to materialist sociological analysis is implicit) in *The Sirens of Titan.* Lessing uses a similar device in *Shikasta,* though with broader import, when she places humankind, and its entire history, as part of one project, amongst many, of the superior culture of Canopus. These comprehend the fracture in terms of historical narrative examined for nonmathematical expositions of Relativity—effectively, it can be argued, Lessing and Vonnegut reduce the diachronicity of human historist discourse into the synchronic discourse of science. The outcome is one of an existentialist sense of the smallness, arbitrariness, dread of human existence; as well as a telling critique of the paucity of all current ideology.

Phase 3 (Futuristic and Fantastic Science Fiction)

Since the appearance of W. Olaf Stapledon's monumental *Last and First Men* (1930) futuristic science fiction (or, to expand the connotation of that, the science fiction of *another* time) has merged into fantasy, and become a composite genre—easily identified as such in the bookshelves of public libraries and retailers' outlets. It is possible to extricate a philosophical or sociological overview of humanity from these. Stapledon's view of the eighteen species of humanity is undeniably an optimistic view of humanity, each successive species moving to higher planes of development. Similarly Asimov's concept of "psychohistory" in the Foundation series presents a necessaristic (and therefore calculable) view of human development. But, in its presentation of detail, in its emphasis on the nuances which dominate the foreground, dominate the immediate events and characters, dominates the *story* in fact, the manner in which science tests ordinary credulity is played up. From the interstices of this appeal to science to asseverate the ordinarily incredible appears the science fiction fantasy genre.

Admittedly, it is difficult to demonstrate how consistently and decisively the details of science fiction fantasy works utilize nonspecialist scientific discourse to challenge ordinary credulity. That would require a necessarily detailed and systematic examination of a range of texts, and would involve discernment of the range of scientific data and nonspecialist scientific expressions being used, and some analysis of the correlation of scientific data (within the appropriate context) and nonspecialist scientific expression. However, a few random examples, which are pertinent to the above reflections on nonmathematical expositions of Relativity, may serve to clarify the point. In this context, for example, the following could be considered. In Orson Scott Card's *Ender's Game* (1985) the key to winning mock space battles in a zero gravity situation was the realization that the idea of "down" is inoperative. One of Piers Anthony's earlier books, *Macroscope* (1969), deals with hijacking alien technology to attain speed of light travel. It goes into some detail in outlining how ideas of existence would have to change in order to accomplish this. For instance, in order to withstand large accelerations one would need to turn one's body into some sort of gelatin and then reconsitute it afterwards. Larry Niven's *Ring World* (1970) describes a ring which has been constructed around the world, of a radius that is the same as the radius of an earth orbit. Much of the book is devoted to describing how living on the ring world changes one's perspective. In *Rendezvous With Rama* (1974) Arthur C. Clarke explores the laws of physics in environments of different degrees of weightlessness.

Obviously, such details operate much as examples and metaphors operated in the nonmathematical expositions examined above. The kind of fracture observed there, and the fantastical remedy that examples and metaphors provided there, are merely dislocated and focused in the science fiction fantasy. The effect is of drawing out the "stuff of fantasy," so to say, from the nonspecialist scientific exposition. If, in turn, these details of science fiction fantasy were displaced and posited in the context of a serious nonspecialist exposition of Relativity (or the appropriate area), they could effectively be reduced to examples or metaphors too. It is probably not too tenuous to suggest that, in its attention to detail, science fiction fantasy could and does provide the reification-mediation function between lay or nonspecialist perceptions of science and specialist scientific discourse that one observes in nonspecialist expositions for a specific area in the sciences—arguably, a process initiated through nonmathematical expositions of Relativity.

Phase 4 (Fantasy to Reality)

An extended appreciation of this phase doesn't really belong to this study, and I will consequently keep this short. A sense of symmetry does tempt me to make a quick and final point however, to draw a "Phase 4."

Science fiction fantasy derives, in some sense, from a formulated scientific reality; but its displacement from the context of the actual scientific exposition of an existing state of knowledge can have a regressive impact. It has become customary, in some measure, to assess the perspicacity of futuristic science fiction fantasy by gauging the actual degree of realization in *retrospective.* A fairly common assessment of Jules Verne's work is to enumerate the number of technological predictions therein which have been realized. In *Brave New World Revisited* (1959) Huxley produced his own assessment of the possibile validity of the *Brave New World* scenario by his reflections on scientific advances in the fifties. I recall distinctly the large number of self-congratulatory articles which appeared in 1984 about the ways in which Orwell's *1984* had fallen short of the truth. To put it glibly, science fiction is in a sense seen as retaining some of the prophetic qualities that was traditionally allocated to poetry. Disturbingly, the retrospective perspective that is implied in such assessments could, through a simple *volte face,* assume a *prospective* character. I believe it is becoming clear that science fiction fantasy, through its increasingly wider and more effective dissemination, could assume an autonomous "reality," more fantastic than scientific, and occupy the darker recesses of our social psyche. The burgeoning industry of UFOlogy; the growing hysteria of alien abductees and psychological experts (scientists again) who validate their claims; the numerous texts, internet sites, audio-visual material on the Roswell incident and the evasive record of the Photographer, on Bob Lazarus's claims and other "scientific" observers of his sort (texts in which reality is nightmarish and nightmares are reality) testify to this.

However, I need take that final phase no further than the above gestural statement. As far as this part is concerned, the exempla of the cautious literary text extending to ostensibly nonliterary disciplines are done.

Notes

1. Terry Eagleton, "Introduction to Wittgenstein," *Wittgenstein: The Terry Eagleton Script, The Derek Jarman Film* (London: British Film Institute, 1993), p. 12.

2. "The decimal numbers assigned to the individual propositions indicate the logical importance of the propositions, the stress laid on them in my exposition. The propositions n.1, n.2, n.3, etc. are comments on proposition no. n; the propositions n.m1, n.m2, etc. are comments on proposition no. n.m; and so on." Ludwig Wittgenstein, *Tractatus Logico-Philosophicus,* trans. D. F. Pears and B. F. McGuiness (London: Routledge and Kegan Paul, 1961), p. 5.

3. Terry Eagleton, "The Terry Eagleton Script," *Wittgenstein,* pp. 23–26.

4. Ibid., p. 26.

5. Ibid., p. 47.

6. Ibid., p. 55.

7. Ibid., pp. 32–35.

8. Ibid., p. 40.

9. Ibid., pp. 32–33.

10. Ibid., pp. 24–25.

11. Henry Staten, *Wittgenstein and Derrida* (Lincoln: Univ. of Nebraska Press, 1984), p. 75.

12. Ibid., p. 104.

13. Terry Eagleton, "Introduction to Wittgenstein," p.9.

14. Thomas C. Singer, "Riddles, Silence and Wonder: Joyce and Wittgenstein Encountering the Limits of Language," *ELH,* 57, no.2, Summer 1990, p. 460.

15. David A. White, "The Labyrinth of Language: Joyce and Wittgenstein," *James Joyce Quarterly*, 12, no.3, Spring 1975, p. 295.

16. Stanley Fish, *Is There A Text In This Class?* (Cambridge, Mass.: Harvard univ. Press, 1980), p. 241.

17. Richard Wollheim, *Art and Its Objects* (New York: Harper and Row, 1968), p. 90.

18. Jean-François Lyotard, *The Postmodern Condition*, trans. Geoff Bennington and Brian Massami (Manchester: Manchester Univ. Press, 1984), p. 10.

19. Terry Eagleton, "The Terry Eagleton Script," p. 7.

20. For a discussion on biographies as response statements see Suman Gupta, "On Literary Biography and Biografiends," *New Literary History*, 24, no.3, Summer 1993, pp. 683–95.

21. In Part I of *A Discourse on Method*, trans. John Veitch (London: Everyman, 1986), René Descartes made a synthetic survey of knowledge, and in Part II he renounced synthesist approaches in favour of a creative methodological approach which was characterised by four decisions (pp. 15–16).

22. Terry Eagleton, "Wittgenstein's Friends," *Against the Grain* (London: Verso, 1986), pp. 99–129.

23. Paul Riceour, *Interpretation Theory* (Fort Worth: Texas Christian Univ. Press, 1976), pp. 76–78.

24. Wayne Booth, *Critical Understanding* (Chicago: Univ. of Chicago Press, 1979), pp. 244–46; and Paul Armstrong, *Conflicting Readings* (Chapel Hill: Univ. of N. Carolina Press, 1990), pp. 13–15.

25. Jürgen Habermas, *The Theory of Communicative Action, Vol.I*, trans. Thomas McCarthy (Boston: Beacon, 1984), pp. 22–23.

26. Stephen Toulmin, *The Uses of Argument* (Cambridge: Cambridge Univ. Press, 1958), pp. 44–93.

27. Jürgen Habermas, *The Theory of Communicative Action, Vol.I*, p. 31.

28. Ibid., pp. 34–35.

29. Stephen Toulmin, *The Uses of Argument*, pp. 94–95.

30. Ibid., pp. 44–93.

31. Ludwig Wittgenstein, *Tractatus Logico-Philosophicus*, prop.6.552, p. 73.

32. Ibid., Bertrand Russell's Introduction, p. xxi.

33. Ibid., prop. 4.0312, p. 22.

34. Ibid., 6.124, p. 63.

35. Ibid., 4.03, p. 22.

36. Ibid., 6.123, p. 62.

37. Ibid., 5.4731, p. 47.

38. Ludwig Wittgenstein, *Culture and Value*, trans. Peter Winch (Oxford: Basil Blackwell, 1980), p. 10 (1931 note).

39. *Tractatus Logico-Philosophicus*, 5.6, p. 56.

40. Ibid., 7, p. 74.

41. Ibid., 4.115, p. 26.

42. Ibid., 4.114, p. 25.

43. Ibid., 6.41, p. 71.

44. Ibid., 5.54, p. 74.

45. Stephen Toulmin, *The Uses of Argument*, p. 39.

46. Ibid., p. 123–27.

47. Ibid., p. 248–52.

48. Ludwig Wittgenstein, *Philosophical Investigations*, trans. G. E. M. Anscombe (Oxford: Basil Blackwell, 1958), Section 3, p. 3.

49. Ibid., section 7, p. 5.

50. Ludwig Wittgenstein, *Blue and Brown Books* (Oxford: Basil Blackwell, 1958), p. 17.

51. *Philosophical Investigations*, sec.635, p. 167.

52. Ludwig Wittgenstein, *Last Writings on the Philosophy of Psychology, Vol.I*, trans. C. Luckhardt and Maximilian A. E. Aue (Oxford: Basil Blackwell, 1982), sec.121, p. 18.

53. *Philosophical Investigations*, sec.65, p. 31.

54. Ibid., sec.66, p. 32.

55. Ibid., sec.71, p. 34.

56. Ibid., p. 226.

57. Saul A. Kripke, *Wittgenstein on Rules and Private Language* (Oxford: Basil Blackwell, 1982).

58. Dwight Bolinger, *Language—The Loaded Weapon* (London: Longman, 1980), Chapter 1.

59. Thomas Sprat, *History of the Royal Society* (1667), ed. Jackson I. Cope and Harold Whitmore Jones (Missouri: Washington Univ. Press, 1958), p. 113.

60. William Gilman, "The Language of Science," *The Language of Science* (London: The English Universities Press, 1961), p. 7.

61. Ibid., pp. 14–15.

62. N. Katherine Hayles, "Introduction," *Chaos and Order*, ed. N. Katherine Hayles (Chicago: Univ. of Chicago Press, 1991), p. 5.

63. William Gilman, "Popularization (and Honesty)," *The Language of Science*, p. 213.

64. Martin Green, *Science and the Shabby Curate of Poetry* (London: Longman, 1964), pp. 32–33.

65. Bertrand Russell, *The Autobiography of Bertrand Russell, Vol.III* (London: George Allen and Unwin, 1969), p. 15.

66. To do this one will have to take into account the formation, and subsequent questioning, of their *Principia Mathematica* (Cambridge: Cambridge Univ. Press, 1927).

67. The work of Gottlob Frege, Ludwig Wittgenstein, Rudolf Carnap, and W. V. O. Carnap (among others) would have to figure if I did.

68. Samuel Alexander, *Space, Time and Deity* (Vol.I) (London: Macmillan, 1927), p. 37.

69. Bertrand Russell, *The ABC of Relativity* (London: Kegan Paul, Trench and Trubner, 1925), pp. 4–5.

70. For a comparative discussion of the Chomskyan and Greenbergian approaches to the issue of Language Universals, see Bernard Comrie, *Language Universals and Language Typology* (Oxford: Basil Blackwell, 1981).

71. Roland Barthes, "Einstein's Brain," *Mythologies*, trans. Annette Lavers (St.Albans: Paladin, 1972), pp. 68–69.

72. A. N. Whitehead, *Science and the Modern World* (Middlesex: Penguin, 1926), p. 34.

73. Ibid., p. 35.

74. Albert Einstein, *Relativity: The Special and the General Theory*, trans. Robert W. Lawson (London: Methuen, 1920), p. v.

75. Ibid., p. 59.

76. Ibid., p. 96.

77. Ibid., pp. 32–34.

78. Ibid., pp. 55–57.

79. Ibid., pp. 87–90.

80. Dedre Gentner and Michel Jeziorski, "The Shift from Metaphor to Analogy in Western Science," *Metaphor and Thought*, ed. Andrew Ortony (Cambridge: Cambridge Univ. Press, 1993), p. 452.

81. Ibid., pp. 448–49.

82. Arthur Eddington, *The Nature of the Physical World* (Cambridge: Cambridge Univ. Press, 1928), p. 342.

83. L. Susan Stebbing, *Philosophy and the Physicists* (London: Methuen, 1937), p. 47.

84. Ibid., pp. 50–51.

85. Bertrand Russell, *The ABC of Relativity*, pp. 126–29.

86. Ibid., p. 129.

87. Bertrand Russell, *The ABC of Relativity* 3d edition, ed. Felix Pirani (London: George Allen and Unwin, 1969), pp. 120–21.

88. Albert Einstein, *Relativity*, p. 114.

89. James L. Kinneavy, *A Theory of Discourse* (New York: W. W. Norton, 1971), p. 85. I have deleted all the references from this passage: there are, in fact, references to Israel Scheffler, *The Anatomy of Inquiry* (1963); Carl G. Hempel, *Philosophy of Natural Science* (1966); Paul Oppenheim, "Studies in the Logic of Explanation" (1948); Peter Alexander, *Sensationalism and Scientific Explanation* (1963); and Stephen E. Toulmin, *The Philosophy of Science* (1953).

90. Albert Einstein, *Relativity*, pp. 31–32.

91. Ibid., p. 66.

92. A. N. Whitehead, *Science and the Modern World*, Chapters I and II.

93. Ibid., p. 66, p. 74.

94. Ibid., Chapters III to VIII.

95. Ibid., Chapter VII.

96. Ibid., p. 137.

97. Ferdinand de Saussure, *Course in General Linguistics*, trans. Wade Baskin (London: Peter Owens, 1974), p. 80.

98. Ibid., p. 83.

99. Ibid., pp. 99–100.

100. Roman Jakobson and Krystyna Pomorska, "Dialogue on Time in Language and Literature," *Verbal Art, Verbal Sign, Verbal Time* (Oxford: Basil Blackwell, 1985), p. 12.

101. C. K. Ogden and I. A. Richards, *The Meaning of Meaning* (London: Kegan Paul, Trench and Trubner, 1923), particularly Chapter 2, "The Power of Words."

102. Ferdinand de Saussure, *Course in General Linguistics*, pp. 65–66.

103. Stuart Chase, *The Tyranny of Words* (New York: Harcourt, Brace and World, 1938), p. 119.

104. Ibid., p. 130.

105. Wyndham Lewis, *Time and the Western Man* (London: Chatto and Windus, 1927), pp. 3–4.

106. Ibid., see particularly pp. 13–18, and the larger part of Book II, Part I.

107. Edouard Dujardin, "Interior Monologue", *The Bays are Sere and Interior Monologue*, trans. August Suter (London: Libris, 1991), p. 113.

108. L. C. Hartley, "The Sacred River, Stream of Consciousness: The Evolution of a Method," *The Sewanee Review*, Vol.39, Jan.–March 1931, p. 84.

109. Mary Colum in "The Confessions of James Joyce," *James Joyce: A Critical Heritage Vol.I 1907–1927*, ed. Robert Demming (London and Henley: Routledge and Kegan Paul, 1970), p. 234. Her conviction that Joyce drew on psychoanalysis

in writing *Ulysses* is repeated in *From These Roots* (London: Jonathan Cape, 1938), p. 317; and in collaboration with Padraic Colum in *Our Friend James Joyce* (New York: Doubleday, 1958), pp. 132–33. C. G. Jung, "Ulysses: A Monologue," trans. W. Stanley Bell, *Nimbus*, Vol.2, No.1, June–Aug. 1953, 7–20.

110. Leon Edel, *The Psychological Novel: 1900–1950* (London: Rupert Hart-Davis, 1955), pp. 14–22. Erwin Steinberg, *The Stream of Consciousness and Beyond in* Ulysses (Pittsburgh: Univ. of Pittsburgh Press, 1958), p. 3.

111. Melvin Friedman, *Stream of Consciousness: A Study in Method* (New Haven: Yale Univ. Press, 1955); Robert Humphrey, *Stream of Consciousness in the Modern Novel* (Berkeley: Univ. of California Press, 1958); and Shiv K.Kumar, *Bergson and the Stream of Consciousness Novel* (London and Glasgow: Blackie, 1962).

112. Johannes Söderlind, "The Interior Monologue: A Linguistic Approach," *Studia Neophilologica*, Vol.61, 1989, pp. 169–73.

113. Christopher Caudwell, *The Concept of Freedom* (London: Lawrence and Wishart, 1977), p. 200.

114. Huxley's correspondence with H. L. Mencken (1920–1926) and H. G. Wells (1927–1935), and early reviews, are quoted and examined in the first two sections of David Bradshaw ed. *The Hidden Huxley: Contempt and Compassion for the Masses* (London: Faber and Faber, 1994).

Afterthoughts

The two discussions which follow are not directly connected to the main concerns of the foregoing study, though they are informed by it and follow on from it. More precisely, they are informed by, and follow on from, a part of the foregoing study—Part II specifically, i.e., the examination in the bold text of the status of literary studies and English literary studies, and of the nuances of canonicity. The first discussion concerns the practical implications of questioning the self-evident canon or the accepted canon (I had maintained that these often work in *collaboration*), and the status of specific writers and texts which find their place therein. In this I examine the recent debate in England about T. S. Eliot's anti-Semitism. The second discussion focuses on the pragmatics of the transition from a potential canon to a realized canon in a specific, and still emergent, field of literary creative and critical practice—Indian-English literature. I investigate here a possible program for creating an Indian-English(es) stylistics.

Needless to say, in keeping with Part II of this study, the following discussions assume predominantly the tone of a "bold" text. This is significant: if these discussions were conducted in the cautious text their preoccupations were liable to have appeared irrelevant and the conclusions reached would have been quite different. The issues addressed in these discussions can only be effectively addressed in a predominantly bold text.

Though not directly linked to the argument supporting the theoretical asseverations of Part II, these discussions can be viewed as pragmatic illustrations of points regarding accepted canons and potential canons made there. It might be useful to think of the following as appendices for Part II—though the connection is more vital than that of an appendix, and more in the spirit of a clarification. These discussions also demonstrate, I believe, that the conclusions reached in this study are not merely offered as clarifications of a state of affairs (a so-called crisis in English literary studies) but may also open up specific modes of critical and creative practice.

Discussion I
T. S. Eliot's Anti-Semitism: The Pragmatics of Assessing the Aesthetic and Social Value of a Canonised Poet's Works

The recent (1996–97) debate in England about T. S. Eliot's anti-Semitism in the wake of the publication of Anthony Julius's *T. S.*

Eliot, Anti-Semitism and Literary Form[1] has yet again drawn attention to one of the obvious blind spots in literary criticism: the relation between social-cultural and aesthetic-literary value (am I echoing Paul de Man here?[2]). The outcome of the debate appears to have reached the consensus that these measures of value should be kept distinct. This discussion offers a clarification about the relation between the two measures of value and hopes that this would both contribute to specific debates of this nature and to the theory and practice of literary criticism generally.

The debate has taken up a fair amount of space recently in the literary papers and national dailies in England and has been unsurprisingly joined by reputed contemporary poet-critics like Craig Raine, Tom Paulin, and James Fenton, amongst others. One infers that when contemporary poet-critics feel called upon to differ from or endorse a, on the whole, just and necessary but critically unremarkable book it is probably because their own creative and critical values are somehow called into question. They have all clearly admired T. S. Eliot's poetry and hated anti-Semitism. They have understood their aesthetic-literary values in terms of Eliot's poetry and distanced their social-cultural values as far as possible from anti-Semitism. While these two measures of value could be kept comfortably separate all were at peace. The comparatively mild gestures towards Eliot's anti-Semitism in Erik Svarny's *'The Men of 1914': T. S. Eliot and Early Modernism*[3] as early as 1988 could be disregarded because they were mild. The less than convincing and convoluted defence of T. S. Eliot against this charge in Christopher Ricks's *T. S. Eliot and Prejudice*,[4] also in 1988, gained easy approbation because it was commensurate with the dual value-system. But Anthony Julius's book obliges the descendants of T. S. Eliot and his literary establishment to actively juxtapose social-cultural value and aesthetic-literary value and this has clearly been a disturbing experience. On the whole the liberal standpoint, shared by Anthony Julius, which has now emerged is the action-replay of one that has emerged all too often in the latter half of this century: social-cultural values needn't affect aesthetic-literary evaluation. T. S. Eliot was an anti-Semite and it's best to face up to it but he is still a great poet. Very similar to saying Ezra Pound was fascist but a great poet. Or Rudyard Kipling was racist and an apologist for imperialism but an excellent writer.

This easy retreat into divided value systems fails to address the main issue. We know it is comfortable to carry on admiring T. S. Eliot's poetry and be able to asseverate our distaste for any form of anti-Semitism or racism at the same time. The main issue of the debate is not how this can be achieved or how soon it can be achieved but whether it can be achieved at all. The disquiet expressed, particularly by Eliot's literary descendants, at the juxtaposition of aesthetic-literary value and social-cultural value in the Eliot and anti-Semitism debate indicates that there is doubt. It is clearly felt that should Eliot's anti-Semitism become common knowledge his reputation as a poet would somehow be tarnished. It is no use just asserting that it won't. One would simply have to address a series of questions which are implicit in the situation. As it happens these questions can be posed in the specific terms of the Eliot and anti-Semitism debate but cannot be answered except by engaging with broad theoretical and practical issues. All the parties involved in this debate have failed before they began by confining themselves to the individual personality and achievement of T. S. Eliot and his literary institution. They have failed because of their unwillingness to spell out the presumptions of their critical-creative theory and practice.

At any rate, the questions can be posed in terms of the Eliot and anti-Semitism debate and it is necessary that this be done with all possible expediency. In trying to answer them the scope of this discussion would naturally have to be extended. The questions are:

1. When one makes a statement like: "Eliot was an anti-Semite but a great poet," does one mean "Eliot was both an anti-Semite *and* a great poet, though the former is an undesirable quality and the latter an admirable quality," or does one mean "Eliot was a great poet *despite* being an anti-Semite; i.e., his racism might have affected his aesthetic achievement but didn't"?

2. If one accepts the first sense of the statement, i.e., "Eliot was both an anti-Semite and a great poet," one implies thereby that Eliot's aesthetic-literary achievement is *not* related to his social-cultural perspective. In that case, one would have to clarify what the distinct criteria of aesthetic-literary evaluation and of social-cultural evaluation are.

3. If one accepts the second sense of the statement, i.e., "Eliot was a great poet despite being an anti-Semite," one thereby implies that there is a link between aesthetic-literary evaluation and social-cultural evaluation but in the case of Eliot the latter hasn't seriously affected the former. If that is so, then one would natu-

rally have to elucidate what precisely is the link between the two evaluative systems, and how come the link fails in the specific instance of Eliot's poetic achievement.

4. And finally, is it possible that on closer examination of the links between the two evaluative systems one might disagree with the statement: "Eliot was an anti-Semite but a great poet," itself? Could one come up with a statement like: "Because Eliot was an anti-Semite he was not as great a poet as we had supposed him to be," instead?

5. There are a series of questions attached to the alternative suggested in (4), which can be treated as one large question. If one says, "Because Eliot was an anti-Semite he was not as great a poet as we had supposed him to be," one implies that our estimation of Eliot's stature as a poet has changed though we recognize that *historically* he was recognized as a great poet. What difference does the change from the past evaluation of Eliot as poet to our present evaluation make to literary critical theory and practice? Does it imply that we refuse to acknowledge Eliot any longer or does it mean that we continue to do so but with different imperatives?

Though these questions do concern the convictions and achievements of T. S. Eliot closely these are not, in fact, questions about that. These questions interrogate issues which are more commonly raised in discourse analysis (the nature of a propositional statement, the nuances of syntax, logical discrimination and ambiguity in statements, stylistics and meaning, etc.). More importantly, the above questions have all been raised in a general sense (i.e., not with regard to the specifics of Eliot criticism) by sociologists, philosophers, and critical theorists who rely on a consensual notion of "reason." The answers they have proposed, together with the clarifications which a discourse analyst may offer, could be brought to bear upon the specific debate in question and on literary critical theory and practice generally. And yet, I fear, any effort in this direction, particularly in the specific context of Eliot criticism, would be resisted. It has been recognized for a while that the liberal humanist tradition of English literary criticism, which has dominated and constructed the institutional features of the discipline of English literature, is peculiarly inimical to the influence of "external" disciplines, particularly anything on a "scientific" model.[5] All those who have done sustained sociological research on the English liberal humanist tradition (in which Matthew Arnold, T. S. Eliot, and F. R. Leavis are key figures), beginning with Chris Baldick,[6] have noted its hostility to "science" and other disciplines. Ironically, such research also demonstrates (as Marxist analysis has suggested, with its own peculiar emphasis, even as the liberal humanist tradition was emerging) that this hostility stems from the political vested interests of the liberal humanists and their establishments. That the above questions haven't been asked indicates that the Eliot establishment and Eliot's literary descendants are liberal humanists at heart. Naturally they would be reluctant to ask these questions.

Arguably, the term "liberal humanist" is erroneous in its application to the historical mind-set which it most commonly designates in the sphere of English literary studies.

At any rate, it is best to plunge in and try to set up a theoretical and practical framework within which the above questions could be answered. In attempting this, I do not explicitly demarcate the influence of the entire range of "extra"-literary and literary sources which have been brought to bear on this. My liberal humanist education has persuaded me of the usefulness of lucid, unequivocal, and uncomplicated presentation.

When one makes a statement like: "Eliot was an anti-Semite but a great poet," without any qualifications, both possible interpretations of the statement suggested in question (1) above are equally possible: i.e., "Eliot was both an anti-Semite *and* a great poet, though the former is an undesirable quality and the latter an admirable one," and "Eliot was a great poet *despite* being an anti-Semite; his racism might have affected his poetry but didn't." The two interpretations are generated by exploring the possibilities of the conjunctive "but" in the original statement. The presumptions regarding the relation between aesthetic-literary and social-cultural values implied in the two interpretations of the statement are however different (hence questions (2) and (3)), and should be treated differently.

"Eliot was both an anti-Semite *and* a great poet, though the former is . . ."

Replacing the conjunctive "but" by "and" in the first possible interpretation makes sense because of the coordinate clause "though the former is an undesirable quality and the latter an admirable one." The "and" seems to bring the two qualitative factors (anti-Semite *and* great poet) together, but they are in fact held apart by the coordinate clause. The "and" interpretation is one way of apprehending Anthony Julius's book, which brings the two qualities together in the same object, Eliot. I might as well note here that the tendency of the Christopher Ricks line of argument in *Eliot and Prejudice,* with its agonized attempt to prove Eliot's innocence, assumes a more problematic "or" statement—something like: "a person is either a great poet *or* an anti-Semite." This essay focuses primarily on the liberal consensus which accepts the fact of Eliot's anti-Semitism.

The emphasis of the "and" statement is not actually on bringing the two strata of evaluative criteria together (the social-cultural stigma attached to anti-Semitism to the aesthetic-literary approbation of Eliot's poetry) but on holding them apart. In other words, it rests on the presumption that judgements regarding social-cultural standing needn't influence judgements regarding aesthetic-literary achievement. The question that arises (as in (2) above) is what exactly are the criteria that distinguish the two areas of evaluation so firmly?

Another way of putting that question would be to ask: is there any mode of making aesthetic-literary judgements which doesn't take the social-cultural environment of the author, reader or contexts of transmission of the text, into account? We are aware that there are methods of analyzing texts which are ostensibly independent of context. There have been "art for art's sake" movements, new critical modes of thinking, structuralist analyses of texts, etc. which appear to do this; influential critics like Wimsatt and Beardsley who have maintained that there is both an "intentional fallacy" as well as an "affective fallacy"; hermeneutical exercises by Roman Ingarden, Hans Gadamer, Hans Jauss, and others which have idealized the breadth of "horizons of expectation" and separated the strata of texts till contexts seems to disappear; structuralist poetic principles propounded and put to practise by Roman Jakobson and Michael Riffaterre, for instance, which disregard social, ethical, political, cultural factors. Many other examples can be adduced. Let's call these broadly formalist modes of analysis. Formalist (as an umbrella term) modes of analysis have indubitably contributed much to our understanding of almost every aspect of literature except the evaluative. Purely formalist analyses of texts reveal the inner workings of a text with or without relation to writer and reader, clarify the degrees of complexity which may underlie a text, help to compare two or more texts in terms of technical virtuosity, but none of these necessarily tell us which text is "great literature" and which a "minor work."

A purely formalist reading may enhance our understanding of texts, and allow us to compare and contrast a multiplicity of techniques, but doesn't provide reasons for choosing a systematic hierarchy of value. Riffaterre may contemplate Jakobson's and Lévi-Strauss's analysis of Baudelaire's "*Les Chats*" but not know why Baudelaire is a great poet.[7] Barthes may perform a sustained analysis of *Sarrasine* with a view to uncovering the very subjectivity of reading and never worry about its being great literature.[8] Umberto Eco may demonstrate that James Bond novels are "closed ended" and *Ulysses* is "open ended" and yet in itself this doesn't explain why we value the latter more.[9] The best that a broad-ranging formalist approach may achieve is to show that certain techniques arouse more interest, are more challenging or more pleasurable, in specific contexts or in a range of contexts. But that brings us right back to the area of contexts, and everything that goes with it (ideology, culture, politics, social and ethical values), and therefore outside the scope of the formalist theorist.

Unsurprisingly, the logical outfall of most formalist schools of thinking is the placing of that school in terms of sociological context. Plekhanov put "art for art's sake" theories in their place.[10] Adorno, Benjamin, and Brecht reiterated the findings of formalists in terms of sociological imperatives. Raymond Williams, Terry Eagleton, Fredric Jameson, and Aijaz Ahmad place all forms of literary theory and practice within a Marxist framework. Edward Said, Homi Bhabha, and Gayatri Spivak find that insidiously social values govern narrative practice. The idealized implied reader of Wolfgang Iser is absorbed in the Stanley Fish frame of "interpretive strategies" described in the existence of "interpretive communities." And so on.

Let's ask that question again: is there any mode of making aesthetic/literary judgements which doesn't take the social-cultural environment of the author, reader, or contexts of transmission of the text, into account? Not in terms of purely formalist criticism, seems to be the answer. But one needn't fall back on purely formalist criticism; one could assume an Arnoldian touchstone theory instead. Indeed this forms the spine of the establishment of English literature as an academic discipline at an international level; was developed by T. S. Eliot himself and F. R. Leavis-Q. D. Leavis; had been disseminated almost unopposed in departments of English literature around the world till the seventies at an orthodox estimate; and is being perpetuated to this day in England by conservative politicians cum educationists like Ron Dearing and Brian Cox.[11]

Speaking simplistically, the Arnoldian touchstone theory seems to have two strands: one, discerning and educated readers can recognize great works of literature irrespective of when and where they are produced and read; and two, these great works of literature are replete with moral values which would be apparent, again irrespective of when and where they are produced and read. Both strands rest on a notion of the universal self-evidence of greatness in literature. Cultural and social concerns are withdrawn from specific historical, geographical, and communal contexts and relegated to a realm of universality (by definition, opposed to multiplicity or plurality). There is no rationale behind the realization of universality and therefore the allocation of greatness; it is simply self-evident.

The arbitrariness of the Arnoldian touchstone theory is self-evident. The necessity and plurality of context is proved by the difference in response of the European reader, American reader, Jewish reader, colonial and post-colonial reader, black reader, woman reader, gay reader, etc.[12] to works which are designated and presented as great by the liberal humanists. These are arguments which one would have thought scarcely need reiteration; and yet these presumptions are still being disseminated in classrooms, aired in academic and popular fora (book reviews, literary advertisements, "high-brow" programmes on television and radio, etc.), and crop up, as we have seen, in debates like that about Eliot and anti-Semitism. It has been conditioned into us by years of concordant literary education. Needless to say, the evasiveness regarding context implicit in the touchstone approach has been interrogated successfully in historical and sociological research into the establishment of English literature as an academic discipline (in the work of Chris Baldick, Brian Doyle, John Dixon, Gauri Vishwanathan, Robert Crawford, amongst others[13]). Specific political, social, cultural, and communal imperatives, it has been demonstrated, govern the actual practice of canonical selection. To a large extent these imperatives are geared towards colonial, sexist, and racist discourses. All those working or interested in the field are undoubtedly aware of these views. Countercanonical constructions which interrogate the liberal humanist tradition have gained popularity because they are meant to combat the insidious hold of the latter on the literary establishment and our habits of critical thinking. And yet, paradoxically and ironically, countercanonical constructions are often absorbed into the same, and are validated, promoted, and disseminated within the same frame of irrational self-evidence.

More sophisticated reiterations of the touchstone theory have, of course, evolved since the classical liberal humanists. Harold Bloom's *The Western Canon,*[14] for instance, doesn't depend entirely on the arbitrariness of authoritative canonical selection in terms of self-evidence. He proposes instead a network of creative "misreadings," both weak and strong, to explain the self-evidence of great works of literature. The notions were developed at a theoretical level in *The Anxiety of Influence,* for instance, and *A Map of Misreadings.*[15] The obfuscation which surrounds the terms which describe his concept of creative misreading arguably disguises an implicit notion of inter-textuality. This in turn raises questions (Bloom wouldn't agree) regarding the communication in and the availability of texts, which reintroduces sociological-cultural issues. As it stands, attention is drawn more to the paradox of an inscrutable and absolute notion of misreading than to the mechanics of selection in Bloom's canon of great literary works. Selection becomes an automatic process in the network of misreading, he says, and one is left wondering more about the concept of misreading than about the process involved.

At any rate if we feel justifiably sceptical about evaluative criteria in terms of formalist criticism and touchstone theories, the implicit separation of social-cultural evaluation and aesthetic-literary evaluation asseverated in so much of practical literary criticism today won't do. "Eliot was both anti-Semite *and* a great poet, though the former is an undesirable quality and the latter an admirable one" isn't acceptable.

"Eliot was a great poet *despite* being an anti-Semite; his racism might have . . . "

In the second interpretation of the original statement ("Eliot was an anti-Semite but a great poet") the conjunctive "but" is replaced by "despite." Unlike in the statement with the "and" replacement however the coordinate-clause doesn't work against the grain of the conjunctive; the coordinate-clause here strengthens the implications of the conjunctive "despite." The coordinate-clause in question ("his anti-Semitism might have affected his poetry but didn't") clarifies what is implied in the "despite": there is a relation between aesthetic-literary value and social-cultural value though it is valid to keep these separate in so far as these apply to Eliot's anti-Semitism and his poetic achievement. Three possible surmises follow. One, this is possible because though Eliot was anti-Semitic he had sound opinions in other and more important areas which are reflected to a greater degree in his work and which vindicate him. Two, this is acceptable because though Eliot was anti-Semitic so were many others at that time (in fact it was almost considered natural) and we have to judge aesthetic-literary quality as well as social-cultural standing in terms of the context. Three, this is so because though Eliot might have been anti-Semitic in life one doesn't see any of it in his poetry (perhaps even the contrary).

Before one can engage with these three surmises there are a couple of ancillary questions which have to be cleared up. What exactly is the relation between aesthetic-literary quality and social-cultural standing which the above statement seems to tacitly accept? Since this is not answerable in terms of the statement itself, or the specifics of the Eliot and anti-Semitism debate, we will have to look at the larger canvas of literary theory and practice in general. The other question which will also have to be answered concerns the degree to which a particular aspect of one's social-cultural concerns relates to the many other aspects which constitute one's social-cultural standing.

The relation between aesthetic-literary and social-cultural values: this is in fact the nub of the debate and this section. Aesthetic-literary nuances can be understood and clarified, it has been maintained above, through formalist modes of analyses. But these kinds of clarification cannot help us allocate aesthetic-literary value. It has been demonstrated that the nearest formalist modes of analyses can come to doing so is by showing that in a specific context or in a range of contexts (historical, geographical, communal) a particular sort of formalist feature arouses more interest, curiosity, or pleasure. Let's tentatively define aesthetic-literary value as the degree to which a text can arouse curiosity, interest, and pleasure in a contextual situation (both in a specific context and in a range of chronologically, spatially, and communally defined contexts). This mode of aesthetic evaluation is broadly accepted by theorists of the fine arts; it is implicit, as much in the notions of taste proposed from Winckelmann to Herbert Read, as in the expressionist concepts of art described by Benedetto Croce and R. G. Collingwood, as indeed in the "form of life" concept of aesthetics suggested by Richard Wollheim.[16] If aesthetic-literary value is to be allocated in terms of the above definition we can't help noticing that the degree of value is actually decided at the behest of socially defined context(s). It is because there is a consensus regarding the desirable formalist qualities of a text in one or many socially defined context(s) that aesthetic-literary value can be allocated.

Society defines itself through systems of communicative actions and agreements which necessarily welds the social, political, cultural, economic, technological, etc. into the composite *zeitgeist* of a context. This is a commonplace of sociology and I do elucidate this further below. Society therefore necessarily expresses and fulfils its desires and reaches a consensus only in the terms and possibilities which are available in the contextual *zeitgeist* where a text might appear and be received. That means nothing more complex than the obvious truth that while it was possible, for instance, for the eighteenth-century European to feel enthused by Newton's ideas it was impossible that he would have digested much of Einstein's if, through some curious quirk of nature, he had encountered them. If there is a consensus about the aesthetic-literary efficacy of a certain formalist feature in a certain text it is because in that context it cohered to the desires and possibilities of the *zeitgeist*—i.e., the social-cultural values that are envisagable and contained therein. That is the necessary relation between aesthetic-literary value and social-cultural value.

Let me state it again. I am not endorsing a Ben Jonsonian notion of a good man being a good poet, nor am I following Samuel Johnson in looking for sound moral instruction in literature. Let us not conflate universalist Judeo-Christian connotations of "good" or "great" with aesthetic-literary evaluation and social-cultural evaluation. Aesthetic-literary value and social-cultural value manifest each other by being bound to the *zeitgeist*(s) in which they appear. A text can be considered socially and aesthetically laudable in several contextual *zeitgeist*s but whenever it injures the aesthetic-literary or social-cultural sensibilities of any *zeitgeist* its judgement of both would be affected to some degree. If it injures (or for that matter rewards) either one of the value systems—aesthetic-literary or social-cultural—it means that it thereby inevitably injures (or rewards) the other to some degree as well, because ultimately they manifest each other.

This doesn't mean that the context in which a literary text is less valued aesthetically and socially cannot be cognisant of the higher evaluation it has received in other context(s). This might determine the sense of significance that is allocated to a literary text—historical significance, for instance.

Now that we have a working understanding of the relation between aesthetic-literary value and social-cultural value, let's turn to the other issue: the degree to which a particular aspect of one's social-cultural convictions relates to the many other aspects which constitute one's social-cultural standing. In delineating the idea of a composite *zeitgeist* which comprehends the social, cultural, political, economic, technological, etc. aspects of its context I had mentioned that this is a commonplace of sociology. I had also promised to elucidate that further, and this is the appropriate space to do so. The issue is, how closely are the several strands which constitute the social-cultural values of a context related, and can they be kept separate so as not to necessarily impinge upon each other's sphere.

It seems clear in retrospect that the pioneers and later practitioners of methods of sociological investigation have realised the inter-relatedness of all aspects of society. This inter-relatedness can be charted out usually in terms of the ideological consistency which is manifested in diverse areas of sociological interest (i.e., the areas in which the space between individual and society, constituent parts and society, and society and society, is negotiated). This includes tracing out the inconsistencies and disjunctions in ideological discourses and social practices. The usual method adopted by sociologists and social-historians for assimilating the various aspects of society is to find a quantum of social description or methodological approach (a kind of basic unit in terms of which any aspect of society, in all its diversity, can be described and analyzed). For Karl Marx this is the relation between labor and produce, for Emile Durkheim it is social "things," for Max Weber it is "social acts," for Louis Althusser it is "ideological state apparatuses," for Michel Foucault it is discourse formations and an archaeological method, for Jürgen Habermas it is communicative acts and a concept of reason, for Niklas Luhmann it rests in functional systems theory, and so on. I mention primarily those sociologists who have provided literary theorists with their instruments of social evaluation, as and when they are exercised. It seems to me that the Marxist modes of critique have been, and continue to be, the most potent. The implications of moving from quantum, so to say, to totality is that no particular aspect of the totality is isolated from the others, and no aspect fails to impinge on the others. In the very construction of our sociological realizations and formulations we have an implicit sense that no necessary methodological or theoretical privilege attaches to our particular focus, and no single element of a contextual *zeitgeist* can be touched without somehow touching every other element as well.

With these clarifications in hand (i.e., the relation between aesthetic-literary value and social-cultural value, and the degree of interlinkedness between the elements which constitute social-cultural standing) we can revert to the statement under discussion. As a reminder: the original statement is: "Eliot was anti-Semite but a great poet"; and the second interpretation which we are concerned with now is: "Eliot was a great poet despite being an anti-Semite; his racism might have affected his poetry but didn't". The three surmises which the latter give rise to are as follows. One, this is possible because though Eliot was an anti-Semite he had sound opinions in other and more important areas which are reflected to a greater degree in his work and which vindicate him. Two, this is acceptable because although Eliot was anti-Semite so were many others at that time and we have to judge aesthetic-literary quality as well as social-cultural quality in terms of the context. Three, this is so because though Eliot might have been anti-Semitic in life one doesn't see any of it in his poetry (perhaps even the contrary).

The responses which come to mind apropos these three surmises are best stated briefly and in reverse order. Ré surmise three: Anthony Julius's book demonstrates that Eliot's anti-Semitism was amply visible in his poetry and other published work. That, to a large extent, is what the debate has been about. Ré surmise two: if we are going to say that anti-Semitism was in a sense in-built in his *zeitgeist,* then we will also have to clarify that it isn't so in our's. We can see why he was considered a great poet in his time, but given the necessary linkage between social-cultural value and aesthetic-literary value we can't see why he should continue to be regarded as such now. But we can distinctly perceive the immense historical significance of Eliot's poetry in the development of English literature and literature in English. Perhaps it can be maintained that had Eliot's achievement been less *derived* from his context and more *constructive,* or even *reflexive,* of his context,[17] with its in-built anti-Semitism, our evaluation might have differed. Ré surmise one: Eliot's anti-Semitism cannot be separated from the rest of his social-cultural standing. All elements of one's social-cultural status are linked to each other and impinge on each other just as all elements of a society have a bearing on each other. Eliot's anti-Semitism cannot be separated from the class-consciousness, from the gender biases, from the doctrinaire religiosity, from the formal innovations, from the liberal humanist criticism, from the expatriate parochialism, from the modernist *angst*, indeed from any of the other elements which comprehend Eliot's achievement.

The long and short of it is that if we reason our way through the general issues involved in the Eliot and anti-Semitism debate which has caught public attention recently, we find it difficult to accept the liberal consensus that Eliot might have been an anti-Semite but is still a great poet. None of the senses which could attach to the latter sentiment can be easily justified. Or, at the very least, such justifications as one imagines might be found need to be discussed further, and possibly outside the realm of the literary establishment and the Eliot-specialist. The terms of discussion have to encompass broader issues of literary critical theory and practice, and their relation to other disciplines of knowledge.

Following the argument offered in this paper there is another statement which needs to be made explicit and brought into the discussion: "Because Eliot was an anti-Semite his poetry cannot be considered as great as it has been till recently." This doesn't mean that Eliot will make a sudden exit from the canon and the curriculum. Neither are, as this study has repeatedly implied, about studying "greatness" but about interrogating it, nor are they about getting moral instruction from literature but about examining significance in terms of a diversity of contexts (most importantly, our own). I use "significance" in the particular sense elucidated above. Eliot's significance is undeniable. To proceed from here we would probably have to ask ourselves: "Why?"

Discussion II
Literature in Indian English(es)[18]: Pragmatic Considerations in the Move from Potential Canon to Realised Canon

In R. K. Narayan's *My Dateless Diary* one gets a brief glimpse of an encounter between the Indian creative writer who writes in English and the professional researcher in linguistics:

> As I listened I was appalled at the dryness of the subject of phonetics. The Professor read a paper suppressing a yawn all the time in the mumbling manner of a nervous secretary reading an annual report. I didn't follow a word of what he said; I caught '*phoneme*' or 'phoney' constantly. The audience sat through in dead stillness, in a state of

> morose resignation. [. . .] I felt that I had wasted an evening in sitting through this baffling function [. . .][19]

It fails. It doesn't fail because R. K. Narayan disagrees with the views presented in the paper but because he doesn't really hear them, because he isn't interested in them, because he suspects they are somehow fake (that tactless pun on 'phoneme'), because he brings a predisposition to hostility with him. Why this occurs is a moot question. Possibly this is due to the specialized nature of linguistics research. I suspect that the hostility of literature to science also plays a role: a hostility which has been particularly worked into the liberal humanist roots of English literature[20] (which no doubt fed into Narayan's education), as well as the broader hostility at the scientific language which seems to stress the instrumentality of language rather than liberating it (which Barthes speaks about[21]).

Of late it has become increasingly clear to the Indian English creative and critical writer that R. K. Narayan's sort of disregard of linguistics cannot be taken much further, especially in a complex linguistic context like India's. Unsurprisingly one finds the occasional Indian English poet and anthologist wondering about the relation between an Indian poet's use of English and of the relevant mother tongue—brief, and on the whole unsatisfactory, sections in Arvind Krishna Mehrotra's and K. Ayappa Paniker's anthologies[22] attest to this. And, occasionally, when critical theorists descend from the complexities of post-colonial theory to consider the pedagogic practice of English in India, they do propose interesting negotiations and collisions between the English language and a regional Indian mother tongue. Harish Trivedi's sketchy but, I think, serious idea of a *panchadhatu* system of literary and linguistic education is a case in point;[23] as indeed are the following sentiments expressed by Gayatri Spivak:

> What I am suggesting, then, is that, in the post-colonial context, the teaching of English literature can become critical only if it is intimately yoked to the teaching of the literary or cultural production in the mother tongue(s). In that persistently asymmetrical intimacy, the *topos* of language learning, in its various forms, can become a particularly productive site. I am not speaking here of becoming an "export" of the mother tongue, for the benefit of those who are thoroughly ignorant of it in the metropolis [. . .]. I am speaking of a much less practical thing: becoming "inter-literary," not "comparative," in the presence of long-established institutionalised divides and examination requirements.[24]

There is usually a faint air of incredulity in the literary creative and critical writer's contemplation of the collision of languages in India and the possibilities (for the larger part only very partially realised) that are implicit therein. This is probably because they are essentially insulated, by force of a Narayan-like habit, against linguistics specialists' voices. The latter have conducted over the last three decades an extraordinarily thorough and painstaking investigation of the nuances of Indian English(es) and the only incredible thing here is that, barring a few feeble gestures, very little of this has been wedded to the ever increasing field of the Indian English litterateur's productions.

Some of the responsibility for this division of worlds is undoubtedly also the linguistics researcher's. Discourse analysis, demographic studies, etc. of Indian English(es) are necessarily couched in the specialist vocabulary which comes with the discipline, are largely rigidly academic and inter-textual, and collate and synthesise statistical data and results of empirical research in a manner which the average literary person finds daunting. But the necessity for the Indian English litterateur's (creative and critical) educating himself in this field and bringing it to bear upon Indian English literature can scarcely be stressed enough. It would undoubtedly chart the way forward for Indian English literature as a potential canon. It would also probably clear up, once and for all, the status of the linguistic common denominator of English in Indian English literature with relation to other related literary spaces (English literature, new/commonwealth/postcolonial etc. literature). It would indubitably have a profound effect on the pedagogy and practice of literature in English (in all senses) in India.

To initiate this process I present the following points.

a. A process of delimitation of relevant material in linguistics from the perspective of Indian English literary studies would necessarily have to be conducted first. Understandably, the use of English in India lends itself to a wide variety of considerations, all of which appear to be relevant to some degree. Linguistic research in this area encompasses diverse factors such as levels of competence (pidgins, mesolects, acrolects, for instance); the relation of nonnative varieties of English to native varieties; syntactical, lexical, and contextual features which attach to the above; social attitudes (ranging from attribution of status to being considered pretentious); demographic features (distribution of levels of competence, and change in distribution, for instance); educational imperatives and educational policy; and political imperatives (especially the Hindi-English debate)—a number of excellent overall surveys of the field are available.[25] In recommending delimitation of what is relevant I do not intend to write off any aspect of this range of material as insignificant. I suggest instead a necessary hierarchy of factors: it would be prudent to begin with the basics (the state of Indian English usage in Indian English literature as it is perceived now) and then to proceed to the broader issues (social status, pedagogic practice, reader response, etc.). The following points attempt to propose briefly an appropriate path to follow.

b. In Indian English literature we are looking primarily at English as a second language amongst various regional languages. Two levels of enquiry are relevant here.

One, trying to distinguish the features of a standardized Indian English. This could be posed as a distinction between nonnative and native varieties of English (most of S. C.Bhatia's qualifications about a standardized nonnative Indian English apply[26]); or as possessing features of an acrolect (used, as Kamal K. Sridhar maintains, "by speakers with considerable educational qualifications who are employed as professionals [. . .]. This variety is widely understood throughout the country and abroad, and shows a wider style range, though it is still noticeably distinct from the native English at every level of linguistic organization"[27]); or more broadly as educated English in India. Extensive work on the specific characteristics —syntactical, lexical, registral, stylistic, contextual—which a standardized Indian English in the above sense possesses has been and is being done.[28] It is also worth noting here that in discerning these characteristics Indian linguists have had to create an appropriate theoretical framework, since existing theoretical frameworks till quite recently were not sufficiently equipped to do this.[29]

Two, trying to distinguish the varieties of Indian English (or Indian Englishes) which emerge in distinct geographical and communal contexts due to contact with regional languages. Again, substantial, though by no means exhaustive, empirical data on the interference of specific regional languages on regional varieties of Indian English have been collected and analyzed by linguistic researchers.[30] The necessarily specialized and localized application of such work render these difficult to obtain, and I suspect these are seldom discussed outside the academic communities to whom such material is easily available.

Both levels of enquiry could be brought to bear upon, and would undoubtedly clarify, the efforts of Indian English litterateurs. Voluntarily or otherwise there can scarcely be any Indian English literary work which doesn't manifest features which are analyzable in the above terms. More importantly, Indian English writers have increasingly pondered the status of their linguistic usage and tried to manipulate it in a self-conscious fashion, especially since independence.[31] This is inevitable where writers are expected to maintain a sense of a homologous national identity (where Indian English as a link-language plays a seminal role and English as a language with international currency gains significance), along with a sense of heterogeneous local or regional realities (where the interference of regional languages come into play). The negotiations which Indian English writers perform with regard to these two poles cannot be effectively analyzed or manipulated unless the two levels of linguistic enquiry above are taken into account.

It seems to me that to enable analysis and manipulation in the above sense (for both creative and critical writing) an Indian English literary stylistics would have to be developed. This would necessarily be distinct from the substantial body of work on English literary stylistics which has been developed. An Indian English literary stylistics could not, however, be independent of English literary stylistics since the installation of a liberal humanist English literary education in India, and its postcolonial implications, have had a profound and indelible influence on the development of Indian English literature. Indeed, an Indian literary stylistics would probably best be served by a sense of reference to (using extant tools of stylistic analysis) and an awareness of difference from (by the introduction of the peculiarly Indian linguistic factors involved) English literary stylistics. Works of English literary stylistics do generally leave space for such realizations of contact and difference.[32]

Apart from many differences of detail, an Indian English literary stylistics is arguably a matter of greater urgency in Indian English literary studies than English literary stylistics has been in English literary studies (hence the inertia in its development). This itself is the primary difference. Indian English(es) is English made opaque by a continuous awareness of its linguistic reaccomodations, by its agonizing about its connotations, by its traces of displacement into nonnative contexts and different regional cultures with corresponding regional languages. In a vital sense, Indian English literature is inevitably about writing in English, which English literature doesn't have to be. The development of an Indian English literary stylistics would, therefore, have to be not only an aid to interpretation and canonical evaluation but a necessary interpretive and evaluative act itself.

An understanding of Indian English literary stylistics would, in other words, go a long way towards realizing and confirming its indigenous status, and would possibly have a corresponding impact on state and educational policy, social attitudes, and the publishing-distributing industry which are relevant to its dissemination and absorption. It might prepare the way for answering questions which those interested in the nexus of linguistics and sociology, like Lachman Khubchandani, may raise with regard to Indian English literature. Khubchandani repeatedly asks the following two questions:

> (a) Is it the 'grammar' (inflection-derivation and syntax) in which you write, or is it the symbolic representation of the ancestral heritage that counts in a literary expression? In other words, should the frontiers of a literary tradition be demarcated according to the *verbal* language, i.e. the linguistic structure, or on the basis of the *visionary* language, i.e. the patterns of sensitivity conveyed through symbolism? [. . .]
> (b) What are the problems of creativity in an adopted language? How to express ideas, customs, values, and other human experiences which have no equivalents in the native English-speaking environs?[33]

I am not entirely clear what Khubchandani means by "symbolic" and "visionary": I take these as interrogations of the relation between language and content (question one) and of the methods of linguistic accommodation and transformation (question two) which one finds in Indian English literature.

c. In considering a development of an Indian English literary stylistics (i.e., the manner in which linguistic research in Indian English linguistics can inform Indian English literature) text linguistics would understandably demand most attention. This means that the substantial and more marked distinctions of phonetics and phonemics in Indian English(es) as compared to other nonnative and native varieties of English would by and large be disregarded. This is perfectly justifiable till one comes to literary texts in which aural nuances are tacitly implied in the text, especially in poetry. It follows that the development of an Indian English literary stylistics would have to be followed by the development of a distinct Indian English poetics. A distinct Indian English poetics would be informed by two factors: (i) the manner in which indigenous poetic structures, cadences, themes, and traditions in different regional languages and locales impinge upon Indian English poetry (or poetry in the Indian Englishes); and (ii) the manner in which the particular phonological features of Indian English(es) feed into its formal and structural innovations.

In the context of the present paper the second factor interests me more. I stress the plurality of Indian English*es* here because it is clear to all Indians that the multiplicity of Indian Englishes is more marked from a phonological perspective than in text linguistics. People accustomed to different regional languages in India speak English differently. The development of an Indian English*es* poetics would undoubtedly be a complex and convoluted affair and would depend on how extensive empirical phonological research of the various Indian Englishes is. I suspect this is another area which could be developed further. At any rate, one can visualize what the shape of an Indian English*es* poetics might be by extending such phonological observations regarding standardized Indian English as are available.[34] It is readily comprehensible that the Indian English speaker's system of seventeen vowels (eleven pure vowels and six glides) and twenty-three consonants, as opposed to the twenty vowel (twelve pure vowels and eight glides) and twenty-four consonants system followed by those accustomed to Received Pronunciation (or standard native) English, would have an impact on poetic cadence. The fact that Indian English speakers usually stress words differently from Received Pronunciation speakers would influence the manner in which Indian English poets and readers may scan poetry, or may present or perceive sprung rhythms in *vers libre.* The different tonal groups of Indian English utterances would necessarily create different sets of aural effect (dramatic, soft, lilting, harsh, etc.) from those in poetry heard with Received Pronunciation in mind. An Indian English*es* poetics would simply multiply the range of such differences many more times.

d. And finally when linguistics research in Indian English(es) has informed the development of a distinct Indian English(es) literary stylistics and an Indian English(es) poetics, attention could be turned to the reverse situation. That is, the manner in which Indian English literature contributes to the linguistic enhancement of Indian English(es) could begin to be examined and analyzed. That Indian English literature has begun making such a contribution has been noted by linguists. R. N. Srivastava, for instance, observes that writers like Khushwant Singh, Mulk Raj Anand, etc. introduce neologisms in their writings which are as far outside standard Indian English as James Joyce's or E. E. Cummings's neologisms were outside standard English. He goes on to maintain:

> The fact is that Indo Anglian writers are trying to change the semantics of the English language. Faced with the task of conveying cultural experiences that are alien to it they intentionally distort language so that in a single stroke it would be bleached of its original cultural complexion and would absorb a new one. How successfully or unsuccessfully they do that within the world of their individual work is for the literary critics to judge but whether such deflections or innovations can, outside those works, be considered to be the basis of a standard IE [Indian English], only time will tell.[35]

Time will *confirm,* I feel inclined to believe, and the linguistics specialist in Indian English(es) will tell.

Notes

1. Anthony Julius, *T. S. Eliot, Anti-Semitism, and Literary Form* (Cambridge: Cambridge Univ. Press, 1995).

2. The irony of recalling Paul de Man's position (also interrogating the gap between theoretical convictions and critical practice) at this early stage will, of course, not be lost on the reader. He has himself notoriously been the subject of a similar debate in the not too distant past. It is best to clarify here that this paper understandably takes an opposite direction from de Man's. Where de Man says:

> When modern critics think they are demystifying literature, they are in fact being demystified by it; but since this necessarily occurs in the form of a crisis, they are blind to what takes place within themselves. At the moment that they claim to do away with literature, literature is everywhere [. . .]

in *Blindness and Insights: Essays in the Rhetoric of Contemporary Criticism* (London: Methuen, 1983), p. 18, this paper asserts that at the moment of realizing what takes place within themselves the literary critic is not only subsumed inside literature, but simultaneously inside that which is allegedly extraliterary—which is inevitably social-cultural.

3. Erik Svarny, *"The Men of 1914": T. S. Eliot and Early Modernism* (Milton Keynes: Open Univ. Press, 1988), pp. 182–83.

4. Christopher Ricks, *T. S. Eliot and Prejudice* (London: Faber and Faber, 1988), chapter 2.

5. "Hostility towards science, and fear of its growth, is a constant and indeed constitutive element of the English literary tradition from Arnold through to the Leavises," says Chris Baldrick, *The Social Mission of English Criticism, 1848–1932* (Oxford: Clarendon, 1983), p. 199.

6. See note 13 below.

7. Michael Riffaterre, "Describing Poetic Structure: Two Approaches to Baudelaire's 'Les Chats,'" *Reader-Response Criticism*, Jane Tompkins ed. (Baltimore: Johns Hopkins Univ. Press, 1980).

8. Roland Barthes, *S/Z*, trans. Richard Miller (London: Jonathan Cape, 1975).

9. Umberto Eco, *The Role of the Reader* (London: Hutchinson, 1979).

10. G. V. Plekhanov, *Art and Social Life* (London: Lawrence and Wishart, 1953).

11. Interesting discussions of the influence of these figures is found in Peter Brooker and Peter Humm, eds., *Dialogue and Difference: English in the Nineties* (London: Routledge, 1989); and in Ken Jones, ed., *English and the National Curriculum: Cox's Revolution?* (London: Kogan Page and Institute of Education, 1992).

12. In maintaining this I must make a note on Chris Baldick's reflections on the literary establishment now in his recent book, where it is described as:

> a pluralist 'bazaar' of critical approaches and theoretical schools, sustained by an ethos of 'openness', plurality or heterogeneity which governs attitudes to interpretive legitimacy, canonicity and even aesthetic value. As each of these approaches has constructed self-confirming discourses which render it more or less deaf to critical challenge from its competitors, so the bazaar as a whole has tended to insulate itself from the corrective influences of a secular reading public outside the academy [. . .]

Criticism and Literary Theory 1890 to the Present (London: Longman, 1996), p. 204. One notes with interest the use of the words "bazaar," "even" before "aesthetic value," and "corrective" before "influences of a secular reading public."

13. The references are to the following books respectively: Chris Baldick, *The Social Mission of English Criticism;* Brian Doyle, *English and Englishness* (London: Routledge, 1989); John Dixon, *A Schooling in English* (Buckingham: Open Univ. Press, 1991); Gauri Vishwanathan, *Masks of Conquest* (London: Faber and Faber, 1989); and Robert Crawford, *Devolving English Literature* (Oxford: Clarendon, 1992).

14. Harold Bloom, *The Western Canon: The Books and Schools of the Ages* (London: Macmillan, 1994).

15. Harold Bloom, *The Anxiety of Influence* (New York: Oxford Univ. Press, 1973); and Harold Bloom, *A Map of Misreadings* (New York: Oxford Univ. Press, 1975).

16. Richard Wollheim, *Art and its Objects: An Introduction to Aesthetics* (New York: Harper and Row, 1968).

17. This sentence refers to sentiments expressed by J. Hillis Miller under the influence of Paul de Man (with whom this paper in a sense began):

> Sociological theories of literature which reduce it to being a mere "reflection" of dominant ideologies in fact tend to limit its role to that of passive mirroring [. . .]. In order to understand how it might be the case that a certain kind of language would make what we call history happen it is necessary first to understand what it means, in the case of a given text, to speak of it as a textual allegory with a high level of rhetorical complexity

in "The Function of Literary Theory at the Present Time," Ralph Cohen, ed., *Future Literary Theory* (London: Routledge, 1989).

18. In "Indian English(es)" I try to encapsulate both the aspiration for a homologous Indian identity through a standardized Indian English and the

actuality of a heterogeneous variety of Indian Englishes formed through interference from regional languages and cultures.

19. R. K. Narayan, *My Dateless Diary* (New Delhi: Orient, 1969), p. 104.

20. See, for instance, Chris Baldick, *The Social Mission,* p. 199.

21. Roland Barthes, "Science versus Literature," *Times Literary Supplement,* 28 September 1967, pp. 897–98.

22. Arvind Krishna Mehrotra, "Introduction," *Twelve Modern Indian Poets* (Calcutta: Oxford Univ. Press, 1992), p. 5; K. Ayappa Paniker, "Introduction," *Modern Indian Poetry in English* (Delhi: Sahitya Akademi, 1991), pp. 14–15.

23. Harish Trivedi, *Colonial Transactions* (Calcutta: Papyrus, 1993), pp. 229–51.

24. Gayatri Chakravarty Spivak, "The Burden of English," Carol A.Breckenridge and Peter van der Veer, eds., *Orientalism and the Postcolonial Predicament: Perspectives on South Asia* (Philadelphia: Univ. of Pennsylvania Press, 1993), p. 151.

25. B. B. Kachru, *The Indianization of English* (Delhi: Oxford Univ. Press, 1983); Kamal K. Sridhar, *English in Indian Bilingualism* (Delhi: Manohar, 1989); S. V. Parasher, *Indian English: Function and Form* (New Delhi: Bahri, 1991).

26. S. C. Bhatia, "Towards a Non-Native Standard in Indian English," *Indian Linguistics,* vol.39, no.1–4, 1978, pp. 226–27.

27. Kamal K. Sridhar, *English in Indian Bilingualism,* p. 43.

28. Apart from the obvious lexical, syntactic, registral, stylistic, and contextual differences marked out in the work of the above-mentioned (Kachru, Sridhar, Parasher), the following give interesting insights into the range of detailed differences which more intensive investigations reveal: Omkar N. Koul ed. *English in India: Theoretical and Applied Issues* (New Delhi: Creative, 1992), particularly B. N. Patnaik and K. Geetha, "A Note on the Semantic and Pragmatic Aspects of Indian English," pp. 167–78 ; R. S. Gupta and Kapil Kapoor, eds., *English in India: Issues and Problems* (Delhi: Academic Foundation, 1991), particularly Yamuna Kachru, "Writings in the Other Tongue: Expository Prose in Indian English," pp. 226–46 ; and most essays in R. K. Agnihotri and A. L. Khanna eds., *Second Language Acquisition: Socio-Cultural and Linguistic Aspects of English in India* (New Delhi: Sage, 1994).

29. The reasons why linguistics theories till recently had been inadequate, and the kind of developments which were required and have been made, are briefly and succinctly charted out in S. N. Sridhar and Kamal K. Sridhar, "Indigenized Englishes as Second Languages: Toward a Functional Theory of Second Language Acquisition in Multilingual Contexts," in Agnihotri and Khanna, eds., *Second Language Acquisition,* pp. 41–63.

30. See, for instance, R. S. Gupta, "English and Indian Languages: Code Mixing" in Gupta and Kapoor, eds., *English in India,* pp. 207–15; and Prem Sagar Bhargava, *Linguistic Interference from Hindi, Urdu, and Punjabi and Internal Analogy in the Grammar of Indian English* (Ph.D. Thesis of Cornell Univ., 1968), (Ann Arbor, University Microfilms Inc., 1975).

31. In so far as this refers to Indian English poetry see Suman Gupta, "Reinscribing Nation-People in Anthologies of Indian English Poetry," *Journal of Commonwealth Literature,* vol.XXXI, no.2, 1996. Needless to say, this could easily be demonstrated with regard to novelists as well; the range of references required to do this is too numerous to be summarized in a short space.

32. Usually in the slightly paternalistic fashion found, for example, in Ronald Carter and Walter Nash, *Seeing Through Language: A Guide to Styles of English Writing* (Oxford: Basil Blackwell, 1990), p. 20.

33. These questions appear in Lachman M. Khubchandani, "English in a Plural Milieu," p. 113, in Omkar N. Koul, ed., *English in India;* and again in essays entitled "Polygenesis of English Heritage: Creative Experiments in Non-Native English" (Nilufer E.Barua and Vilas Sarang, eds., *Indian English Fiction 1980–1990* (Delhi: B. R, 1994), p. 223), and "English as a Contact Language" (Agnihotri and Khanna, eds., *Second Language Acquisition,* pp. 81–82). For his interest in sociolinguistics see Lachman M. Khubchandani, "Sociolinguistics and Indian Scene" in Khubchandani, ed., *Language in a Plural Society* (Delhi and Simla: Indian Institute of Advanced Studies, 1988), pp. 8–14.

34. For brief and useful summaries of this complex area see S. V. Parashar, *Indian English,* pp. 57–58; or R. K. Agnihotri, "Sound Patterns of Indian English: A Sociolinguistic Perspective" in Omkar N. Kaul, ed. *English in India,* pp. 175–88.

35. R. N. Srivastava, "Indian English Today," *Applied Linguistics: Studies in Language and Literature* Vol.IV (Delhi: Kalinga, 1995), p. 286.

Bibliography

The books which may be considered to be relevant to a study of this nature, or which have in some way or the other contributed to it, are too numerous to be listed here. What follows is, with a few exceptions, a list of those scholarly works which have been directly referred or evoked.

Adorno, Theodor. *Aesthetic Theory.* London: Routledge and Kegan Paul, 1984.

Agnihotri, R. K., and A. L. Khanna, eds. *Second Language Acquisition: Socio-Cultural and Linguistic Aspects of English in India.* New Delhi: Sage, 1994.

Ahmad, Aijaz. *In Theory.* London and New York: Verso, 1992.

Alexander, Samuel. *Space, Time and Deity.* Vol.1. London: Macmillan, 1927.

Althusser, Louis. *Philosophy and the Spontaneous Philosophy of Scientists.* London and New York: Verso, 1990.

———.*Politics and History.* Trans. Ben Brewster. London: NLB, 1972.

Armstrong, Paul. *Conflicting Readings.* Chapel Hill: University of North Carolina Press, 1990.

———.*The Challenge of Bewilderment.* Ithaca and London: Cornell University Press, 1987.

Arnold, Matthew. *Culture and Anarchy.* Cambridge: Cambridge University Press, 1932.

———. *Essays in Criticism: First and Second Series.* London: Dent and New York: Dutton, 1964.

———. *On Translating Homer.* London: Longman, Green, Longman and Roberts, 1861.

Ayer, A. J. *Wittgenstein.* Harmondsworth: Penguin, 1986.

Baker, G. *Wittgenstein, Frege and the Vienna Circle.* Oxford: Blackwell, 1988.

Baker, G. and P. M. S. Hacker. *Wittgenstein: Rules, Grammar and Necessity.* Oxford: Blackwell, 1985.

———. *Wittgenstein: Understanding and Meaning.* Chicago: University of Chicago Press, 1980.

Baldick, Chris. *Criticism and Literary Theory: 1890 to the Present.* London: Longman, 1996.

———. *The Social Mission of English Criticism, 1848–1932.* Oxford: Clarendon, 1983.

Barnett, Ronald, ed. *Academic Community: Discourse or Discord?.* London and Bristol: Jessica Kingsley, 1994.

Barthes, Roland. *Image-Music-Text.* Trans. Stephen Heath. London: Fontana, 1977.

———. *Mythologies.* Trans. Annette Lavers. St.Albans: Paladin, 1972.

———. "Science versus Literature." *Times Literary Supplement* (28 September 1967), 897–98.

———. *S/Z.* Trans. Richard Miller. London: Jonathan Cape, 1975.

———. *The Pleasure of the Text.* Trans. Richard Miller. London: Jonathan Cape, 1976.

———. *The Rustle of Language.* Trans. Richard Howard. Oxford: Basil Blackwell, 1986.

————. *Writing Degree Zero.* Trans. Annette Lavers and Colin Smith. London: Jonathan Cape, 1967.

Barua, Nilufer E., and Vilas Sarang, eds. *Indian English Fiction 1980–1990.* Delhi: B. R., 1994.

Baudrillard, Jean. *Forget Foucault.* New York: Semiotext(e), 1987.

Becher, Tony. *Academic Tribes and Territories.* Buckingham and Bristol: Open University Press and The Society for Research into Higher Education, 1989.

Benjamin, Walter. *Illuminations.* Trans. Harry Zohn. Glasgow: Fontana/Collins, 1968.

Belsey, Catherine. *Critical Practice.* London: Methuen, 1980.

Bennett, Tony. *Outside Literature.* London and New York: Routledge, 1990.

Berger, Peter L., and Thomas Luckmann. *The Social Construction of Reality.* Harmondsworth: Penguin, 1966.

Bhargava, Prem Sagar. *Linguistic Interference from Hindi, Urdu, and Punjabi and Internal Analogy in the Grammar of Indian English.* Ph.D. Thesis of Cornell University, 1968. Ann Arbor, University Microfilms Inc., 1975.

Bhatia, S. C. "Towards a Non-Native Standard in Indian English." *Indian Linguistics* 39, no.1–4 (1978): 226–27.

Bleich, David. "Intersubjective Reading." *New Literary History* 17, no.3 (spring 1986): 401–22.

———. *Subjective Criticism.* Baltimore and London: Johns Hopkins University Press, 1978.

———. *The Double Perspective.* Oxford and New York: Oxford University Press, 1988.

Bloom, Harold. *A Map of Misreadings.* New York: Oxford University Press, 1975.

———. *The Anxiety of Influence.* New York: Oxford University Press, 1973.

———. *The Western Canon: The Books and Schools of the Ages.* London and Basingstoke: Macmillan, 1994.

Bolinger, Dwight. *Language—The Loaded Weapon.* London: Longman, 1980.

Booth, Wayne. *Critical Understanding.* Chicago: University of Chicago Press, 1979.

Bradshaw, David, ed. *The Hidden Huxley: Contempt and Compassion for the Masses.* London: Faber and Faber, 1994.

Breckenridge, Carol A., and Peter van der Veer, eds. *Orientalism and the Postcolonial Predicament: Perspectives on South Asia.* Philadelphia: University of Pennsylvania Press, 1993.

Broderick, Damien. *Reading by Starlight.* London: Routledge, 1994.

Brooker, Peter, and Peter Humm, eds. *Dialogue and Difference: English in the Nineties.* London: Routledge, 1989.

Carnap, Rudolf. *The Unity of Science.* Trans. M. Black. London: Kegan Paul, 1934.

Carter, Ronald, and Walter Nash. *Seeing Through Language: A Guide to Styles of English Writing.* Oxford: Basil Blackwell, 1990.

Caudwell, Christopher. *The Concept of Freedom.* London: Lawrence and Wishart, 1977.

Chase, Stuart. *The Tyranny of Words.* New York: Harcourt, Brace and World, 1938.

Chinweizu, *et al. Toward the Decolonization of African Literature.* London: KPI, 1985.

Chomsky, Noam. *Knowledge and Language.* New York: Praeger, 1986.

———. *Language and Problems of Knowledge.* Cambridge, Mass.: MIT Press, 1989.

———. *Rules and Representations.* Oxford: Blackwell, 1980.

Clausen, Christopher. "'National Literatures' in English: Toward a New Paradigm." *New Literary History* 25, no.1 (winter 1994).

Cohen, Ralph, ed. *Future Literary Theory.* London: Routledge, 1989.

Colum, Mary. *From These Roots.* London: Jonathan Cape, 1938.

Colum, Mary, and Padraic Colum. *Our Friend James Joyce.* New York: Doubleday, 1958.

Comrie, Bernard. *Language Universals and Language Typology.* Oxford: Basil Blackwell, 1981.

Cook, Guy. *The Discourse of Advertising.* London: Routledge, 1992.

Crawford, Robert. *Devolving English Literature.* Oxford: Clarendon, 1992.

da Vinci, Leonardo. *Treatise on Painting* (Cordex Urbinas Latinus 1270). Vol.1. Princeton: Princeton University Press, 1956.

Deleuze, Gilles. *Foucault.* Trans. Seán Hand. London: Athlone, 1988.

Deleuze, Gilles, and Felix Guattari. *What Is Philosophy?.* Trans. Hugh Tomlinson and Graham Burchill. London and New York: Verso, 1994.

de Man, Paul. *Blindness and Insights: Essays in the Rhetoric of Contemporary Criticism.* London: Methuen, 1983.

———. *The Resistance to Theory.* Manchester: Manchester University Press, 1987.

Demming, Robert, ed. *James Joyce: A Critical Heritage: 1907–1927.* Vol.1. London and Henley: Routledge and Kegan Paul, 1970.

Derrida, Jacques. *Margins of Philosophy.* Trans. Alan Bass. New York: Harvester Wheatsheaf, 1982.

———. *Of Grammatology.* Trans. Gayatri Chakravorty Spivak. Baltimore: Johns Hopkins University press, 1976.

———. *Writing and Difference.* Trans. Alan Bass. London and Henley: Routledge and Kegan Paul, 1978.

Descartes, René. *A Discourse on Method.* Trans. John Veitch. London: Everyman, 1986.

Dixon, John. *A Schooling in 'English'.* Buckingham: Open University Press, 1991.

Doyle, Brian. *English and Englishness.* London: Routledge, 1989.

Dujardin, Edouard. *The Bays are Sere and Interior Monologue.* Trans. August Suter. London: Libris, 1991.

Durkheim, Emile. *Education and Sociology.* Trans. Sherwood Fox. London: Collier Macmillan and New York: Free Press, 1956.

———. *The Evolution of Educational Thought.* Trans. Peter Collins. London, Henley and Boston: Routledge and Kegan Paul, 1977.

———. *The Rules of Sociological Method.* Trans. Sarah Solovay and John Mueller. New York: Free Press and London: Collier Macmillan, 1938.

Eagleton, Terry. *Against the Grain.* London: Verso, 1986.

———. *Criticism and Ideology.* London: NLB, 1976.

———. *Literary Theory.* Oxford: Blackwell, 1983.

———. *Myths of Power.* London and Basingstoke: Macmillan, 1975.

———. *The Ideology of the Aesthetic.* Oxford: Basil Blackwell, 1990).

———. *Wittgenstein: The Terry Eagleton Script, The Derek Jarman Film.* London: British Film Institute, 1993.

Eco, Umberto. *The Limits of Interpretation.* Bloomington and Indianapolis: Indiana University Press, 1989.

———. *The Role of the Reader.* London: Hutchinson, 1979.

Eddington, Arthur. *The Nature of the Physical World.* Cambridge: Cambridge University Press, 1928.

Edel, Leon. *The Psychological Novel: 1900–1950.* London: Rupert Hart-Davis, 1955.

Einstein, Albert. *Relativity: The Special and the General Theory.* Trans. Robert W.Lawson. London: Methuen, 1920.

Fish, Stanley. *Doing What Comes Naturally.* Oxford: Clarendon, 1989.

———. *Is There A Text In This Class?*. Cambridge, Mass.: Harvard University Press, 1980.

———. *Surprised by Sin: The Reader in* Paradise Lost. London: Macmillan and New York: St.Martin's Press, 1967.

Foucault, Michel. *Discipline and Punish.* Trans. A. M. Sheridan Smith. New York: Pantheon, 1977.

———. *Madness and Civilization.* Trans. Richard Howard, New York: Pantheon, 1965.

———. *Power/ Knowledge.* Ed. Colin Gordon. New York: Harvester Wheatsheaf, 1980.

———. *The Archaeology of Knowledge.* Trans. A. M.Sheridan Smith. London: Routledge, 1972.

———. *The Birth of the Clinic.* Trans. A. M. Sheridan Smith. London: Tavistock, 1973.

———. *The History of Sexuality.* Vol.1. Trans. Robert Hurley. New York: Pantheon, 1978.

———. *The Order of Things.* London: Tavistock, 1970.

Frege, Gottlob. *Translations from the Philosophical Writings of Gottlob Frege.* Eds. Peter Geach and Max Black. Oxford: Blackwell, 1952.

Friedman, Melvin. *Stream of Consciousness: A Study in Method.* New Haven: Yale University Press, 1955.

Geertz, Clifford. *Local Knowledge.* New York: Basic, 1983.

Gilman, William. *The Language of Science.* London: The English Universities Press, 1961.

Green, Martin. *Science and the Shabby Curate of Poetry.* London: Longman, 1964.

Gupta, R. S., and Kapil Kapoor, eds. *English in India: Issues and Problems.* Delhi: Academic Foundation, 1991.

Gupta, Suman. "On Literary Biography and Biografiends." *New Literary History* 24, no.3 (summer 1993): 683–95.

———. "Reinscribing Nation-People in Anthologies of Indian English Poetry". *Journal of Commonwealth Literature* 31, no.2 (1996): 101–16.

Guy, Josephine, and Ian Small. *Politics and Value in English Studies: A Discipline in Crisis?*. Cambridge: Cambridge University Press, 1993.

Habermas, Jürgen. *The Philosophical Discourse of Modernity.* Trans. Fredrick Lawrence. Cambridge: Polity, 1987.

———. *The Theory of Communicative Action.* Vol. 1. Trans. Thomas McCarthy. Boston: Beacon, 1984.

Hacker, P. M. S. *Insight and Illusion.* Oxford: Clarendon, 1986.

Hartley, L. C. "The Sacred River, Stream of Consciousness: The Evolution of a Method." *The Sewanee Review* 39 (January–March 1931): 80–89.

Hayles, N. Katherine, ed. *Chaos and Order.* Chicago: University of Chicago Press, 1991.

Hayman, David. *Ulysses: The Mechanics of Meaning.* Englewood Cliffs: Prentice-Hall, 1970.

Heidegger, Martin. *Being and Time.* Trans. Joan Stambaugh. New York: State University of New York Press, 1996.

Holland, Norman. *Five Readers Reading.* New Haven and London: Yale University Press, 1975.

———. *The Dynamics of Literary Response.* New York: Oxford University Press, 1968.

Hume, David. *A Treatise of Human Nature.* Bk. 1. Glasgow: Fontana/Collins, 1962.

Humphrey, Robert. *Stream of Consciousness in the Modern Novel.* Berkeley: University of California Press, 1958.

Husserl, Edmund. *Ideas: General Introduction to Pure Phenomenology.* Trans. W.R.Boyce Gibson. London: George Allen & Unwin, 1931.

Ingarden, Roman. *The Literary Work of Art.* Trans. George Grabowicz. Evanston: Northwestern University Press, 1973.

Iser, Wolfgang. *Laurence Sterne: Tristram Shandy.* Cambridge: Cambridge University Press, 1988.

———. *The Act of Reading.* London and Henley: Routledge and Kegan Paul, 1978.

———. *The Implied Reader.* Baltimore and London: Johns Hopkins University Press, 1974.

Jakobson, Roman, and Krystyna Pomorska. *Verbal Art, Verbal Sign, Verbal Time.* Oxford: Basil Blackwell, 1985.

Jauss, Hans Robert. *Aesthetic Experience and Literary Hermeneutics.* Minneapolis: University of Minnesota Press, 1982.

———. *Toward an Aesthetic of Reception.* Minneapolis: University of Minnesota Press, 1982.

Jones, Ken, ed. *English and the National Curriculum: Cox's Revolution?* London: Kogan Page and Institute of Education, 1992.

Joshi, Svati, ed. *Rethinking English: Essays in Literature, Language, History.* New Delhi: Trianka, 1991.

Julius, Anthony. *T.S.Eliot, Anti-Semitism, and Literary Form.* Cambridge: Cambridge University Press, 1995.

Jung, C. G. "Ulysses: A Monologue". Trans. W.Stanley Bell. *Nimbus* 2, no.1 (June–August 1953): 7–20.

Kachru, B. B. *The Indianization of English.* Delhi: Oxford University Press, 1983.

Kenny, Anthony. *Wittgenstein.* Harmondsworth: Penguin, 1975.

Kermode, Frank. *History and Value.* Oxford: Clarendon, 1988.

Khubchandani, Lachman M., ed. *Language in a Plural Society.* Delhi and Simla: Indian Institute of Advanced Studies, 1988.

King, Arthur R., and John A. Brownell, *The Curriculum and the Disciplines of Knowledge.* New York, London and Sydney: Wiley, 1966.

Kinneavy, James L. *A Theory of Discourse.* New York: W. W. Norton, 1971.

Koul, Omkar N., ed. *English in India: Theoretical and Applied Issues.* New Delhi: Creative, 1992.

Kripke, Saul A. *Wittgenstein on Rules and Private Languages.* Oxford: Basil Blackwell, 1982.

Kuhn, Thomas S. *The Structure of Scientific Revolutions.* 2nd ed. Chicago: University of Chicago Press, 1970.

Kumar, Shiv K. *Bergson and the Stream of Consciousness Novel.* London and Glasgow: Blackie, 1962.

Leach, Geoffrey N. *English in Advertising.* London: Longman, Green and Co., 1966.

Leavis, F. R., and Denys Thompson. *Culture and Environment.* London: Chatto and Windus, 1933.

———. *The Common Pursuit.* London: Chatto and Windus, 1952.

———. *The Great Tradition.* Middlesex: Penguin, 1948.

———. *The Living Principle: 'English' as a Discipline of Thought.* London: Chatto and Windus, 1975.

Leavis, Q. D. *Fiction and the Reading Public.* London: Chatto and Windus, 1932.

Lewis, Wyndham. *Time and the Western Man.* London: Chatto and Windus, 1928.

Lyotard, Jean-François. *The Postmodern Condition.* Trans. Geoff Bennington and Brian Massami. Manchester: Manchester University Press, 1984.

Macherey, Pierre. *A Theory of Literary Production.* Trans. Geoffrey Wall. London, Henley and Boston: Routledge and Kegan Paul, 1978.

Marcuse, Herbert. *An Essay on Liberation.* Boston: Beacon, 1969.

———. *One-Dimensional Man.* London: Sphere, 1964.

Mehrotra, Arvind Krishna, ed. *Twelve Modern Indian Poets.* Calcutta: Oxford University Press, 1992.

Morris, William. *News From Nowhere and Selected Writings and Designs.* London: Penguin, 1962.

Moylan, Tom. *Demand the Impossible.* London: Methuen, 1986.

Nagel, Ernest. *The Structure of Science.* New York: Harcourt Brace, 1961.

Narayan, R. K. *My Dateless Diary.* New Delhi: Orient, 1969.

Ngugi wa Thiong'o. *Decolonizing the Mind.* London and Nairobi: James Currey, Heinemann Kenya and Heinemann, 1986.

———.*Moving the Centre.* London: J. Currey, 1993.

Ogden, C. K., and I. A. Richards. *The Meaning of Meaning*. London: Kegan Paul, Trench and Trubner, 1923.

Ortony, Andrew, ed. *Metaphor and Thought*. Cambridge: Cambridge University Press, 1993.

Palmer, D. J. *The Rise of English Studies*. London: Oxford University Press, 1965.

Paniker, K. Ayappa, ed. *Modern Indian Poetry in English*. Delhi: Sahitya Akademi, 1991.

Panofsky, Erwin. *Idea: A Concept of Art Theory*. New York: Harper and Row, 1968.

Papineau, David, ed. *The Philosophy of Science*. Oxford: Oxford University Press, 1996.

Parashar, S. V. *Indian English: Function and Form*. New Delhi: Bahri, 1991.

Parrinder, Patrick. *Science Fiction*. London: Methuen, 1986.

Parsons, Talcott. *Action Theory and the Human Condition*. New York: Free Press, 1978.

———. *Social Systems and the Evolution of Action Theory*. New York: Free Press, 1977.

Pater, Walter. *The Renaissance*. Oxford: Oxford University Press, 1986.

Peacocke, Arthur, ed. *Reductionism in Academic Disciplines*. Surrey: Society for Research into Higher Education and National Foundation for Educational Research-Nelson, 1985.

Pears, David. *Wittgenstein*. London: Fontana, 1971.

Plekhanov, G. V. *Art and Social Life*. London: Lawrence and Wishart, 1953.

Popper, Karl R. *Conjectures and Refutations*. London: Routledge, 1963.

———. *In Search of a Better World*. London: Routledge, 1992.

———. *Objective Knowledge*. Oxford: Clarendon, 1972.

———. *The Logic of Scientific Discovery*. New York: Basic, 1959.

Pound, Ezra. *Literary Essays*. London: Faber and Faber, 1954.

Rajan, Rajeshwari Sunder, ed. *The Lie of the Land*. Delhi and Oxford: Oxford University Press, 1992.

Richards, I.A. *Principles of Literary Criticism*. London: Kegan Paul, Trench, Trubner & Co., 1930.

Ricks, Christopher. *T. S. Eliot and Prejudice*. London: Faber and Faber, 1988.

Ricoeur, Paul. *Interpretation and Theory: Discourse and the Surplus of Meaning*. Fort Worth: Texas Christian University Press, 1976.

Riffaterre, Michael. "Describing Poetic Structures: Two Approaches to Baudelaire's '*Les Chats*'." In *Reader Response Criticism*, ed. Jane Tompkins. Baltimore and London: Johns Hopkins University Press, 1980: 26–40.

Robinson, Andrew, and Dipankar Home. "The Mathematician and the Mystic". *The Times Higher Education Supplement*, issue no.1164 (24 February 1995): 18.

Russell, Bertrand. *Human Knowledge*. New York: Simon & Schuster, 1948.

———. *The ABC of Relativity*. London: Kegan Paul, Trench and Trubner, 1925.

———. *The ABC of Relativity*. 3rd edition. Ed. Felix Pirani. London: George Allen and Unwin, 1969.

———. *The Autobiography of Bertrand Russell*. Vol.3. London: George Allen and Uniwin, 1969.

———. and A. N. Whitehead. *Principia Mathematica. Cambridge: Cambridge University Press, 1927.*

Sartre, Jean-Paul. *Being and Nothingness.* Trans. Hazel E.Barnes. New York: Washington Square Press, 1956.

———. *What is Literature?.* Trans. Bernard Frechtman. London: Methuen, 1967.

Saussure, Ferdinand de. *Course in General Linguistics.* Trans. Wade Baskin. London: Peter Owens, 1974.

Scholes, Robert. *Science Fiction.* New York: Oxford University Press, 1977.

Searle, John R. *The Construction of Social Reality.* Harmondsworth: Penguin, 1995.

Sherif, Muzafer, and Carolyn Sherif, eds. *Interdisciplinary Relationships in the Social Sciences.* Chicago: University of Chicago Press, 1969.

Showalter, Elaine. *A Literature of Their Own.* Princeton: Princeton University Press, 1977.

Singer, Thomas C. "Riddles, Silence and Wonder: Joyce and Wittgenstein Encountering the Limits of Language." *ELH* 57, no.2 (summer 1990): 459–84.

Slawinski, Janusz. "Reading and Reader in the Literary Historical Process". *New Literary History* 19, no.3 (Spring 1988):521–39.

Sluga, Hans, and David G.Stern, eds. *The Cambridge Companion to Wittgenstein.* Cambridge: Cambridge University Press, 1996.

Snow, C. P. *The Two Cultures.* London: Cambridge University Press, 1969.

Söderlind, Johannes. "The Interior Monologue: A Linguistic Approach." *Studia Neophilologica* 61 (1989), 169–73.

Sprat, Thomas. *History of the Royal Society* (1667). Ed.Jackson I. Cope and Harold Whitmore Jones. Missouri: Washington University Press, 1958.

Sridhar, Kamal K. *English in Indian Bilingualism.* Delhi: Manohar, 1989.

Srivastava, R.N. *Applied Linguistics: Studies in Language and Literature.* Vol.4. Delhi: Kalinga, 1995.

Staten, Henry. *Wittgenstein and Derrida.* Lincoln: University of Nebraska Press, 1984.

Stebbing, L. Susan. *Philosophy and the Physicists.* London: Methuen, 1937.

Steinberg, Erwin. *The Stream of Consciousness and Beyond in* Ulysses. Pittsburgh: University of Pittsburgh Press, 1958.

Svarny, Erik. *"The Men of 1914": T. S. Eliot and Early Modernism.* Milton Keynes: Open University Press, 1988.

Toulmin, Stephen. *The Philosophy of Science.* London: Hutchinson, 1953.

———. *The Uses of Argument.* Cambridge: Cambridge University Press, 1958.

Trivedi, Harish. *Colonial Transactions.* Calcutta: Papyrus, 1993.

Vishwanathan, Gauri. *Masks of Conquest.* London: Faber and Faber, 1989.

Waddington, C. H., ed. *The Future as an Academic Discipline.* Amsterdam: Radopi, 1975.

Weber, Max. *Economy and Society.* Vol. 1. Berkeley: University of California Press, 1968.

Weinberg, Steven. *Dreams of a Final Theory.* London: Vintage, 1993.

Welleck, René. *The Attack on Literature and Other Essays.* Brighton: Harvester, 1982.

White, David A. "The Labyrinth of Language: Joyce and Wittgenstein." *James Joyce Quarterly* 12, no.3 (Spring 1975): 294–304.

Whitehead, A. N. *Science and the Modern World.* Middlesex: Penguin, 1926.

Wicke, Jennifer. *Advertising Fictions.* New York: Columbia University Press, 1988.

Wilde, Oscar. *Intentions and the Soul of Man.* London: Dawson, 1969.

Williams, Raymond. *Problems of Materialism and Culture.* London: NLB, 1980.

Williamson, Judith. *Decoding Advertisements.* London: Marion Boyars, 1978.

Wittgenstein, Ludwig. *Blue and Brown Books.* Oxford: Basil Blackwell, 1958.

———. *Culture and Value.* Trans. Peter Winch. Oxford: Basil Blackwell, 1980.

———. *Last Writings on the Philosophy of Psychology.* Vol. 1. Trans. C. Luckhardt and Maximilian A. E. Aue. Oxford: Basil Blackwell, 1982.

———. *Philosophical Investigations.* Trans. G. E. M. Anscombe. Oxford: Basil Blackwell, 1958.

———. *Tractatus Logico-Philosophicus.* Trans. D. F. Pears and B. F. McGuiness. London: Routledge and Kegan Paul, 1961.

Wollheim, Richard. *Art and Its Objects.* New York: Harper and Row, 1968.

Wolmark, Jenny. *Aliens and Others.* New York and London: Harvester Wheatsheaf, 1993.

Index